CYCLOPEDIA OF SERMON OUTLINES FOR SPECIAL DAYS AND OCCASIONS

A COMPREHENSIVE COLLECTION OF SUGGESTIVE
MATERIAL FOR THE OUTSTANDING DAYS AND
SEASONS OF THE ENTIRE CHURCH YEAR, ALSO
FOR FRATERNITIES, ETC.

COMPILED AND EDITED BY

REV. G. B. F. HALLOCK, D.D.
EDITOR OF *The Expositor*

NEW YORK
GEORGE H. DORAN COMPANY

*Copyright, 1925,
By George H. Doran Company*

*Cyclopedia of Sermon Outlines for Special
Days and Occasions
— B —
Printed in the United States of America*

FOREWORD

The lot and life of the writer and compiler of this set of books have been cast amid busiest and most pressing pastoral demands. Forty years of need and of experience lie enshrined within their covers. Would that some one had presented me with such volumes when I was a young minister, or at any time along the way! I needed them; would have prized them; would have used them—as a source of inspiration, of pastoral methods, and as ready reference manuals for innumerable occasions.

This is the third of three works written to fill this long-felt want. The books are purely pastoral, intended for ministers only. They are unique, supplying a demand no one has yet attempted to meet. They are comprehensive, aiming to be cyclopedic in contents. One would need go to the table of contents of each volume to find the full inclusion. Without going into minutiæ, but referring only in barest outline, in the Cyclopedia of Pastoral Methods are aids to the worthy conduct of public devotions, including all special days and occasions, with salutations, invocations, pastoral prayers, offertory sentences and prayers, intercessions for special persons and objects; here too are numerous ceremonies for weddings, funerals, communion services, baptisms, confirmations, ordinations, for the adoption of children, and for the sending out of missionaries; also services for the installation of Elders, Deacons, Deaconesses and of Bible School officers and teachers. In addition, and possibly even more valuable because harder to find, are many choice and fitting forms for corner-stone layings, dedication of churches, re-openings, setting apart of parish houses, educational buildings, hospitals, private homes, manses, towers and church spires, organs, windows, bells, chimes, choir stalls, paintings, pulpits, fonts, communion tables and communion sets, pulpit lamps and Bibles, church decorations, flags, monuments, memorial tablets, an illuminated cross, hymn books, for mortgage burnings, etc.

FOREWORD

The second volume, Cyclopedia of Commencement Sermons and Baccalaureate Addresses, solves the problem of preparing for the occasional yet important call in the service of educational institutions. Not alone ministers, but college presidents, principals of schools, teachers, school officials, parents and citizens are called upon for timely Commencement and Baccalaureate addresses. It is sure they cannot but welcome aid for this duty and privilege, and in this volume, definitely intended to be a ministrant in behalf of all who are expected to prepare for such occasions, will be found a vast collection of suggestive material from the very best sources.

This third volume is a Cyclopedia of Sermon Outlines and Sketches for Special Days and Occasions, being a compendious assortment of suggestive material for the outstanding days and seasons of the entire church year, also for fraternities, etc.—a sermon suggestor and inspirer, offering welcome help amid pressing days and duties. One of its most valuable features is a selection of more than fifteen hundred suggestive texts and themes especially appropriate to the various days and seasons and exceptional occasions.

These books are intended for use by ministers of all bodies. They are non-denominational; or, to be more exact, inter-denominational.

The aim has been to make these associated volumes practically indispensable to every preacher, pastor and theological student.

G. B. F. H.

BRICK CHURCH,
Rochester, N. Y.

CONTENTS

Part I: Christmas Texts and Themes 19
Part II: Christmas Sermon Outlines 22–41

	PAGE
Under the Christmas Star	22
The Geometry of the Angels' Song	22
No Room in the Inn	23
Christmas, the Surprise of God	23
Back to Work with Joy	25
The Rising Star	25
The Unspeakable Gift	26
The Meaning of the Incarnation	27
The Calendar of God	27
The Christmas Gift of Life	29
Legend of the Christmas Rose: Talk to Children	30
The Story That Never Grows Old	31
The First Christmas Service	32
What the Shepherds Saw in the Cradle	34
A Christless World	34
Christ's Advent	36
The Dayspring from on High	36
God's Revelation in Christ	36
All Men Shall be Blessed in Him	37
The Kingdom of Christ	37
The Wonderful Christmas Gift	37
The Christmas Saviour	38
"God with Us"	38
Christ the World's Sun	38
The Design of the Saviour's Advent	39
Rejoicing in Christ's Reign	39
The Good Tidings of God	40
The Day-Spring	40
The Story of the Star	41
Why Jesus Came	41

CONTENTS

Part III: New Year Texts and Themes 42
Part IV: New Year Sermon Outlines 44–55

	PAGE
The Christian a Sojourner	44
Over a New Road	45
New Year Accompaniments	45
The January Inventory	46
Visiting the Great Yesterdays	46
A New Year Exhortation	48
The Path Unknown	48
The Guide Through the Gate	49
Go Forward!	50
The Open Door	50
Under Sealed Orders	51
Lest We Forget	52
The New Path	53
The New Date	54
A Happy New Year Problem	55
Shifting Scenery	55

Part V: Evangelistic Texts and Themes 56
Part VI: Evangelistic Sermon Outlines 59–72

Making Excuse	59
A New Creation	60
Steps to Christ	60
What Time Is It?	61
"Remember Jesus Christ"	61
Care for Souls	61
Church Prosperity	62
Giving the Heart	62
The Great Question	63
The Seeking Shepherd	64
Acquaintance With God	64
Excuses	65
Price of Redemption	66
Christ Waiting	67
A Spirit-Filled Life	67
A Blessed Whosoever	68
The Worth of the Soul	69
Our Best Helper	69
Continuing	69
Three Conditions of Soul	70

CONTENTS

	PAGE
The Calls of Christ	70
Almost a Christian	70
"We Bear the Name of Christians"	70
Christ at the Door of the Heart	71

Part VII: Lincoln's Birthday Texts and Themes 73

Part VIII: Lincoln's Birthday Sermon Outlines 75–78

Lincoln	75
Patriotism	75
The American Great-Heart	76
The Greatness of Lincoln	76

Part IX: Washington's Birthday Texts and Themes 79

Part X: Washington's Birthday Sermon Outlines 81–88

The Living Washington	81
Washington as a Leader	82
Washington Ever Our First Citizen	83
Washington a Man of Loftiest Purposes	83
The Ever-Growing Influence of Washington	84
The Character of Washington	84
A Study in Heroes	85
Washington	88
Washington as a National Asset	88

Part XI: Palm Sunday Texts and Themes 89

Part XII: Palm Sunday Sermon Outlines 91–97

The Kingship of Christ	91
The Triumphal Entry	92
The Lord Hath Need of You	92
The Triumphal Entry	93
Popular Attractions	93
Songs or Silence	94
The Conquering King	95
Lessons for To-day from Christ's Triumphal Entry	96
Garment Givers	96

Part XIII: Good Friday Texts and Themes 98

Part XIV: Good Friday Sermon Outlines 100–108

The Cross of Christ	100
Watchers by the Cross	101

CONTENTS

The Watchers Around the Cross	101
The Group Around the Cross	101
Behold the Man!	102
Lessons from the Crucifixion	102
The Seven Words from the Cross	103
The Three Crosses at Calvary	106
The Scene of Our Saviour's Execution	106

Part XV: Easter Texts and Themes 109
Part XVI: Easter Sermon Outlines 112–125

The First Easter Sermon	112
Endless Power for Endless Living	113
The Risen Christ	114
The Empty Grave	114
Mary's Joy in Her Risen Lord	115
The Resurrection a Fact	116
And Peter	117
The Lesson of Easter	117
The First Gospel Sermon	118
Easter Talk to Children	119
The Power of His Resurrection	120
Rolling Away the Stone	121
Easter Gladness in Seeing the Lord	121
The Spiritual Parable of Christ's Crucifixion, Resurrection, Ascension and Return	122
The Power of Christ's Resurrection	123
The Risen Christ	124

Part XVII: Lord's Supper Texts and Themes 126
Part XVIII: Lord's Supper Sermon Outlines 130–142

Stirring to Remembrance	130
Christ Expected at the Feast	130
The Duty and Obligation to Keep the Feast	131
Communion	131
Empty Places at the Lord's Table	132
Invited Nearer: A Communion Meditation	132
Preparatory Service	133
Love Made the Supper	134
The Value of Spiritual Dreaming	135
Communion Continued	136
The Lord's Supper	136
The Friendship of Jesus	137

CONTENTS

	PAGE
The Scene of Calvary	137
Lessons from the Names of the Ordinance	138
Lessons from the Nature of the Ordinance	138
Lessons from the Design of the Ordinance	138
Meditation	139
"Come and Dine"	139
Communion Address	140
Self-Examination	141
Communion a Meditation	142

Part XIX: Arbor Day Texts and Themes 143
Part XX: Arbor Day Sermon Outlines 145–153

Men and Trees: Arbor Day Talk	145
Gideon Under the Oak, Or a Hero Commissioned	146
Perpetual Arbor Day	146
The Seed We Are Sowing	146
Trees of the Lord	148
A Sermon for Boys and Girls	150
A Message from Springtime	151
A Springtime Lesson	153

Part XXI: Ascension Day Texts and Themes 154
Part XXII: Ascension Day Sermon Outlines 155–161

Lessons from the Ascension	155
Heaven's Ascension Day Message	155
An Ascended Yet Ever-Present Lord	156
Captivity Led Captive	156
Carried Up into Heaven	157
Christ's Ascension	158
The Ascended Lord	160
The Ascension of the Lord Jesus Christ	160

Part XXIII: Mother's Day Texts and Themes 162
Part XXIV: Mother's Day Sermon Outlines 165–171

The High Mission of the Mother	165
Mother	165
Our Debt to Motherhood	166
The Encircling Love and Loyalty of Mother	169
The Mother Love	170
Our Mothers: An Appreciation	171

CONTENTS

Part XXV: Memorial Day Texts and Themes 172
Part XXVI: Memorial Day Sermon Outlines 175–189

- The Memorial of Liberty 175
- Gestures of Progress, Personal and National . . 175
- Forget-Me-Nots Gathered from God's Acre . . 176
- Flowers for Memorial Day 176
- The Oriflamme of God 177
- Spicery for Our Dead 178
- War Deprecated 179
- The Reign of the Dove 179
- Bringing Back the King 180
- The Veteran as an Oracle 180
- Our Memorial Day 181
- The Day of Memory 182
- The Incomparable Day 185
- New Issues Call for New Courage . . . 185
- Lessons of Memorial Day 185
- Sharing the Hero Spirit 186
- The Supreme Gift of Patriotism . . . 186
- The Inspiration of Heroic Memories . . . 187
- A New Memorial Day 188

Part XXVII: Children's Day Texts and Themes . 190
Part XXVIII: Children's Day Sermon Outlines . 194–212

- The Eyes of Your Heart 194
- Things to Watch 195
- A Bright Pin 195
- The Blessedness of Childlikeness . . . 197
- The Ministry of Children 198
- Manners 200
- The Message of the Flowers 202
- Six Minds 203
- The Swans' Dinner Bell 203
- Children's Day Talk 204
- Rhoda, A Girl Christian 205
- A Children's Sermon with White Mice as a Text . 206
- Watch Your Steps 207
- Making Faces 208
- Candle Sermon for Children's Day . . . 209
- The Pony Engine 210
- Lessons from the Dandelion 211

CONTENTS

Part XXIX: Commencement Texts and Themes 213
Part XXX: Commencement Sermon Outlines 214–222

   Passing Dividends 214
   Democracy and Education 215
   True Education 216
   "Pressing Toward the Mark" 216
   Address to the Graduating Class 217
   For Such a Time 218
   The Garden of Life 220
   The Teacher and His Pupil 221
   To Young Women Graduates 221

Part XXXI: Independence Day Texts and Themes 223
Part XXXII: Independence Day Sermon Outlines
                                                         226–236

   The Nation's Greatest Need 226
   The Blessing of Liberty 227
   The Bible and Christian Citizenship . . . 227
   Righteousness Exalteth a Nation 228
   The Land We Love 229
   Love of Liberty 230
   Foes of Our Country 231
   Influence of the Declaration 231
   The Duties of an American Citizen . . . 233
   What the Liberty Bell Said: Talk to Children . 235

Part XXXIII: Texts and Themes Concerning Vacation 237
Part XXXIV: Sermon Outlines Concerning Vacations 239–245

   Vacation Rest 239
   Come Ye Apart 240
   Perils of the Summer 241
   The Value of an Eddy in the Stream of Life . 243

Part XXXV: Texts and Themes on the Sabbath 246
Part XXXVI: Outlines of Sermons on the Sabbath
                                                         248–255

   Sunday Rest in the Twentieth Century . . 248
   Sabbath Benefits 248
   Our Need of the Lord's Day 248

CONTENTS

	PAGE
Sanctify the Sabbath: How?	249
The Sabbath a Necessity	250
The Sabbath a Delight	250
Made for Man	251
The Need for the Sabbath	251
The Sabbath a Reminder	252
Civil Stewardship	252
How We Should Keep the Sabbath	253
Sabbath Keeping in Christ's Way	253
The Spirit of Sabbath-keeping	254
How to Enjoy Sunday	255

Part XXXVII: Labor Day Texts and Themes 256
Part XXXVIII: Outlines of Labor Day Sermons 259–264

The Meeting Place of Manhood	259
The Battle for Bread	260
God's Law of Labor	261
Work as a Means of Grace	263

Part XXXIX: Armistice Day Texts and Themes 265
Part XL: Armistice Day Sermon Outlines 267–268

Armistice Day Instituted	267

Part XLI: Prison Sunday Texts and Themes 269
Part XLII: Prison Sunday Sermon Outlines 270–272

The Sighing of the Prisoner	270
Our Duty Toward Prisoners	270
Christianity and the Prisoner	271
A Moral Earthquake	271
A Saint in Prison	272

Part XLIII: Good Citizenship Day Texts and Themes 273
Part XLIV: Good Citizenship Day Sermon Outlines 275–281

Putting Religion Into Politics	275
The Christian and His Ballot	276
Christian Citizenship	277
Christian Democracy	278
Christian Principles in Politics	279
The Best Government	280

CONTENTS

Part XLV: Election Day Texts and Themes 282
Part XLVI: Election Day Sermon Outline 283–284
   The Divine Election 283

Part XLVII: Thanksgiving Day Texts and Themes 285
Part XLVIII: Thanksgiving Day Sermon Outlines
                                                         288–299
   Gratitude for God's Remembrance 288
   Thanksgiving Day 288
   Thanksgiving 289
   Special Reasons for Thanksgiving 289
   Joyful Thanksgiving 289
   Volcanic Thanksgiving 293
   Feast of Ingathering 293
   Real Thanksgiving 293
   The Dower of a Nation 294
   The Goodness of God 295
   Excellent Loving-kindness 295
   Praise God 296
   Olden Time Appreciation 297
   Why Give Thanks? 297

Part XLIX: Outlines of Sermons on Special Occasions and to Fraternities 300–325
   A Pastor's Installation Sermon 300
   The Christian's Confidence 302
   Freemasonry Triumphant 304
   The Three Links of the Independent Order of
      Odd Fellows 307
   Royal Arcanum Fellowship 309
   Fraternal Life Insurance 312
   Love and the Mysteries: Sermon for Fraternal
      Organizations 314
   Independent Order of Foresters 317
   The Supremacy of Love: Sermon to Odd Fellows 320

CYCLOPEDIA OF SERMON OUTLINES
FOR SPECIAL DAYS AND OCCASIONS

PART I: CHRISTMAS TEXTS AND THEMES

The Disclosure of the Star: Matt. 2:10. 1. Christ the eternal. 2. Christ the creator. 3. Christ the light. 4. Christ the man. 5. Christ the Saviour.

The Christmas Spirit: Isa. 9:2-7. 1. The spirit of goodwill. 2. The spirit of sacrifice. 3. The spirit of service.

The Glory of Immanuel: "The Word was made flesh, and dwelt among us, and we beheld his glory, the glory of the only begotten of the Father, full of grace and truth." John 1:14.

The Song of the Angels: "And the angel said unto them, Fear not; for, behold, I bring you good tidings of great joy, which shall be to all people." Luke 2:10.

The Joy That Jesus Brings: "Behold, I bring you good tidings of great joy." Luke 2:10.

Messiah's Rightful Dominion: "And the government shall be upon his shoulder." Isa. 2:10.

The Song in the Night: "There were shepherds abiding in the fields, keeping watch over their flocks by night." Luke 2:8. The first Christmas song was sung in the night. The glory broke over the world when the world was dark. That is a comforting fact this year.

The First Peace Convention: "Glory to God in the highest and on earth peace." Luke 2:14. It is still true that the ultimate aim of the principles promulgated at that first year peace convention between earth and heaven was peace to the whole world.

The Song That Never Dies: Luke 2:46-55.

The Quest for the King: "Where is he that is born king of the Jews? for we have seen his star in the east, and are come to worship him." Matt. 2:2.

The Manger Cradle: "And this shall be a sign unto you." Luke 2:12.

The Rising Star: "There shall come a star out of Jacob, and a scepter shall rise out of Israel," etc. Num. 24:17.

Christmas with Christ Left Out: "What think ye? Will he come up to the feast?" John 11:56.

The Day-Star in the Heart: 2 Pet. 1:19.

The Incarnation: "For ye know the grace of our Lord Jesus Christ, that, though he was rich, yet for our sakes he became poor, that ye through his poverty might be rich." 2 Cor. 8:9.

The Bethlehem of the Heart: "Until Christ be formed in you." Gal. 4:19.

Lessons from the Shepherds: "The Shepherds said one to another, Let us now go even unto Bethlehem, and see." Luke 2:15.

The Gift That Transforms the World: 2 Cor. 9:15; Luke 1:46-55.

The Child Jesus: "Set for the fall and rising again of many in Israel." Luke 2:34. 1. His destiny. 2. His development. 3. His wisdom. 4. His coming rule.

The Christmas Offering: "They offered unto him gifts." Matt. 2:11. Christ has only one reason for desiring gifts from us, and that is in order that he may give gifts to us. He can give only to givers.

The Greatest Quest: "Where is he?" Matt. 2:2. Never be afraid to ask your way to Christ. Never think that you can find your way to Christ alone. You need all the help you can get on the quest of quests.

Inquirers for Christ: "He inquired." Matt. 2:4. Herod as well as the wise men is inquiring, it seems. Some inquire about truth to worship it; others, to murder it.

The First Advent: "So Christ was once offered to bear the sins of many." Heb. 9:28.

The Second Advent: "Unto them that look for him shall he appear the second time without sin unto salvation." Heb. 9:28.

The Nearness of Christ: "The Lord is at hand." Phil. 4:5.

A Prevision of the Christ: "Behold a virgin shall conceive and bear a son and thou shalt call his name Immanuel." Isa. 7:14.

Pondering of the Christ: "But Mary kept all those things and pondered them in her heart." Luke 2:19.

Proclaiming the Christ: "And the angel said unto them,

Fear not; for behold I bring you good tidings of great joy," etc. Luke 2: 10, 11.

Endowing the Christ: "And when they had opened their treasures, they presented unto him gifts, gold," etc. Matt. 2: 11.

An Apocalypse of the Christ: "For unto us a child is born . . . and his name shall be called Wonderful," etc. Isa. 6: 7.

Hailing the Christ: "And suddenly there was with the angel a multitude of the heavenly host, praising God," etc. Luke 2: 13, 14.

The Pedigree of the Christ: "Concerning his Son Jesus Christ our Lord, which was made of the seed of David according to the flesh," etc. Rom. 1: 3, 4.

PART II: CHRISTMAS SERMON OUTLINES

UNDER THE CHRISTMAS STAR

"We have seen his star in the east, and are come to worship him." Matt. 2:2.

I. Underneath the star of Bethlehem lay a visible token of the love of God. "And they called his name Jesus."

II. Power lay beneath the star. And where Christ is, there is power now for us all.

III. Hope lies waiting for us beneath the star of Bethlehem—a new hope of a better life.

IV. Beneath the Bethlehem star lay faith, that first Christmas night. The men from afar saw only a child, yet they knew the child for a King. They had faith—in the years that would bring him to manhood. Have we as much faith in Christ, in ourselves, in other people?

V. Beneath the star lay unselfishness—in the Wisemen; in Mary, the mother; in Jesus, the willingly earth-born Son of God; and in God, the Father of him. And every Christmas that is worth the name is marked by a spirit of unselfishness—even to-day.

VI. Beneath the Bethlehem star there was found a combination of sorrow (there was no room for them in the inn) and joy, but the sorrow was quite overwhelmed in the joy. Always it is so for those who find the Lord Jesus.

VII. When we follow the star we find a starting point and a terminus; a beginning of all that is worth while for ourselves and the end of all our longing; the Beginning and the End; the Alpha and Omega.—REV. PAUL FARIS.

THE GEOMETRY OF THE ANGELS' SONG

"And suddenly," etc. Luke 2: 13, 14.

1. The Gospel in miniature.

2. The angels, unconscious geometricians.

I. Their vertical ascription of praise. "Glory to God in the highest." Ours is a canopying gospel—of tip-top concern—and lifting in one direction, uplifting.

II. Their horizontal target of desire. "On earth peace." "Heavenly host"—army anticipating universal peace. Symbolizing peace in responsive song.

III. Their centrical convergence in the soul of man. "To men of good-will." The gospel is centric. An intense Jesus—"Saviour, Christ, the Lord—seeks an intense work in man and by man.

Conclusion: How far is the Christianity of this Christmas season thus geometrical?—REV. S. B. DUNN, D.D.

NO ROOM IN THE INN

"There was no room for them in the inn." Luke 2:7.

There was no room for Jesus then. Is there now?

I. Among the nations. In governments, in politics, in army and fleet.
II. In society. Luxury, show, infidelity, sin.
III. In business. Ideals of Christ in the market.
IV. In church. Does church meet test, "Follow me"?
V. In homes. Place of Bible and religion in home.
VI. In our sinful hearts:

> "Dear little stranger
> Slept in a manger,
> No downy pillow under his head,
> Only the darkness his cradle caresses,
> Only a manger, lowly, his bed,
> Blinded and selfish, the world in its sin.
> No room in the Inn!
> No room in the Inn!"

CHRISTMAS, THE SURPRISE OF GOD

"Now when Jesus was born in Bethlehem of Judea," etc. Matt. 2:1.

Goodness, which is essentially love, is full of glad surprises. We may gild the gold of Christmas with grudging remembrances; we may even tarnish it with unworthy motives. Yet Christmas remains the token of God's surprise for the human race, the surprise of his unsearchable goodness.

I. Think of how many surprised ones there were that first Christmastide. The mother and Joseph, the shepherds; and, after a while, the Magi from the East. The crowded inn was also doubtless surprised when there passed from lip to lip the word that a child had been born in the lowly manger. Finally, Israel was surprised—and Rome and the ends of the earth; and the surprise is not over. The goodness of God broke through every barrier, overflowed every channel and became incarnate in the only Begotten Son.

II. By common consent we insist that the children must have a Christmas surprise. For the rest of us, we are not so much concerned. We are missing the meaning of it all, however, if we are not still overawed by the glad surprise of goodness that seeks us on Christmas day.

III. How many ways there are of letting goodness have its surprising way on this festival day! Little but loving fingers can weave a royal robe for those who have taught them how and whom to love. Every parent knows that the rarest Christmas gifts are those that come from the simple store of children's love.

IV. The surprise of love is not exhausted, however, by children's gifts. Husbands may give their wives such assurances of unbroken trust and fidelity that diamonds will become lusterless in comparison. Wives may renew their vows of loving and chaste allegiance in such a variety of ways that the holiday will become a glorified honeymoon.

Friendships may be made to glow with a radiance that is not earthly as each friend brings to the other some hitherto unrevealed gift of strength or patience, confidence or courage. Masters and servants, in every modern relationship of our toiling life, may seal the prosperity of the enterprise in which both are engaged, by the gift of each to the other for the weal of all.

The wayward boy may bring to a heart-broken mother his own broken heart and in the glad surprise of the gift both his heart and hers will be healed.

The far away child of God may draw near "with full assurance" and find pardon and peace so sweet and so satisfying that the sorrows of sin will be lost in the joy of the Saviour.—REV. WILLIAM HIRAM FOULKES, D.D.

BACK TO WORK WITH JOY

"And the shepherds returned, glorifying and praising God for all the things that they had heard and seen, and as it had been spoken unto them." Luke 2:20.

The shepherds had just seen angels and heard their marvelous music, and had seen the Christ. After that experience we read that they "returned." Back to their sheep. With joy they returned to their common duty.

The difference between Christian joy and the world's pleasure is in this: the one fits for duty, while the other unfits. Three thoughts are suggested in this.

I. Christ brings joy. The angels sang when Christ was born. Simeon and Anna returned thanks. Andrew shouted "Eureka." A man may rejoice indeed when he finds the Saviour.

II. Christ would turn joy into the performance of duty. The shepherds went back to work gladly. Christ brought the disciples down from the mountain to where the demoniac child was. Paul exhorts Christians to live contentedly where they are. Onesimus was sent back to his earthly master. Our joy in Christ is to fit us for the every-day duties.

III. Christ would have gratitude expressed in work. The best way to praise God is by our lives. There is not much spirituality in the man who won't work. The birds praise God by their songs, the flowers by their beauty, the stars by their shining and their motion in their spheres. We can best "adorn the doctrine" and praise God by our lives.

THE RISING STAR

"There shall come a star out of Jacob, and a scepter shall rise out of Israel," etc. Num. 24:17.

Balaam caught the first faint beams of the Star-rise of the reign of Christ.

I. The rising Star brings light. On the deepest mysteries —on immediate duties—on human destiny.

II. The rising Star has a scepter-quality. The light is instinct with celestial authority. Is charged with a quickening and governing dynamic.

III. The rising Star is born of the humanity lying back of it—of the chosen race—of our flesh and blood—of the needs that our human nature feels.

Star-rise to Balaam is Sun-rise to us.—Rev. S. B. Dunn, D.D.

THE UNSPEAKABLE GIFT

"Thanks be unto God for his unspeakable gift." 2 Cor. 9:15.

I. It is the best of gifts. The heart naturally yearns for love. "Greater love hath no man than this," etc. "Herein is love, not that we loved God," etc. "God so loved the world," etc.

II. Because it includes other gifts. Have you Christ? If you trust and serve him you have the guarantee of all.

III. Because it improves other gifts. The presence of one possession may add to the worth of all else. Example, sight. Thus it is with the gift Christ. All we have seems better for it. It improves everything.
 1. We value nature more.
 2. We value human nature more.
 3. We value the Bible more.

IV. Because it makes us givers. When we receive it we become like it.

V. Because it is a gift to all. "To all people."
 1. A gift, not a loan.
 2. A gift, not a purchase.

> " 'Tis only God that is given away,
> 'Tis only Heaven may be had for the asking!"

 3. How shall we express our "thanks"?
  (a) By giving this gift to others.
  (b) By giving ourselves to the Giver.
—Rev. Thomas R. Stevenson.

THE MEANING OF THE INCARNATION

"Now when Jesus was born in Bethlehem of Judea." Matt. 2:1.

I. When Jesus was born there was the realization of the supernatural. The birth of Christ was no ordinary birth. It brings us face to face with the supernatural. It means the visitation of God. For Christ is God manifested in the flesh. The incarnation signifies not the coming of an absent God into the world, but the manifestation of an ever-present Father. Christ was not a revealer of God, he was the revelation of God, and he alone could say, "He that hath seen me hath seen the Father."

II. When Christ was born in Bethlehem there was also the working out of God's eternal plan of salvation. The Incarnation of Christ is the first great earthly event in connection with this divine purpose. The angels sang a heavenly truth when they said, "Unto you is born a Saviour." Christ did not come into the world merely as a teacher, a lawgiver, or a reformer, but primarily as a Saviour. Man's redemption is wrapped up in Christ's incarnation. Humanity must pin its hope of salvation to him and him alone.

III. When Jesus was born in Bethlehem there was also the culmination of an eternal process. As Christ was the Incarnation of God, the advent makes possible the Incarnation of Christ in men. It is now possible for us to be made partakers of his divine nature. If that is so, then there must be a likeness between our redeemed nature and his divine nature. When we are most like him we think less of self and more of others. As the world grows more and more Christlike, it grows less and less selfish. The nearer we come to him in the likeness of our lives, the more practicable become his teachings.—REV. W. W. BUSTARD.

THE CALENDAR OF GOD

"When the fulness of the time was come, God sent forth his Son." Gal. 4:4.

Christmas is witness to the timekeeping of a calendar-making God. It echoes the mightiest clock stroke ever resounding from the chronometer of the universe. Each new celebration of the day is a reminder of the unfailingly timed program forever in the thought of the divine Governor of creation—a graphic refutal of all skeptic imaginations which picture his story as the sport of chance.

For the word says it was "when the fulness of time came" that "God sent forth his Son."

I. The need of the world was ancient when Christ appeared to answer it. In the judgment of men the redeeming Messiah was far overdue. Impatient faith had been crying for centuries: "How long, O Lord, how long?" But God waited. The "times" he had appointed for Messianic preparation were not complete. Imperative necessities of each passing age he met with gracious supply of prophets and teachers calling the people to himself. He ever made plain the way of righteousness for those who desired to walk therein. But he would not hasten his working plan.

Sending his Son into the world to inaugurate the era of the kingdom of heaven was an enterprise far too vast to risk its success by inadequate readiness or inopportune introduction.

II. The hour of the first Christmas was no doubt the first hour when God had looked down on a world where the good news of Jesus the Saviour could be proclaimed with surety of its being retold till all nations heard. As God's great Missionary to man, the Christ could not inaugurate his work among men until the stuff out of which missionaries are made had been developed in the earth. There are many reasons for believing the age of his advent was the earliest age of history in which the missionary impulse could have been evoked from the human soul.

III. To-day's singularly dynamic democracy of the kingdom of God, this spontaneous stir of the mass of the church's common people, this uplifting of the general spirit of religious folk, is a phenomenon that no previous age of Christianity has quite paralleled. What if for the moment it does not seem to be coming to any very definite head of tangible results? What if there are many uncertain gropings which betray doubt of where to turn or what to do? May not all these things prove none the less to be God's preparation of times which shall ere long make possible vaster triumphs than the Master's cause has yet seen? If so, may we not believe that the leader or leaders whom God appoints to be captains of that greater victory will not fail to appear when his clock, still running true, strikes again his chosen hour?—C.

THE CHRISTMAS GIFT OF LIFE

"God so loved the world that he gave his only begotten Son," etc. John 3:16.

I. The motive was love. The gift, an expression of love, was the gift of a life.

That first Christmas gift was not a gift to a child; it was the gift of a child. Love prompts gifts to those near and dear. Greater love, unbounded love, prompts gifts of self and gifts of those nearest and dearest in order that the world may be blessed.

II. How has it happened, one wonders, that through all the years of its observance Christmas Day has not been counted as the one day of all the year for the giving of life in Christian service? It is a day set to celebrate the manifestation of God's wondrous gift to mankind. How better could that manifestation be celebrated than by the full consecration of life to the same ends for which the life of Jesus was given?

III. The gift of life is the most costly gift that can be made. The man who gives millions does not give as much as the man who gives himself—fully, unreservedly, with oneness of purpose—as a servant of mankind. The father and mother who gives stocks and bonds and silks and satins do not give a fraction of that given by the parents who give their sons and daughters for the world's weal. All other gifts are but toys and tinsel as compared with the kind of gift which is celebrated on Christmas day—the gift of life. Yet why should it not be that, in Christian homes, Christmas should come to be the one day of all the year when the young of the family face the question: Shall I make to the world the greatest gift within my power, the gift of life? Why should it not be the day when parents consider most seriously the giving of their sons and daughters in Christian service? It's a costly gift when father and mother give the young life upon which they might lean when their own steps falter. But—"God so loved that he gave his only begotten Son." Has the familiar declaration of fact no appeal to the love that has been kindled in us by that first Christmas gift?

The supreme need of the world to-day, as always, is sacrificing service, and only through such Christ-like service will it find its full life. The gift most like that first gift is the gift of a life of sacrificing service.

LEGEND OF THE CHRISTMAS ROSE: TALK TO CHILDREN

Many, many years ago the roses had a meeting. They met to decide at what season they would best like to blossom. There were ever so many varieties, large and small, double and single, white and pink, and red and yellow. Nearly every one of the many kinds chose to blossom in June. There was here and there a straggler who preferred the later summer or early autumn. The majority said: "June! June! June is surely the most beautiful month, and the rose is surely the most beautiful flower. The month and the flower belong together."

But there was one little plant, the leaves of which were not yet unfolded. It thought it was a rose, but it was so small it hardly knew. None of the proud flowers paid it the least attention. It wasn't asked for an opinion, and it never said a word. But it had its own sweet thoughts. They were something like this: "It seems too bad that all the roses should bloom when the world is already full of beauty without them. I should like to have blossoms that would cheer when things were dreary. I should like to bloom in winter. I wonder if I could!" The little plant did not yet know what power there was in a kind purpose.

The year sped around. The beautiful roses enjoyed their time of blossoming, and had all passed away. The snow was heavy on the ground. Men said that in many years there had not been such a snowfall. Christmas Day came, and on that day a young woman went to live with him who was once the Christ-child. "How sad that there are no flowers," one said.

"She was so fond of flowers." But another said: "I know a bush which has blossoms under the snow. It is in the far corner of the garden."

They dug away the white drifts, and, sure enough, deep down below the brave plant had done its best. Dozens and dozens of roses bloomed sturdily, daintily, white with pale pink frills, many more than were needed for the friend who appreciated flowers.

In a house near by, a new baby came on this joyous day. "The mother must find a flower on her pillow, when she wakens from her sleep." So a spray of the pale pink-edged blossoms lay there to welcome the new life.

In still another house, on this Christmas Day there was a gay wedding. The bride's table was adorned with a bowl of the delicate winter rose blossoms. All the guests praised their exquisite perfection. "To think they blossomed for my wedding!" the bride exclaimed. Happy rosebush, for it had given beauty and gladness to the great events of life!

But there was something better for the rose. The Lord of the garden knew all about it. He said: "Because this little plant grew and blossomed unnoticed, unpraised, content to wait and bring its small meed for others' happiness, glad to be of use when other roses failed, it shall be named for me. Now and always, it shall be the Christmas Rose."

Think of others. Do not be selfish. Christmas means unselfishness. Love came down at Christmas, love all lovely, love Divine. Children, young people, bring all the love you can into the world—all the beauty, all the kindness, all the happiness.—H.

THE STORY THAT NEVER GROWS OLD

"Behold I bring you good tidings of great joy which shall be to all people." Luke 2:10.

There is no story that has so stirred the heart of humanity as the story of the birth, life and labors of Jesus Christ, born of the Virgin Mary, in Bethlehem of Judea, in the days of Herod the Great. The story has been told oftener than any other story, and yet it is still full of charm, and men tell it in all lands, and joy over it as if it were an event of yesterday. It is new at every Christmas, and the whole world lays aside its cares and its labors to listen to it once again.

Why has this story such a hold upon the world?

I. The hero of this story was a babe. The babyhood of heroes is usually thought unworthy of chronicle, but the babyhood of Jesus has a significance which sacred historians think worthy of mention, for in this baby was the incarnation of God in human form.

II. The hero of this story was a King. He had no royal trappings, and lived in no royal palace, but he was "King of kings and Lord of lords." All things in heaven and in earth recognized his sovereignty.

III. He was a priest. He brought men to God, he revealed God to men, for the priest is one who makes the connection between God and man.

IV. He was a perfect example. He challenged men to convict him of sin, but they were silent. There was found no fault in him as even his enemies testified.

V. He was a perfect friend. He loved men. He lived with them. He never forsook those who needed him. The world is singing yet with increasing fervor, "What a Friend We Have in Jesus."

VI. He was a counselor. His words are the wisdom of life. He pointed out to men the way of life, and warned them against the danger that beset their paths.

VII. He was a comforter. No sorrowing one ever approached him who did not find in him a comforter.

VIII. He was a Saviour. He gave hope to the hopeless. No sinner was beyond redemption who came to him for cleansing. The witnesses of his saving power are everywhere in the world to-day. The invitation of salvation is borne on every breeze to every land. "Look unto me and be ye saved, all ye ends of the earth."

THE FIRST CHRISTMAS SERVICE

Luke 2: 8-17.

I. The place. The first Christmas service was not held in temple or synagogue, but out of doors; not under the glowing sun, but beneath the silent stars.

II. **The time.** Although it was night, yet it was not dark, for a great light—"the glory of the Lord"—shone all around and lighted the place of the assembly.

III. **The congregation.** The congregation was small, but there was no vacant place. So far as we know, it was composed wholly of men, not of the rich and great, but of the poor and lowly. They were shepherds "abiding in the field, keeping watch over their flocks by night." They were not gathered for worship, but for a round of common duty; but being faithful, were accounted worthy of the highest privilege and richest blessing.

IV. **The preacher.** The preacher came from "the land that is very far off," from "the better country," and was a notable one, even "the angel of the Lord." Nothing is said of his personal appearance or dress, and we are not told whether he stood before them or above them in the air. But what is vastly better, we are told what he said.

V. **The sermon.** The sermon is short, but every word is full of meaning. It has three parts.

1. In the first, the preacher puts his hearers at ease by saying, "Fear not"; excites their interest with, "Behold, I bring you good tidings of great joy"; and suggests the duty of publishing the good tidings by the words, "Which shall be to all people."

2. The second part is the heart of the angel's sermon. Here it is: "For unto you is born this day, in the city of David, a Saviour, which is Christ the Lord." It is as if he had said: "The long line of prophecy is fulfilled; that for which ears have listened and hearts have hungered is now come to pass; the City of David has at last received her king; the Christ is born; God is manifest in the flesh: Emmanuel." He is born "this day"; not yesterday, for God's love for men is so great that he cannot withhold the "good tidings of great joy" for a single day. And lest in their humility the shepherds might think that the "good tidings" were not for them, the preacher made it personal: "Unto you"—shepherds—"is born this day—a Saviour."

3. The third part of it is by way of confirmation and assurance. The shepherds need not rely wholly on the preacher's declaration, for somewhere in the City of David,

the babe, wrapped in swaddling clothes, was lying in a manger, and they could go and see for themselves.—REV. J. C. ROBINSON.

WHAT THE SHEPHERDS SAW IN THE CRADLE

"And the shepherds said one to another, Let us now go even unto Bethlehem and see this thing which is come to pass, which the Lord hath made known unto us." Luke 2:13-15.

We are told what the shepherds said: "Let us go even now unto Bethlehem, and see this thing which is come to pass." And what did they see when they got there? This is the question we should ponder this Christmas morning.

I. They saw a Child through whom had come to man the greatest revelation of man.

II. They saw a Child born to give earth the greatest revelation of man.

III. They saw him who was born to be the world's Saviour.

IV. They saw a Child who was born to be earth's greatest Teacher.

V. They saw a Child who alone had the right to the sovereignty of the world. Lowly, but King! Jesus, Son of man, Son of God! We worship thee this morning. Amen.

A CHRISTLESS WORLD

There is a strange old legend of a world that grew colorless in a single night. The clouds became lifeless, spongy vapors; the waves turned pale and motionless; the fire fled from the diamond, and light from every gem. The world turned into a sculptor's world, and all was animated stone. Those that dwelt upon it were saddened and bewildered at the change, and never ceased to mourn for the beautiful tints of flowers and grasses, and the vanished hues of the sunset clouds. All Nature was in mourning, and wore a leaden-colored robe. Nevermore should diamonds sparkle, nor rubies shine, nor dewdrops glisten in the morning light. Nevermore should there be a rainbow on the cloud, or a silver in the falling raindrops. The expanse of lake or ocean should nevermore reflect a blue heaven, nor the stars nor the sun. The world had passed into eclipse,—into the shadow of death.

This old legend is a parable. It suggests to us a picture of the world without the Christmas Christ. What a dark, dead, dismal world this would be, what an awful world it would be if in that total eclipse of a Christless condition! What if there had been no Saviour?

We celebrate the day of Christ's birth—Christmas, the gladdest, brightest, happiest day of all the year; but will it not be all the happier if we prepare for it by at least for a little time thinking of what the world would be if there had been no Saviour? The bright scene will be all the brighter for having in the background this heavy, dark curtain of the thought of a Christless world.

Others have had this thought. Job had it. He saw man a sinner, and asked how it was possible for him to be justified before God. The apostle John had it, and said: "He that believeth not is condemned already." The writer of the epistle to the Romans had it, when he told of the awful sins of men, and added that God would render to every man according to his deeds. The apostle Paul had it when he told the Ephesian Christians that before they had been quickened by Christ they were "dead in trespasses and in sin." A Christless world! If there had been no Saviour! No eclipse could be so dark as that.

I. It would mean a heathen world. Read Pagan history.

II. It would mean a hopeless world. Christ put hope into the world. Christmas Day has well been called "The Birthday of Hope."

III. It would mean a paralyzed world, for where there is no hope there is no action.

IV. It would mean a lost world. Lost! A lost world! If there had been no Saviour!

Are you ready to appreciate the Christmas message? The good news of the Gospel? Are you ready to yield yourself wholly, heartily, gladly to Christ and let him be your Saviour?—H.

CHRIST'S ADVENT

Luke 1:78, 79.

I. The state of mankind before he came. "In darkness and the shadow of death." Ignorant (1) Of moral character of God; (2) Of the purity of his law; (3) Of the evil nature and dreadful consequences of sin; (4) Of the true source of happiness; (5) Regarding the future state.

II. The remarkable description of the Saviour. "The Dayspring from on high." The great source of (1) Life; (2) Light; (3) Glory.

THE DAYSPRING FROM ON HIGH

Luke 1:78, 79.

I. A declaration of a blessed fact. "The Dayspring from on high hath visited us."

II. The source and origin of that fact. "Through the tender mercy of our God."

III. Its divine fruits and consequences. "To give light to them that sit in darkness and in the shadow of death; to guide our feet into the way of peace."

GOD'S REVELATION IN CHRIST

"For unto you is born this day in the city of David, a Saviour, which is Christ the Lord." Luke 2:11.

Bethlehem's manger holds the profoundest thought of theology, the grandest theme of song, the cheerfulest hope for humanity, the answer to man's imperious cry.

I. Incarnation. God coming to dwell in man.

II. Revelation. In that cradle man looks upon the face of the King and the soul is satisfied.

III. Presence. "Emmanuel—God with us," the living root of Christian faith—the foundation and superstructure of the church.

IV. Power. Outward reach of God to help his children up. 1. By his power—regenerating and sanctifying. 2. By his teachings—loftiest and most practical. 3. By his example—"He went about doing good."—C. A. T.

CHRISTMAS SERMON OUTLINES

ALL MEN SHALL BE BLESSED IN HIM

"His name shall endure forever; his name shall be continued as long as the sun; and men shall be blessed in him; all nations shall call him blessed." Ps. 72:17.
  I. The renown which the Saviour shall acquire.
    1. The sources from which it is derived.
        (1) It is derived from the constitution of his person.
        (2) It is derived from his work.
        (3) It is derived from his reward.
    2. The duration through which it shall last.
  II. The influence which the Saviour shall exert.
        (1) Its beneficial nature.
        (2) Its universal extent.
        (3) Its unworldly methods.

THE KINGDOM OF CHRIST

"Thou sawest till that a stone was cut out without hands, which smote the image upon his feet that were of iron and clay and brake them in pieces," etc. Dan. 2:34, 35.
  I. The kingdom of Christ is divine in its origin.
  II. The kingdom of Christ is humble in its beginnings.
  III. The kingdom of Christ is progressive in its tendency.
  IV. The kingdom of Christ is triumphant in its course.
  V. The kingdom of Christ is universal in its extent.
  VI. The kingdom of Christ is eternal in its duration.

THE WONDERFUL CHRISTMAS GIFT

"Thanks be unto God for his unspeakable gift." 2 Cor. 9:15.
  Bethlehem is the goal of man's weary march. Here we receive the gift of the Child-Christ, who is to become our Saviour from sin, our hope from despair and our life from the dead.
  I. The door of the stable opens into the pathway to the palace of the King. The humblest is the holiest place.
  II. The child of Bethlehem's manger, the poorest and weakest of earth, one day will be King of the universe,

crowned with many crowns. Angels are his attendants; wise men his worshippers. A new star is the finger pointing to his birthplace, the shepherds are his watchers and all the future his realm.

III. The wonderful Christmas Gift is yours, if you will take the Christ into your heart; but if the door to your being, like the inn, is closed against him, if there is no room for him in your darkened soul, you will suffer regret, disgrace and sorrow. The greatness of the gift is indescribable, because with him you have all other treasures—all other needs supplied.

Human language fails to portray more than the fringe of his robes, the beginnings of his power, the touch of his fingers. The unspeakableness of his infinite love will ever invite the affectionate approach of his followers.—REV. E. W. CASWELL.

THE CHRISTMAS SAVIOUR

"Thou shalt call his name Jesus; for he shall save his people from their sins." Matt. 1:21.

Contrast between Jesus and other saviours or deliverers.
I. Their salvation was secular. His is spiritual.
II. Theirs was instrumental, his personal.
III. Theirs was local. His universal.
IV. Theirs was temporary. His everlasting.

"GOD WITH US"

"They shall call his name Emmanuel; which, being interpreted, is, God with us." Matt. 1:23.

Explain the title. "Emmanuel. God with us."
I. God in our nature.
II. God on our side.
III. God in our heart.
IV. God with us in heaven for ever.

CHRIST, THE WORLD'S SUN

"But unto you that fear my name shall the Sun of righteousness arise with healing in his wings." Mal. 4:2.

CHRISTMAS SERMON OUTLINES

I. Illustrate the comparison of our Lord Jesus Christ to a sun.
   1. His unapproachable preëminence.
   2. His benignant influence.
   3. His relation to the whole world.
II. Describe his restorative or remedial efficacy.
   1. In the world.
   2. In the country.
   3. In an individual.
III. Consider the persons to whom his efficacy is confined.
   1. Who are they?
   2. Why are they the sole recipients of the promised blessing?
IV. Regard Christ as the sun of righteousness.
   1. Christ is the center of the spiritual world.
   2. Christ is the source of light.
   3. Christ is the source of heat.
   4. Christ is the object of attraction.

THE DESIGN OF THE SAVIOUR'S ADVENT

"I am come that they might have life, and that they might have it more abundantly." John 10:10.

I. The design of the Saviour's advent.
   1. As a Priest, he procures life.
   2. As a Prophet, he reveals it.
   3. As a King, he dispenses it.
II. The amplitude of the design.
   1. More abundantly than Adam.
   2. More abundantly than the saints under the law.
   3. More abundantly than our former selves.

REJOICING IN CHRIST'S REIGN

"Rejoice greatly, O daughter of Zion." Zech. 9:9.

I. The character under which the Saviour is here presented to us.
   1. As just.
   2. As powerful.
   3. As lowly.

II. The grounds of rejoicing in his reign.
  1. The peacefulness of his government.
  2. The extent of his empire.
  3. The privileges of his subjects.

THE GOOD TIDINGS OF GOD

"And the angel said unto them, Fear not; for, behold, I bring you good tidings of great joy, which shall be to all the people." Luke 2:10.

I. The Gospel may be called good tidings, because it is so beneficial.

II. The Gospel may be called good tidings, because it is so appropriate.

III. The Gospel may be called good tidings, because it is so personal.

IV. The Gospel may be called good tidings, because it is so unexpected.

THE DAY-SPRING

"Through the tender mercy of our God, whereby the day-spring from on high hath visited us, to give light to them that sit in darkness and in the shadow of death, to guide our feet into the way of peace." Luke 1:78, 79.

I. The condition of the world previous to the advent of Christ.
  1. A state of ignorance.
  2. A state of danger.

II. The mercy of God toward the world in that condition.
  1. Undeserved.
  2. Unsolicited.
  3. Seasonable.

III. The manner in which the mercy of God was manifested.
  1. He sent his Son to enlighten it in its ignorance.
  2. He sent his Son to guide it in its danger.

THE STORY OF THE STAR

"For we have seen his star in the east and are come hither to worship him." Matt. 2:2.

I. The story. It is of the Christ Child. What was the star? Ample ground for speculation. But in any event it was the guide divine to these Eastern inquirers. Nor will the serious seeker to-day be left without a pilot to the Saviour.

II. Its teachings.
1. There is an East to every one in which this star appears.
2. When this star is recognized it is the part of true wisdom to follow where it leads.
3. If rejected, the conditions of guidance fail, and the conjunctive planets separate.
4. The terminus of the guiding star is to the adoration of the God-man.

WHY JESUS CAME

"The Son of man is come to seek that which was lost." Luke 19:10.

I. That which was lost. Mankind.

II. Son of man. He is the Wonderful, Counsellor, Mighty God, etc. Yet out of love for a fallen race he lays aside his glory and becomes the Son of man. This is the title which Christ appropriates to himself.

III. He came. Was not forced, compelled; he chose to come.

IV. To seek. It is interesting to study how Jesus sought for souls. The Good Shepherd,—"Jesus sought me when a stranger."

V. To save. He came because there was something to save, something that was precious in his eyes, something worth saving.

PART III: NEW YEAR TEXTS AND THEMES

Seasonal Opportunity: "There is a time to every purpose under the heaven." Eccl. 3:1.

The Life That Lasts: Eccl. 12:1-7.

Secrets of Happiness: "Happy is the man that findeth wisdom." Prov. 3:13.

This Year Also: "A certain man had a fig tree planted in his vineyard," etc. Luke 13:6-9.

Untrodden Ways: "Ye have not passed this way heretofore." Josh. 3:4.

The Divine Leader: "And the Lord went before them," etc. Ex. 13:21, 22.

God the Way: "Thus saith the Lord, which maketh a way," etc. Isa. 43:15-21.

Another Opportunity: "He made it again." Jer. 18:4.

Resolutions for the New Year: "I am resolved what to do." Luke 16:4.

Out of the Old and into the New: "He brought thee out to bring thee in." Deut. 4:37, 38.

Need of Haste: "Brethren, the time is short." 1 Cor. 7:29.

Peace by the Way: "See that ye fall not out by the way." Gen. 45:24.

New Year Optimism: "To-morrow the Lord will do wonders among you." Josh. 3:5.

Shifting Scenery: "The fashion of this world passeth away." 1 Cor. 7:31.

New Year Wisdom: "So teach us to number our days that we apply our hearts unto wisdom." Psa. 90:12.

Over a New Road: "Ye have not passed this way heretofore." Josh. 3:4.

A New Man in a New Year: "If any man be in Christ he is a new creature," etc. 2 Cor. 5:17.

New Books Opened: "The books were opened." Rev. 20:12. Book of Providence. Book of God's Law. Book of God's Remembrance. Book of Individual Memory.

Follow Your Leader: "And he led them on safely, so that they feared not." Psa. 75: 53.

Our Need of a Guide: "O Jehovah, I know that the way of man is not in himself; it is not in man that walketh to direct his steps." Jer. 10: 23.

A Brave Woman's Resolve: Ruth 1: 16.

A Forward Look: Phil. 3: 12-14.

Set Thine House in Order: "Set thine house in order, for thou shalt die and not live." Isa. 38: 1.

The Flood of Years: "The Lord sitteth upon the flood." Psa. 29: 10.

The Perpetuity of the Good: "Their works do follow them." Rev. 14: 13.

New Year Voices: "Remember." Acts 20: 31.

A Pleasant Prospect: "My presence will go with thee." Ex. 33: 14.

Prayer for the New Year: "Hold up my goings in my paths, that my footsteps slip not." Psa. 17: 5.

A Year's Work Reviewed: "Then I looked at all the work that my hands had wrought, and on the labor I had labored to do; and behold all was vanity and a striving after wind, and there was no profit under the sun." Eccl. 2: 11.

The Unknown Future: "Our cattle also shall go with us; there shall not a hoof be left behind; for thereof must we take to serve Jehovah our God; and we know not with what we must serve Jehovah, until we come thither." Ex. 10: 26.

The Assurance: "I will never leave thee." Psa. 139: 1-17.

A Happy New Year: "If they hearken and serve him, they shall spend their days in prosperity, and their years in pleasures." Job 36: 11.

Untrodden Ways: Joshua 3: 1-17. 1. The Divine Leader. 2. God, the way-maker. 3. The Lord's highway. 4. Peace by the way. 5. The excellent way. 6. Trust for each day.

The New Year: "Behold, I make all things new." Rev. 21: 5.

The Consecration of Time: Psa. 90.

The Source of True Happiness: "Whoso trusteth in the Lord, happy is he." Prov. 16: 20.

Strength for the Day: "Thy bars shall be iron and brass; and as thy days, so shall thy strength be." Deut. 33: 25.

PART IV: NEW YEAR SERMON OUTLINES

THE CHRISTIAN A SOJOURNER

"Pass the time of our sojourning here in fear." 1 Peter 1:17.

A sojourner is one who dwells in a strange country, and has no possession in it of his own. Thus, "Abram went down to Egypt to sojourn there." He felt himself a stranger and a pilgrim, and by his unsettled state, he was kept in mind of the city which hath foundations—that is permanent and stable, whose builder is the living God. See Heb. 11:8, 9.

So a Christian is absent from his native country. He is born from above. His home is heaven. The body is but the house of the soul's pilgrimage, in which she is confined during her exile from home. This is our New Year theme.

I. A sojourner is at a distance from his relatives. Some of these may be with him, but how many have departed to the land of the blest!

II. A sojourner is sometimes exposed to rough treatment from the natives. His principles, pursuits, exertions, and hopes are hated by the wicked.

III. A sojourner is but little known. His friendship, his companionship, are not courted. He has pleasures and bright anticipations of future bliss, to which sinners are strangers.

IV. A sojourner has no inheritance in the country through which he is traveling. He seeks a "better country"; that is, a heavenly one. Why fix his affections on earthly things, which are transient and unsatisfying.

V. His pilgrimage here is but short and fleeting. He is in this world for a certain season, and for some certain end; he has his work to do, and his measure of suffering to endure. Christ has called him to work in his vineyard, and he will soon call him to his reward.

VI. The Christian must pass the time of his sojourning here in fear. Not in slavish fear, for there is no necessity for that. Rom. 8:15. But in reverential fear—in fear of sin—in fear of offending God—in fear of temptation.

OVER A NEW ROAD

"Ye have not passed this way heretofore." Josh. 3:4.

I. "Ye have not passed this way heretofore." Therefore do not go until you be assured of the divine presence and protection.

II. "Ye have not passed this way heretofore." It is quite right, consequently, to take new ways and untried paths in life.

III. "Ye have not passed this way heretofore." There are some particulars in which this must be true even of the least eventful life.

IV. "Ye have not passed this way heretofore." The suggestion is not human but divine. It is God himself that proposes to guide and defend the lives of man.—Rev. Dr. Joseph Parker.

NEW YEAR ACCOMPANIMENTS

"And the prophet came to the King of Israel, and said unto him, Go strengthen thyself . . . for at the return of the year the King of Syria will come up against thee." 1 Kings 20:22.

What will the new year bring?

I. A renewal of life's battle. The nobility of the life conflict.

II. The return of the same old antagonists. The same old Syrians, with new faces possibly, but certainly with reënforcements.

III. The need for adequate preparation. In strength; in alertness; in self-possession.

IV. The same victorious leadership. To whom hill or valley battlefield is alike, and with whom menacing numbers and parading chariots do not count.

V. The call for individual loyalty and fidelity.—Rev. S. B. Dunn, D.D.

THE JANUARY INVENTORY

"Forgetting the things which are behind and stretching forward to the things which are before." Phil. 3:13.

Here is a practice in which nearly every business man engages about this time of year. Disposing of old stock and antiquated apparatus, he rearranges and directs energies toward the coming year. Is it not well for souls to do likewise? The text:

I. Implies incompleteness; there is room for something better.

II. Permits progress. "The way of life is wonderful; it is by abandonment," e.g., the runner in the stadium puts behind him all preceding successes as well as failures; also superfluous possession.

III. Centers upon greater things:

> "Build thee more stately mansions,
> O my soul,
> As the swift seasons roll;
> Leave thy low-vaulted past."
> —C. R. S.

VISITING THE GREAT YESTERDAYS

"Ask now of the days that are past." Deut. 4:32.

Yes, but what shall we ask about, and what kind of spoil shall we bring back from the treasures of the past? What have we in our purses or in our wallets when we return?

In the life of Lord John Russell I came upon a phrase which set me inquiring about my own habits. In a speech which he made in the House of Commons he said: "We talk too much, I think a great deal too much, of the wisdom of our ancestors. I wish we would imbibe the courage of our ancestors." It is a very suggestive word, and one which may justly lead us to overhaul our ways. For it too often happens that when we go seeking for the wisdom of the past we bring back its prudence and reluctance. We go for counsel and we return with caution. We seek advice on our own new outlook and then we stand in the "good old ways." Now suppose we take Lord John Russell's suggestion, and visit our ancestors in order that we may imbibe their courage, what sort of courage should we bring back to the new demands of our own time?

I. Well, first of all, I think we should have courage to make new trails over untrodden country. That was one of their most shining characteristics. They were not afraid to break new ground. They would even obey the grip of a dumb imperative, not seeing the distant scene. They went forth, "not knowing whither they went"! They were not afraid to take risks with God. They were not afraid to be pioneers into more scrupulous rectitude and larger freedom. They marched out, with trumpets blowing, over the roadless moors, trusting to the guidance of the Lord they served.

II. We, too, are face to face with untraversed country. We have new ground to break. The wilderness is before us, but we think we hear the call of the garden in the very realm of the desert! Shall we venture? Let us imbibe the courage of our ancestors and dare to leave their ways behind as they left the ways of those who had gone before.

III. If we drink the valor of our ancestors we shall have courage to stand by the Truth even when the crowd has gone another way. We can go to the past and talk with Mr. Worldly-Wisdom, or we can have fellowship with Mr. Valiant-for-the-Truth. Mr. Worldly-Wisdom is always in favor of safe measures, and he would go with the majority in the hope of something turning up, "you never know what!" His offered "wisdom" is always small prudence and compromise. But we need the courage of our great ancestors, courage to march with Truth in little companies, courage to "rejoice with the truth," in the absolute assurance that, in spite of all appearances, she marches to inevitable triumph. It is the courage which believes that Truth is God's leaven of the kingdom and therefore indestructible.

IV. And we must imbibe the courage that sees the Captain, and is comparatively careless about everything else. Where is the Lord Jesus Christ in this business? There! Then forward into hardships, forward into light!—REV. JOHN HENRY JOWETT, D.D.

A NEW YEAR EXHORTATION

"Redeeming the time." Eph. 5:6.
I. How time is lost.
  1. By idleness.
  2. By excessive amusements.
  3. By unprofitable talk.
  4. By exclusive attachment to worldly pursuits.
II. How is the time to be redeemed.
  1. By guarding against its loss.
  2. By acting according to rule or method.
  3. By specially attending to the parts of our time that are most precious.
  4. By being habitually engaged in doing good.
III. Why is time to be redeemed.
  1. Because it is short and uncertain.
  2. Because the work to be done in it is important.
  3. Because the days are evil.

THE PATH UNKNOWN

"I will lead them in paths that they have not known." Isa. 42:16.

To God's servants who had forsaken and forgotten him, but who had returned and were penitent. The promise is similar to that in the Epistle to the Romans: "As many as are led by the Spirit of God, they are the children of God." So the benefit of the promise is limited, conditional. The universe is governed according to law. It is not otherwise in religion. Two great laws govern the life of faith, human agency and divine potency. We need guides, because of the perils of the way.

I. Our greatest peril is the possible loss of faith. Men are eagerly inquiring, "Is the universe friendly?"

II. Another peril to our souls is the possible loss of enthusiasm. Wise was that French philosopher who, speaking to young people, said, "Cherish well your enthusiasm, for life robs us of so many we are likely to reach the end of the race without them." Wise, too, that English philosopher who gives us this saying: "No heart is pure until it is passionate; no virtue is safe unless it is enthusiastic."

III. What can save us from loss of faith and loss of fervency? The very thing which God promises in these words, infallible guidance in the ways of life: "Thou wilt show me the path of life." Overconfidence is characteristic of youth. Underconfidence is characteristic of the disillusioned soul. Rational confidence, spiritual boldness, wealth of motive, plenitude of power, undiminished and undiminishing hope—these are the heritage of all who consent to be led along unknown paths by Infinite Wisdom.—REV. CHARLES CARROLL ALBERTSON, D.D.

THE GUIDE THROUGH THE GATE

"So teach us to number our days, that we may apply our hearts to wisdom." Psa. 90:12.

"The longest day at last bends down to evening." On Thursday begins the new year of hope and victory. May we carry no hatred, no evil habit, across the threshold of 1920. All enmities should lie in the grave of the buried past.

I. Every to-morrow should be better than yesterday, crowning the soul with pardon and peace. It is thus that sorrow will be turned to praise, gloom to gladness, the false to the true.

II. One should never neglect or forget the presence of the Unchangeable One who walks with us all the way, leading us over dangerous places and guiding amid the mazes of mystery to his palace home. Continued communion with him can never exhaust the resources of his love, nor reach the limit of his thought, nor measure the beauty of his holiness. Infinity is his dwelling-place; without him there is no being inviting you to an eternal ideal, no face revealing the glory of the Father, no person who can tell you the secret of life, the purpose of the universe, or the way to heart satisfaction amid the unrest and disappointments of time.

III. He alone can preserve thy going out and thy coming in from this time forth and even forevermore. He is the bread of life for soul hunger, the water of life for thirst. In him we are filled with all the fullness of God.

> So, hope-lit New Year, with thy joys uncertain,
>   Whose unsolved mystery none may foretell,
> I calmly trust my God to lift the curtain;
>   Safe in his love, for me 'twill all be well.
>   —Rev. E. S. Caswell, D.D.

GO FORWARD!

"Speak unto the children of Israel, that they go forward." Ex. 14:15.

No word of admonition was oftener heard during the great war than this: "Carry on." It became an almost universal watchword among the English-speaking Allies. A gifted Englishwoman, left a widow with three children, lost two of her dear ones, but wrote to an American friend, "But we must go on."

I. The command, "Go forward!" is of the very essence of victory. This is true in life as in war. "Faint, yet pursuing," is the apostolic resolution. Unnumbered foes may surround us. Siren voices may sing their song of dalliance. Our native inertia may dispose us to cease effort. But the prize is still before us, and so long as earth tempts us or eternity beckons with its perfect hope, our only safety is to keep our loins girded and go forward, however laboriously, however painfully, making sure that in our progress we leave behind no good that can be taken on with us.

II. In the process of spiritual evolution God allows nothing good in old forms to be forsaken—all that is best is incorporated in the new. The best of Judaism is in Christianity. The best in the Old Testament is confirmed in the New.

III. The best things in our earthly life are to be preserved for us in the life to come—faith and love. "Speak unto the children of Israel, that they go forward."—Rev. Charles C. Albertson, D.D.

THE OPEN DOOR

"Behold, I have set before thee an open door." Rev. 3:8.

Endless ideals are open to every man, calling for his consecration and endeavor. No enemy can shut the doors of opportunity our Father has built into his household of worlds.

I. Every door seems larger than the last, opening into vistas vaster and richer. Nothing is impossible or impassable with one who is girded by divine strength.

In nature, the scientist is entering open doors of wondrous vision. How much more the Christian sees in the realm of the supernatural. To-day, womanhood is passing over the threshold of greater usefulness and activity in larger life. Reformers are also realizing ideals that once were in the dim distance. Governments are anticipating grander achievements than ever before accomplished. Out of the lion-eater of war is coming forth sweetness and light.

II. No human can shut God's open doors. In heathendom, not doors but walls, whole sides, are falling down, inviting missionary effort, educational privileges in the whole Christian civilization.

God reveals to the human mind the secret of the telegraph, the telephone and the wireless, that we may speak to each other as we whisper to him. What a wonderful privilege to enter this gallery of communication and fellowship with the world of mankind!

III. Man is God's pioneer, educated and endowed so he can discover his Maker and the mighty forces of His creation. Let us at this New Year time look for the far spiritual horizon, the possible attainments of man in morals, devotion and heroism, more magical and marvelous than the human mind can picture. Infinite possibilities are waiting our coming, glad to be entered upon, discovered and enjoyed.—C.

UNDER SEALED ORDERS

"And he went out, not knowing whither he went." Heb. 11:8.

We know why Abraham was called out of Ur. It is easy to perceive the philosophy of history after four thousand years. But they who find the first paths across the mountains do not know the configuration of the country. They make the maps and we read them. The soldiers who fight in a great battle know little about it until it is over. It is easy for us now to see that it was God's plan to select and train a special race of people for purposes of righteousness; that some one man must be the father of a family whose descendants were to be kept apart from the heathen world, until at last, educated in the worship of God, in the apprehension of his spirituality, his holiness, and his love, they should be capable of furnishing the human ancestry of the Messiah. This was God's purpose in calling Abraham out of Chaldean idolatry. It was impossible for Abraham to see it, but it was not necessary for him to see it. He had faith in God, faith in the invisible world, faith in the future, faith in the hidden reason of his appointed pilgrimage. And so must we have faith in God, and loyally follow our Leader, who says, "What I do, thou knowest not now, but thou shalt know hereafter."

We start out into this new year—year of tremendous possibilities for us individually and for the race—under sealed orders. Have faith in God. Loyally obey his commands. Be courageous and be true.—H.

LEST WE FORGET

"So teach us to number our days, that we may apply our hearts unto wisdom." Psa. 90:12.

Time is a part of eternity. If we are in eternity now, and we are, it is very easy to see that the character of eternity depends upon our use of time.

I. To-day is the only hold we have upon eternity. This hour is a little fragment of eternity. So, eternal issues flow out of our actions now. When shall we ever learn the value of time? A great English scientist who never willingly wasted an hour said, "He who wastes so much as an hour of time has no proper sense of the value of life." The career of every notable man or woman in the world is marked by this characteristic if not explained by it—a keen sense of the value of time.

There is the story of a king, who, unlike most kings, was distinguished for his philosophic view of life. He said, "I count that day lost in which I have done no good thing."

II. We may count that day lost which does not add to our knowledge of God and of his Word, the knowledge of God's habits and his thoughts.

III. That day is lost which leaves no record of word of praise, no prayer of thanks, no thought of gratitude to God.

IV. What is true of prayer is true of praise, that he who prays but rarely, prays not at all. Prayer and praise are not occasional notes in the organ of life, but pipes in the organ, absence of which means serious loss to the music, discord instead of harmony. Here and now we are to work out what God has wrought in us by his Holy Spirit, the passion for goodness and the quest for truth. Only as we redeem the time do we prove ourselves worthy the great redemption. Let us make the great work of the New Year the effort to use time—to improve time.—H.

THE NEW PATH

"Ye have not passed this way heretofore." Josh. 3:4.

I. "Ye have not passed this way heretofore." We are all continually entering upon new paths, which afterwards turn out to be old ones in a new form. Religious experience moves by crises. Israel had not many years before gone across this same desert and been abruptly turned back to Sinai again, because of rebelliousness in their will. Now they were to go to Canaan, but by another route altogether. We are always beginning new experiences. But we should remember that in the year to come we shall find ourselves traveling over much the same road as last year. There will not be anything extraordinary, surprising. Differences will be in details.

II. "Ye have not passed this way heretofore." Then, in the fresh chance God is giving, he offers to be himself our Helper and Friend. We failed last year. The chances of life are still open. Our parts may be played over again.

III. "Ye have not passed this way heretofore." Then, surely, the gifts of God's love have not been appropriated by others, nor exhausted by ourselves.

IV. "Ye have not passed this way heretofore." But, it is well to remember that the ark has not passed this way, either. The Israelites were to accept God's guidance implicitly. They were to bear the ark to the front and follow it without any question. It makes life a new thing to put the ark on before it.

V. "Ye have not passed this way heretofore." Now, with

the ark in front, "the joy of the Lord is your strength."—
Rev. Charles S. Robinson, D.D.

THE NEW DATE

"This month shall be unto you the beginning of months; it shall be the first month of the year." Exodus 12:2.

We have here a new event, a new starting point—a new epoch, and therefore, a new era. That event was emancipation, a redemption, an exodus. There were centuries behind of exile and servitude; of that experience which has been so characteristic of Israel, a sojourning which was no naturalization, a dwelling amongst, without becoming of, another nation; estrangement, therefore isolation, solitude, even in populous cities, and amidst teeming multitudes. Now, all this is behind them. They are to quit the homeless home. Egypt behind, Sinai before, Canaan beyond, this is the exact account of the position of Israel when the words of the text were spoken. Redemption was the starting point of the new; from it all that follows shall take a new character, and a new life.

I. The idea of a new start is naturally attractive to all of us. We are fatigued, we are wearied, we are dissatisfied, and justly so, with the time past of our lives. We long for a gift of amnesty and oblivion.

II. There are senses in which this is impossible. The continuity of life cannot be broken. There is a continuity, a unity, an identity, which annihilation could only destroy.

III. "The beginning of months" is made by an exodus. Redemption is the groundwork of the new life. If there is in any of us a real desire for change, we must plant our feet firmly on Redemption.

IV. When we get out of Egypt we must remember that there is still Sinai in front, with its thunderings and voices. We have to be schooled and disciplined by processes not joyous but grievous. These processes cannot be hurried, they must take their time. Here we must expect everything that is changeful, and unresting, and unreposeful, within as without. But he who has promised will perform. He who has redeemed will save. He who took charge will also bring through.—Rev. C. J. Vaughan.

A HAPPY NEW YEAR PROBLEM

"Be ye steadfast, unmovable, always abounding in the work of the Lord." 1 Cor. 15:58.

The beginning of the year is the occasion for new policies in business. Why not new programs in life? Here is one which is truly "happy" because of:

I. Tight Adjustment of Life. Original idea of "happy"? "Happily married." Lot failed in adjustment, while Abraham grew into closer blissful friendship with God.

II. Increasing Stability. Tranquil life journey. President Wilson not afraid of "unlucky" thirteens because of his poise.

III. Fruitfulness. Abounding life always follows right planting (adjustment).

IV. Companionships in higher and more congenial vocation: "Work of the Lord."

V. Certain outcome guaranteed by divine integrity.

SHIFTING SCENERY

"The fashion of the world passeth away." 1 Cor. 7:31.

The image is drawn from a shifting scene in a play represented on a stage. Human life, indeed, is a drama, and its conditions and mutations are merely the stage-settings that are ever shifting.

I. The New Year season is a good time to consider the serious import of living. To be actors in earnest in a play that is real.

II. The New Year season is a good time to discriminate between what is essential and what is stage-setting and scenery.

III. The New Year season is a good time to play a part fitting to the scenery of the occasion. To repent, to resolve, to renew as the personal need demands.—REV. S. B. DUNN, D.D.

PART V: EVANGELISTIC TEXTS AND THEMES

Bring Them In: "Go out and compel them to come in." Luke 14:23.

Knowing and Doing: "To him that knoweth to do good and doeth it not, it is sin." Jas. 4:17.

Christ First, and Christ Forever: "Seek first the kingdom of God and his righteousness." Matt. 6:33. Make this the motto of your life. 1. Christ first in your intellectual life. 2. Christ first in your emotional life. 3. Christ first in your domestic life. 4. Christ first in your social life. 6. Christ first in your civic life. 7. Christ first in your church life. 8. Christ first in your personal religious life. Crown him Lord. Crown him Lord of all.

Personal Work: John 1:29. 1. Responsibility of personal work. 2. Advantages of personal work. 3. Hindrances to personal work. 4. Opportunities for personal work. 5. Equipment for personal work. Will you now resolve and act upon Isa. 6:8?

All Sinners May be Saved: John 6:37. 1. Saved from sin. 2. Saved by Christ. 3. Saved for service.

Poverty to Plenty: Isa. 55:1-7. This chapter describes the pilgrimage from Poverty to Plenty via Pardon. 1. The land of spiritual poverty. 2. The land of spiritual plenty. 3. Pardon the way from poverty to plenty.

Become a Christian—Why Not? Matt. 4:17.

How to Help the Unsaved: "Behold the Lamb of God, which taketh away the sin of the world." John 1:29.

When to Believe: "Choose you this day whom you will serve." Josh. 24:15.

The Gracious Invitation: "Come, for all things are now ready." Luke 14:17.

The Very Best Time: "Behold, now is the accepted time, behold, now is the day of salvation." 2 Cor. 6:2.

What is True Penitence? Psa. 51. 1. Repentance is sor-

EVANGELISTIC TEXTS AND THEMES

row. 2. Repentance is humility. 3. It involves confession. 4. It is turning from sin. 5. It leads to God.

Incentives to Work: 1. Without Christ men are lost. 1 John 5:1. 2. Save a soul from death. James 5:20. 3. Shine as the stars. Dan. 12:3. 4. Crown of life. Rev. 2:10.

God's Grace: Eph. 2:4-7. God is a God. 1. Rich in mercy. 2. A God of great love. 3. A God of salvation. 4. A God of grace. 5. A God of kindness.

The Source of Power: "But ye shall receive power, when the Holy Spirit is come upon you." Acts 1:8.

The Self-Complacent Church Member: "What doth it profit, my brethren, if a man say he hath faith, but have not works? Can that faith save him?" Jas. 2:14.

Why Decide Now? "And while they went away to buy, the bridegroom came; and they that were ready went in with him to the marriage feast; and the door was shut." Matt. 25:10.

The House of the Wide-Open Door: Isa. 55:1-13.

Done Suddenly: 2 Chron. 33:26.

Begin Now: 2 Cor. 6:1-10.

An Invitation Slighted: "But they made light of it." Matt. 22:5.

An Open Confession: "I will declare what he hath done for my soul." Psa. 66:16.

Christ's Call for You: "The Master is come and calleth for thee." John 11:28.

The Heart Asked For: "My son, give me thy heart." Prov. 23:26.

Strange but True: "Yet there is room." Luke 14:22.

Prayer a Good Sign: "Behold he prayeth." Acts 9:21.

A Good Resolution: "I will arise and go to my father." Luke 15:18.

Conditions of Discipleship: Luke 9:23. Deny self. Take up cross daily. Follow me.

Acquaintance with God: "Acquaint now thyself with him and be at peace; thereby good shall come unto thee." Job 22:21.

The Supreme Question: "What shall I do to be saved?" Acts 16:30.

Making Excuse: "And they all, with one consent, began to make excuse." Luke 14:1.

Come! Come! Come! "The Spirit and the bride say, Come." Rev. 22:17.

God's Quiet Work: "Whose heart the Lord opened." Acts 16:14.

Seeking the Lord Our Immediate Duty: "It is time to seek the Lord." Hosea 10:12.

The Feast Prepared: "Come, for all things are now ready." Luke 14:17.

The Spirit of Adoption: "And because ye are sons, God hath sent forth his spirit into your hearts, crying, Abba, Father." Gal. 4:6.

The Common Salvation: "Beloved, when I gave all diligence to write unto you of the common salvation," etc. Jude 3.

Seeking God: "O God, thou art my God, early will I seek thee." Psa. 63:1.

The Day of Salvation: "Behold now is the accepted time; behold now is the day of salvation." 2 Cor. 6:2.

Christ Knocking at the Heart: "Behold, I stand at the door and knock," etc. Rev. 3:20.

PART VI: EVANGELISTIC SERMON OUTLINES

MAKING EXCUSE

"And they all, with one consent, began to make excuse." Luke 14: 1.
I. Notice the provision made—"All things are now ready."
 1. On earth. Redemption provided—promise recorded—Holy Spirit prepared to sanctify.
 2. In heaven. Glory secured.
II. The invitation addressed. "Come."
 1. Who are bid to come? All to whom God sends the message. A great privilege.
 2. What does it invite us to do? Not to prepare a feast, but to come to one already provided and receive it as a blessing to be desired.
III. The conduct too generally pursued. "To make excuse."
 1. The Jews. Did not find in him what they expected in the Messiah.
 2. The Gentiles. Did not like the want of philosophy in the gospel; and esteemed it foolishness.
 3. The world. Men of the world are too busy to give religion serious thought.
 4. The young and the frivolous. It forbids their pleasures.
 5. The middle aged, etc. Have too many cares and troubles to attend to it.

Then, if we fail to find mercy at last, it will not be God's fault. He has provided and invited, but we have neglected. What a mercy that the invitation still says, "Come."

A NEW CREATION

"If any man be in Christ, he is a new creature." 2 Cor. 5:17.

I. His judgments are new. His judgment of himself, of God, of the purpose of life, of happiness, is formed by truth.

II. His purposes are new. His great purpose is to serve God. Every other purpose is subservient to this one grand master-purpose of his being new.

III. His desires are new. "Whom have I in heaven but thee?" etc.

IV. His conversation is new. He spake of things above.

V. His actions are new. He walks in Christ.

STEPS TO CHRIST

"I will arise and go to my Father." Luke 15:18.

Let us consider a few of the steps necessary for the sinner in turning to God.

I. Conviction. He must feel his guilt, that he is a sinner, that he has sinned against God, and as such has no part in his kingdom. Do not mistake conviction for conversion. We have often seen souls buried in tears through conviction, who, through acceptance into church fellowship or the partaking of the Lord's Supper, were considered "consecrated to God." Conviction is nothing more than the opening of the eyes to behold the condition and real danger of the soul.

II. Being convicted of the error of his way, it requires action. He must have a desire for forgiveness; a willingness to seek redemption in Jesus Christ. This evidence he shows by coming to the altar of prayer, or some other such step.

III. Faith. He must have faith in Jesus Christ, that his blood is sufficient to cleanse from all sin.

IV. A complete surrender to God. Not for a day, nor for a night, but once and for all: "From this day on until death will I serve thee." No hidden sins or pleasures of this life can be withheld from God; it requires a full surrender, and then, and then only, the blessing will come.—REV. J. F. GRUBE.

WHAT TIME IS IT?

"It is time to seek the Lord." Hos. 10:12.

I. It is time to seek the Lord. A call to the sinner.

II. It is high time to awake out of sleep. Rom. 13:11. A warning to the saint.

III. It is time for thee, Lord, to work. Psa. 119:126. A prayer to the Lord.

> Time was is past, thou canst not it recall;
> Time is thou hast: employ the portion small;
> Time future is not, and may never be;
> Time present is the only time for thee.
> —Rev. Charles Edwards.

"REMEMBER JESUS CHRIST"

I. Why? Because Jesus Christ loves you and died for you. "This is a faithful saying and worthy of all acceptation, that Jesus Christ came into the world to save sinners." 1 Tim. 1:15.

II. How?
1. By receiving him. "As many as received him, to them gave he power to become the sons of God." Jno. 1:12. To receive Christ means to accept the sacrifice that he made for you by his death on Calvary.
2. By confessing him. "If thou shalt confess with thy mouth the Lord Jesus, and shalt believe in thine heart that God hath raised him from the dead, thou shalt be saved." Rom. 10:9.

CARE FOR SOULS

"No man careth for my soul." Psa. 142:4.

I. What is it to care for the souls of others.
1. To have a firm conviction of the value of their souls.
2. To feel apprehension of the danger to which their souls are exposed.

3. To cherish tender solicitude for the welfare of their souls.
4. To make zealous exertion to bring them to the Saviour.

II. Who are they who ought to care for the souls of others?
1. The ministers of the Gospel.
2. The members of the Church.
3. Heads of families.
4. Sabbath School teachers.

III. What are the evils of not caring for the souls of others?
1. How cruel!
2. How ungrateful!
3. How criminal!
4. How fatal!

CHURCH PROSPERITY

"O Lord, I beseech Thee, send now prosperity." Psa. 118:25.

I. God is the source of church prosperity.
II. God is the source of church prosperity through prayer.
III. In what does church prosperity consist?
1. An earnest membership.
2. A learning membership.
3. A membership that conscientiously uses the means of grace.
4. A working membership—all at it and always at it.
5. A membership possessing a missionary spirit.
6. A membership that heartily supports the institutions of religion at home.
7. A membership that walks in separation from the world.

GIVING THE HEART

"My son, give me thine heart." Prov. 23:26.
I. What is implied in the giving of the heart to God?
1. That it is given sincerely.

2. That it is given entirely.
3. That it is given freely.
4. That it is given forever.

II. Why the heart should be given to God.
  1. He is worthy of it.
  2. He has a title to it.
  3. He demands it.
  4. He will bless it.

THE GREAT QUESTION

"Dost thou believe on the Son of God?" John 9:35.

The chapter relates the extraordinary cure of the man born blind. By this miracle Jesus declared himself to be the Son of God with power. Great was the miracle for the body—but a greater miracle was effected for the soul.

I. The object of faith. "The Son of God." His Divinity and Godhead appear from the following considerations: From the express declarations of scripture. From the perfections ascribed to him, which are peculiar to deity. Eternity; "Before Abraham was I am." Unchangeableness; "Jesus Christ, the same yesterday," etc. Heb. 13:8.

Almighty power; "Christ the power of God." 1 Cor. 1:24. Infinite wisdom; "Light of the world"; "the only wise God." Infinite love; "Ye know the grace," etc. 2 Cor. 8:9. Creation is ascribed to him. And so is redemption. From the works which he did. These could not have been done by a person inferior to God. Such as searching the heart, and perceiving what was in it, healing the sick and raising the dead, the forgiving of sins.

II. The nature of faith. "Dost thou believe?" It is not merely giving credit to the Scriptures. It is not merely confessing the doctrines of any particular creed. It is not a mere professing of faith. Faith is confidence, trust or reliance upon the sacrificial death of Christ for salvation and everlasting Life. It is the act of the heart by which we heartily welcome him into our souls. The scriptures figuratively represent this grace, as beholding him, or looking to him; it is coming to Christ, laying hold of him, receiving him, resting on him, etc.

III. The effects of faith. "Dost thou believe on the Son of God?" It does not relate to others, but to ourselves. It does not refer to mere information or opinion, but to faith. It refers not either to past or future, but to the present: "Dost thou believe?"

THE SEEKING SHEPHERD

Luke 15:3, 7.
I. What is sought? The straying sheep. V. 4. Isa. 53:6 is true of you. There is an inborn tendency in you that leads you away from God. How long you have strayed; how far you have strayed; how often you have strayed; prevents not the Good Shepherd from seeking you.

II. How many are sought? One. V. 4. Only one sheep lost, but that one calls forth all the love of the seeking shepherd. Love counts not by numbers, but by worth.

III. Why he seeks. The sheep is his own; and without him it is fatally and finally lost.

IV. How long he seeks. "Until" he find it. The shepherd sought "until" he found his sheep; the woman swept her house "until" she found her silver; the father loved and looked "until" his son returned.—Rev. T. S. Henderson.

ACQUAINTANCE WITH GOD

"Acquaint now thyself with him, and be at peace; thereby good shall come unto thee." Job 22:21.

I. The nature of acquaintance with God. "Acquaintance" implies not mere personal knowledge, but that intimacy and familiarity which subsists between one friend and another. Psa. 55:15; 101:4.

II. The means of acquaintance with God. Enlightenment by the Spirit. Faith in the sacrifice of Christ. Believing prayer. Constant supplications to God through Christ will produce real and precious intimacy with him. The constant cherishing of the Spirit's influences. The study of God in his word, in his house, etc. By frequent intercourses with Christians.

III. The season for commencing acquaintance with God. "Now."

The present time is the best. The present time is claimed by God himself. "To-day, if ye will hear his voice," etc. It is the only time of which you are certain.
  IV. The happy results of acquaintance with God.
    1. Peace. God is the God of peace, and all his people enjoy it.
    2. Good. Temporal good. Providential goodness. Spiritual good. The gifts and graces of the Spirit. Divine support in every trial, etc. Heavenly good. Eternal good.

EXCUSES

"They all with one consent began to make excuse." Luke 14: 18.

I. An excuse implies guilt. It is the acknowledgment of an unperformed duty, with a request for pardon. Our capacity for action in a life full of limitations is such that we are occasionally forced to leave undone or defer doing what we ought to do. In such a case we feel justified in asking to be excused. But our excuses become insults to the party to whom they are offered when we exalt a minor duty above a great and essential one, when by our very excuses we minimize the importance of the one thing needful.

II. In the parable of the great supper earthly interests are set against the divine call of grace by the unwilling guests. Does the Lord, then, mean that in order to become Christians we must let weeds grow on our farms, suffer our cattle to perish, and break a lawful marriage engagement? Indeed not; all these things have the divine approval and do not in themselves conflict with the profession and practice of Christianity. Peter was engaged in plying his trade as a fisherman when the Lord asked for the loan of his boat, and Peter incurred no loss by suspending for a season his regular occupation.

III. Godliness is profitable unto all things, and has the promise of this life and that which is to come. But foolish shortsightedness, carnal indifference, and plain aversion to holy things make men misunderstand completely in which direction their best interests lie.

IV. It is this materialistic, thoroughly secular spirit that the Lord attacks in the present parable. As a servant of the Lord and rejoicing in God's favor, how much better would the farmer have enjoyed his new field, the cattle-raiser his oxen, the newly-married the holy estate of matrimony! Justly the Lord of the banquet is angry at such ruthless contempt of his gracious overtures to sinners.—D.

PRICE OF REDEMPTION

"For ye are bought with a price." 1 Cor. 6: 20.

I. "Jesus paid it all" is welcome news to insolvent debtors. When we were slaves to sin, he purchased our pardon. When we were stained with guilt, he opened the fountain of cleansing. Wanderers in a far country, he himself became our way home; yea, he walks with us in sweet companionship and blessed guidance.

II. What can we do for him who bankrupted himself, became poor that we through his poverty might become rich? Shall we despise our benefactor, refuse his gifts, deny his loving-kindness, reject his offer of liberty? Such ingratitude would be indescribable folly. What child could thus push aside the mother who bore him, loved and reared him, and ever watched over him? But a mother may forget her child—he will not forget thee.

> "I gave my life for thee;
> What hast thou given for me?"

III. We have peace by his blood, ransom by his cross, heaven by his love. Your freedom is purchased, but, alas, you may love slavery better than freedom, the serfdom of Egypt better than the glory of Canaan, the bondage of Satan better than the liberty of the sons of God.

Well may we acclaim, "Blessed Jesus, who bore our sins, carried our sorrows, was touched with the feelings of our infirmities, endured the cross for us, was glad to pay the price of our redemption that we might live unto him and with him in the everlasting life."—C.

CHRIST WAITING

"Behold, I stand at the door and knock," etc. Rev. 3:20.

These words are addressed to careless professors. However applicable to sinners, they are not addressed to them. These words produce widely different emotions. Sorrow, that the door is shut. Joy, that he knocks and waits. Wonder.

I. What bars the door? The 17th verse answers: 1. Riches. Prosperity in the world too often makes the heart callous to the voice of Christ. "If riches increase," etc. 2. Indolence, verse 15. Beware of lukewarmness. Earnest hearts alone give Christ a hearty welcome. 3. Pride. "I have need of nothing." Self-satisfaction is incompatible with devotion. He who prays aright, prays as a pensioner.

II. Why is it not opened? Is it that they do not hear his voice? Have they no desire to see him? Why is your heart shut? Is it not because you have dwelling within that which Christ abhors, that you are loth to part with? Darling sins. Unworthy motives. Sinful desires. Oh, let him in; he will, he must, drive out these polluters of the Holy Spirit's temple.

III. Who knocks without? Thy Friend! thy Saviour! thy God! On him are marks of what he has borne for you. In his hand are blessings he intends for you.

IV. What is his errand? 1. He seeks communion. He would speak to you and have you speak to him. 2. He seeks refreshment. For himself, for you. The heart when Christ dwells therein knows no want. Here Jesus sees of the travail of his soul, and is satisfied.

V. Is he to be admitted? 1. If so, it must be at once. 2. With a hearty welcome.

Jesus knocks; listen. Open.

A SPIRIT-FILLED LIFE

"Be filled with the Spirit." Eph. 5:18.

The Holy Spirit is mentioned 90 times in the Old Testament, and 264 times in the New Testament. There are some distinctions to be borne in mind.

I. There is a difference between being indwelt of the Spirit and being filled with the Spirit. Every Christian is in-

dwelt of the Spirit, but every Christian is not infilled with the Spirit.
  II. The infilling of the Spirit is always subsequent to the indwelling of the Spirit.
  III. The infilling of the Spirit is always one of degree.
  IV. It is for all Christians.
  V. There is a difference between being full of the Spirit and being filled with the Spirit.
  If you are living a Spirit-filled life the following things will be true of you:
    1. You will have an increased knowledge.
       (a) Of your own salvation.
       (b) Of the will of God as it pertains to what he would have you do.
       (c) Of the Word of God. The Bible will be illuminated.
    2. You will have increased development of character.
    3. You will have an increased power of service.
—From a sermon by REV. WM. E. BIEDERWOLF, D.D.

A BLESSED WHOSOEVER

"For whosoever shall call upon the name of the Lord shall be saved." Rom. 10:13.
  I. The Blessing.
    1. Salvation from guilt.
    2. Salvation from sin.
    3. Salvation from misery.
  II. The Duty.
    1. Call on the proper object.
    2. Call through the proper medium.
    3. Call by the proper aid.
    4. Call with the proper dispositions.
  III. The Person.
    1. Of whatsoever nation.
    2. Of whatsoever rank.
    3. Of whatsoever age or sex.
    4. Of whatsoever mental ability or culture.
    5. Of whatsoever moral character.

THE WORTH OF THE SOUL

"For what shall it profit a man, if he shall gain the whole world, and lose his own soul?" Mark 8:36.
  I. The value of the soul.
   1. Its power and capacities.
   2. Its immortality.
   3. The plan of its redemption.
   4. The conflict it occasions in the universe.
  II. The loss of the soul.
   1. Its nature;—the loss, not of being, but of holiness, of happiness, of heaven, of hope.
   2. The ways in which it may be incurred;—through open infidelity, through gross vice, through formal profession, through sheer carelessness.
  III. The impossibility of compensating for the loss of the soul by the gain of the world.
   1. The gain is problematical; the loss is unavoidable.
   2. The gain is ideal; the loss is real.
   3. The gain is temporary; the loss is final and irretrievable.

OUR BEST HELPER

"I will help thee." Isa. 41:10.
I and thee. Two persons. The person speaking is Jesus our God who can help, and the person spoken to means everybody who needs his help and seeks it.
  I. He is always near to help.
  II. He is always able to help.
  III. He is always willing to help.
  IV. He is always kind in helping.

CONTINUING

  I. In the love of Christ. John 15:9.
  II. In the Word of Christ. John 8:31.
  III. In the grace of God. Acts 13:43.
  IV. In the faith. Acts 14:22. 2 Tim. 4:2, 6-8.
  V. In the things learned. 2 Tim. 3:14-15.

THREE CONDITIONS OF SOUL

Psalm 63.
I. My soul thirsteth—desire. V. 8.
II. My soul shall be satisfied—decision. V. 15.
III. My soul followeth hard—devotion. V. 24.

THE CALLS OF CHRIST

I. Follow me. John 1:43.
II. Come to me. Matt. 11:28.
III. Learn of me. Matt. 11:29.
IV. Abide in me. John 15:4.

ALMOST A CHRISTIAN

"Thou art not far from the kingdom of God." Mark 12:34.

To the almost-a-Christian:
I. Describe him.
  1. He may have a considerable knowledge of religion.
  2. He may have strong convictions of sin.
  3. He may have a good reputation among men.
  4. He may have freedom from many of the vices by which he was once enslaved.
  5. He may have a liking for the public and private exercises of devotion as forms.
II. Warn him.
  1. He will not, in his present state, attain the blessings of salvation.
  2. If lost, his ruin will be all the greater because of his attainments.

"Not far from" is not "in" the kingdom. But it is a hopeful condition, a condition of present and blessed opportunity. Enter. Enter now.

"WE BEAR THE NAME OF CHRISTIANS"

"And the disciples were called Christians first in Antioch." Acts 11:26.

I. The origin of the name.
   1. If it was imposed by God, it shows that he is solicitous to fix the proper aspect in which his people are viewed.
   2. If it was assumed by the disciples, it shows that they regarded Christ as the center of their religion.
   3. If it was affixed by the Jews or heathen, it shows that the natural mind has no just appreciation of spiritual excellence.
II. The import of the name.
   1. A believer in Christ.
   2. A lover of Christ.
   3. An imitator of Christ.
   4. A servant of Christ.
   5. An expectant of Christ.

CHRIST AT THE DOOR OF THE HEART

"Behold! I stand at the door and knock; if any man hear my voice, and open the door, I will come in to him, and will sup with him, and he with me." Rev. 3:20.

I. Consider what Jesus Christ does. He "stands at the door." He displays wonderful patience—he stands and knocks. Many do not hear. They are insensible. They are negligent and undetermined. They fear the world. They are influenced by ambition.

II. What Jesus Christ promises. "If any man hear my voice."
   1. The characters interested in the promise. They who by the influence of his Spirit hear his voice, and open the door, i.e., who repent, obey his word, and by faith receive him into their hearts.
   2. The promise itself. "I will come in to him," i.e., be reconciled, grant him pardon and acceptance, comfort, strengthen, and fill him with all spiritual graces. When Christ comes he brings peace, for he is the prince of peace; joy, for he is the source of joy; hope, for he is the foundation of hope; life, for he is the cause of life; salvation, for he is the author of salvation.

"I will sup with him and he with me." By this is intended the mutual joy which he has with the believer and the believer with him. "He will sup with me." Christ will cause the believer to experience that joy which his grace sheds upon the souls who love him, and which arises from a sense of the pardon of sin, reconciliation with God, adoption, complete redemption, perfect deliverance and eternal glorification.—P. D.

PART VII: LINCOLN'S BIRTHDAY TEXTS AND THEMES

Great by Great Service: "Whoever will be great among you, let him be your minister, and whosoever will be chief among you, let him be your servant." Matt. 20:26, 27.

The Serviceable Life: "Remember unto me, O my God, for good, all that I have done for this people." Neh. 5:19.

Lincoln, the American Great-Heart: "Moreover thou shalt provide out of all the people able men, such as fear God, men of truth, hating covetousness; and place such men over them." Ex. 18:21.

Lincoln Was Blest to Bless: "The Lord raised up a deliverer." Judges 3:9.

Lincoln Longed to Promote Peace: "My soul hath long dwelt with him that hateth peace. I am for peace, but when I speak, they are for war." Psa. 34:14.

Lincoln a Lover of Peace: "Be of good courage, and let us play the man for our people, and for the cities of our God; and the Lord do that which seemeth him good." 2 Sam. 10:12.

Lincoln's Faith: "He endured as seeing him who is invisible." Heb. 11:27.

The Character of Lincoln: "As a man is, so is his strength." Judges 8:21.

Lincoln and His Life Lessons: "The memory of the just is blessed." Prov. 10:7.

Lincoln's Growth Under Pressure: "Cast down, but not destroyed."

Prayer for the Nation: "Do good in thy good pleasure unto Zion, build thou the walls of Jerusalem." Psa. 34:14.

Lincoln's Patriotism: "Zebulun was a people that jeoparded their lives unto the death." Judges 5:18.

Lincoln, a Lover of Peace: "Seek peace and pursue it." Psa. 34:14.

Lincoln, the Emancipator: "The same did God send to be a ruler and deliverer." Acts 7:35.

The Memory of Lincoln: "The memory of the just is blessed." Prov. 10:7.

Lincoln's Counsel of Courage: "Be of good courage, and let us play the men for our people, and for the cities of our God; and the Lord do that which seemeth him good." 2 Sam. 10:12.

Lessons from War-Times: "I will hear what God the Lord will speak; for he will speak peace unto his people and to his saints; but let them not turn again to folly." Psa. 85:8.

Social Peace: "See that ye fall not out by the way." Gen. 45:24.

The Citizen Prophet: "I have ordained thee a prophet unto the nations." Jeremiah 1:4.

Lincoln: the Man and the Message: "The memory of the just is blessed." Prov. 10:7.

The Achieving Life: "The same did God send to be a ruler and deliverer." Acts 7:35.

The Price of Liberty: "With a great sum obtained I this freedom." Acts 22:28.

Lincoln as a Leader: "Moreover thou shalt provide out of all the people, able men, such as fear God, men of truth, hating covetousness; and place such over them, to be rulers of thousands, and rulers of hundreds, rulers of fifties and rulers of tens." Exodus 18:21.

PART VIII: LINCOLN'S BIRTHDAY SERMON OUTLINES

LINCOLN

"Commit thy way unto Jehovah: trust also in him, and he will bring it to pass." Psa. 37:5.

I. The greatness of his work. Seen in: 1. Victory in great Civil War. 2. Emancipation of the slaves. 3. Preservation of the Union.

II. In and for all this—his reliance upon God for accomplishing his work (see extract from his letter to Quakers of Iowa, and inaugural address).

III. The elements which such reliance furnishes for all lives. 1. Strength.—Sir Galahad:

"My strength is as the strength of ten,
Because my heart is pure."

2. Determination. The spirit in which the power is used. 3. Courage, especially moral courage. 4. Hope; see Lincoln's second inaugural.

PATRIOTISM

"Zebulun was a people that jeopardized their lives unto the death." Judges 5:18.

I. What is patriotism? Love of country, even to the utmost of self-sacrifice.

II. How cultivated? 1. By observance of days which commemorate deeds. Patriots' Day, Independence Day, Memorial Day. 2. By study of heroic lives; Lincoln, Washington, Nathan Hale. 3. By national songs—the "Marseillaise," "Watch on the Rhine," "America," "God Save the King." 4. By appreciating our national advantages. 5. By entering into the spirit of our national mission.

III. How expressed? 1. By loyal support of a righteous government. 2. By contending against any great public evil. 3. By supporting the movement for good citizenship. 4. By home missions. 5. By fostering a true, world-wide mission.

THE AMERICAN GREAT-HEART

"Moreover, thou shalt provide out of all the people able men, such as fear God, men of truth, hating covetousness; and place such over them." Ex. 18:21.

I. Lincoln was a man with a great heart, full of human affection, sympathizing with the sorrowing and oppressed, humble, God-fearing, believing, prayerful. His parents and grandparents had been members of the church, religious and devout. Mr. Lincoln was outspoken as to his faith in God, and in the power of prayer. He said that he gave his heart to the Saviour when Gettysburg came. He had laid all before God at that crisis as Washington had at Valley Forge.

II. He was a man who loved righteousness and hated injustice and oppression. God gave him an opportunity, such as few men have ever had, for striking down iniquity, and before his blow it fell to its death. Most masterfully he executed the duties of his office as chief executive of the nation. The trials and sorrows of the people almost broke his heart, and the heavy burdens almost pressed him to the ground. He was a man whom God mightily used, and whom the people tenderly loved and revered. As was said of William of Orange: "While he lived he was the guiding star of a whole brave nation, and when he died the little children cried in the streets."

THE GREATNESS OF LINCOLN

I. Lincoln was great as a common citizen among the common people. His humanitarian heart, ready wit, genuine honesty, and practical common sense commanded their confidence and esteem. He loved the common people, believed in them, and was proud to be reckoned as one of them. His quaint utterance, "God must be a lover of the common people, or he would not have made so many of them," is proof of this.

LINCOLN'S BIRTHDAY SERMON OUTLINES

II. Lincoln was great in his magnanimity and patriotism. In evidence of this the words of President Roosevelt are to the point. He said: "In reading his works and speeches, his addresses, one is struck by the fact that as he went higher and higher all personal bitterness seemed to die out of him. In the Lincoln-Douglas debates one can still catch now and then a note of personal antagonism. The man was in the arena, and as the blows were given you could see now and then that he had a feeling against his antagonist. When he became President and faced the crises that he had to face, from that time on I do not think that you can find an expression, a speech of Lincoln's, a word of Lincoln's, written or spoken, in which bitterness is shown to any man. His devotion to the cause was so great that he neither could nor would have feeling against any individual."

III. Lincoln was great in his firm conviction that God rules in the kingdoms of men, and that in the great crises which come to nations he interposes and directs to certain results in vindication of truth and righteousness. In proof of this take the closing sentences of his second inaugural address: "Earnestly do we hope, fervently do we pray that this terrible scourge of war may soon be removed, yet if God wills that it be prolonged until all the wealth piled by the bondman's two hundreds years of unrequited toil be sunk, and every drop of blood drawn by the lash be atoned for by one drawn by the sword, yet as was said three thousand years ago, so must it still be said: 'The judgments of the Lord are true and righteous altogether.'"

IV. Lincoln was great as a master in the simple, eloquent use of the English language. In this respect his addresses and state papers commanded the plaudits of the best critics. As a sample we have but to mention his ever memorable Gettysburg address, which has taken, and will ever hold, its place as a classic wherever the language is spoken.

V. Lincoln was great as President. Of his ability as such, James Ford Rhodes puts the case admirably as follows: "Lincoln is the ideal President, in that he led public sentiment, represented it, and followed it. 'I claim not to have controlled events,' he said, 'but confess plainly that events have controlled me.' During his term of office he was one day called 'very weak,' and the next 'a tyrant'; and when his whole work was done, a careful survey of it could bring one only to the conclusion that he knew when to follow and when to lead. He was in complete touch with popular sentiment, and divined with nicety when he could take a step in advance. He made an effort to keep on good terms with Congress, and he differed with that body reluctantly, although, when necessity came, decisively. While he had consideration for those who did not agree with him, and while he acted always with a regard to proportion, he was nevertheless a strong and self-confident executive."

The good and the great, the patriotic, and the God-fearing still cherish, and will ever continue to cherish his memory and esteem his character as long as men love liberty, truth and honesty and the great Republic he saved holds its place among the nations of the earth.—R. T.

PART IX: WASHINGTON'S BIRTHDAY TEXTS AND THEMES

The Good Ruler: "Thou shalt provide out of all the people able men, such as fear God, men of truth, hating covetousness, and placing such over them to be rulers." Ex. 18:21.

A Christian Man in Public Life: 2 Chron. 17:3,4; 29:27-29.

The Greatest Greatness: "He that is slow to anger is better than the mighty; and he that ruleth his spirit than he that taketh a city." Prov. 16:32.

Washington's Combination of Strength and Beauty: "Upon the top of the pillars was lily work." 1 Kings 7:32.

Patriotic Men the Prop of the Nation: "How is the strong staff broken and the beautiful rod!" Jeremiah 48:17.

The Nation's Deliverer: "The men of Israel said unto Gideon, rule thou over us, both thou and thy son also, for thou hast delivered us from the hand of Midian." Judges 8:22.

Washington's Wisdom: "Now, there was found a poor wise man, and he by his wisdom delivered the city." Eccl. 9:15.

The Just Ruler: "And all Israel feared the king, for they saw that the wisdom of God was in him to do judgment." 1 Kings 3:28.

A Great Man: "There was none like me before me, neither after me shall any rise like unto me." Solomon.

A Man of Understanding: "By the good hand of God upon us, they brought us a man of understanding." Ezra 8:18.

Sent of God: "The same did God send to be a ruler and deliverer." Acts 7:35.

The Discreet and Wise Ruler: "Look out a man discreet and wise, and set him over the people." Gen. 41:33.

Washington the Model Citizen: "Wherefore then were ye not afraid to speak against my servant Moses?" Num. 12:8.

Washington as a National Asset: "And I will make of thee a great nation, and I will bless thee, and make thy name great; and thou shalt be a blessing." Gen. 12:2.

The Foresight of Washington: "Yea, thou shalt see thy children's children, and peace upon Israel." Psa. 128:6.

Washington as a Leader: Moreover, thou shalt provide out of all the people able men, such as fear God, men of truth, hating covetousness; and place such over them." Ex. 18:21.

Washington a Man of Loftiest Purposes: "The Lord spake with Moses face to face." Ex. 33:11.

The Ever-growing Influence of Washington: "The path of the just is as the shining light, that shineth more and more unto the perfect day." Prov. 4:18.

The Living Name: "The memory of the just is blessed, but the name of the wicked shall rot." Prov. 10:7.

A Study of Heroes: "Not by might, nor by power, but by my Spirit, saith the Lord of Hosts." Zech. 4:6.

Washington Our First Citizen: "Wherefore then were ye not afraid to speak against my servant Moses?" Num. 12:8.

PART X: WASHINGTON'S BIRTHDAY SERMON OUTLINES

THE LIVING WASHINGTON

Washington is not dead. He has risen to greater influence and higher service and by his life will influence thousands for their good.

Washington is invisible, yet potent, and stands to-day behind senators and representatives. His words are uttered in legislative halls and his thoughts are voiced with emphasis in many public addresses amid the turbulence of political campaigns. As often as we have looked into his benign face and listened to his fraternal counsels, our sectional discords have disappeared, petty ambitions have subsided, timid doubts have vanished and selfish purposes have receded. He stands to-day above the din and confusion of the earth's battlefield and the turmoils and contentions of civic strife and life and speaks to the heated and scrambling throng and bids us all to be manly, thoughtful, patient and considerate, not "like dumb driven cattle, but heroes in the strife."

I. As a man, pure and simple, he was many-sided, not without faults but was richly endowed in the intellectual grasp of great questions and possessed rare ability for the solution of difficult problems. He understood human nature to a remarkable degree and easily secured the unfaltering confidence of men.

II. As a patriot he combined enthusiasm with sagacity. The flame of his enthusiasm burned with ever-increasing light upon the altar of his heart. He was not impatient with old things and he was not headstrong concerning new ideas.

III. As a statesman he possessed rare executive ability. To handle men is a great gift, but he marshaled his forces with remarkable skill. The combination of dignity and intimacy that prevailed in his attitude toward his followers won for him their highest regard and affection, gave him a high quality of leadership which made him intrepid in the face of the greatest dangers and enabled him to lead where few would dare to follow.

IV. As a soldier he met the best tests. He was never rash, but always brave. He was considerate but energetic. He was never heard to boast of his own heroism, but his record shows nothing but unremitting valor. He never drew a sword except in defense of liberty and independence and he never sheathed it in the presence of tyranny.

V. As a Christian he was a happy combination. He united morality and piety. He recognized the Christian sources of inspiration and guidance and believed in being a faithful and loyal disciple of the meek and lowly Nazarene, and an earnest and efficient follower of the great Captain of our Salvation.
—Rev. H. C. Hinds, D.D.

WASHINGTON AS A LEADER

"Moreover, thou shalt provide out of all the people, able men, such as fear God, men of truth, hating covetousness; and place such over them, to be rulers of thousands, and rulers of hundreds, rulers of fifties, and rulers of tens." Exodus 18:21.

No lesson of Washington's natal day is louder than the call for leadership.

The need for the Washington type of leadership is found in every sphere of modern life.

I. In a democracy leadership must spring from the ranks—"out of all the people."

II. Leadership must have its basis in ability wedded to character—"able men such as fear God," etc.

III. The rule exercised must be scaled according to competence—"rulers of thousands," etc.

Washington helped to make it possible for every American to attain to influential and honorable leadership in manifold forms of service.

The newest field for leadership is among our immigrants.

WASHINGTON EVER OUR FIRST CITIZEN

"Wherefore then were ye not afraid to speak against my servant Moses?" Num. 12:8.

America gave to France a statue of Lafayette of heroic size, but she gave to the world the character of Washington in its colossal proportions, and the world has erected its lofty pedestal.

I. It is high. Gladstone said: "If among all the pedestals supplied by history for eminent public characters I saw one higher than all the rest, and if I were asked to name its fittest occupant, I should at once name Washington."

II. He incarnates our loftiest patriotic thought. Great forces focus in a person, and from him radiate with clearer power, and thus great men are at once the effect and cause of the events of their time. They mediate between principle and practice; between ideas and actions. Of such leaders of the world's thought and action, Washington was preëminent.

III. His eminence, being from inherent worth, is more and more readily acknowledged, not with the hero worship of a myth, but with the deliberate judgment of careful history.

IV. The balance and poise of his character were perhaps his most striking characteristic. A lifelong aristocrat, he was beloved by the people; with very decided opinions on government, he was twice elected President unanimously.—REV. FREDERICK NOBLE.

WASHINGTON A MAN OF LOFTIEST PURPOSES

"The Lord spake with Moses face to face." Exod. 33:11.

The secret of Washington's abiding hold upon the popular imagination and his abiding influence is, first of all, in the moral seriousness of his life.

I. While he was a man of eminently practical habit of mind, yet life and life's work were to him matters of solemn concern.

II. He carried this seriousness into all his multifarious occupations. Nothing was little or trifling to him.

III. This made him do his best in everything to which he set his hand, and when his power and influence became manifest, he was kept from the possibility either of trifling or of self-seeking.

THE EVER-GROWING INFLUENCE OF WASHINGTON

"The path of the just is as a shining light, that shineth more and more unto the perfect day." Prov. 4:18.

While strong in his own generation, Washington is stronger even in the judgment of the generations which have followed. After the lapse of a century he is better appreciated, more perfectly understood, more thoroughly venerated and loved than when he lived.

I. He remains an ever-increasing influence for good in every part and sphere of action of the republic.

II. He is recognized as not only the most far-sighted statesman of his generation, but as having an almost prophetic vision.

III. He built not alone for his own time, but for the great future; and pointed the right solution of many of the problems which were to arise in the years to come.

THE CHARACTER OF WASHINGTON

"As the man is so is his strength." Judges 8:21.

Though in many respects Washington was not different from other men, for he was but a man, and his virtues common virtues, yet these virtues were so many and so combined as to make a wonderfully well-rounded and symmetrical character. As Emerson said: "He stood four-square to every wind that blew."

I. Consider, first, some of the elements that entered into the forming of his character.
1. He had good home training. A man asked the secret of his success, replied: "I had a friend." Washington could say, "I had a mother."
2. He made the most of himself. He believed in downright hard work. He sought an education and got it. His success was the result of no sudden flash of luck or triumph of genius, but of work.

3. He had the physical and material qualities needed for his providential work. Nature gave him a powerful frame, a clear eye, a quick hand.
4. He was a man of intense vigor. There is such a thing as strength without vigor. But real vigor characterized his whole make-up. This it was which helped him to meet privations, and which sustained him in the face of opposition.

II. Consider, secondly, some of the traits or qualities of his character.
1. His modesty. He always felt that his countrymen rated him too high. When chosen Commander-in-Chief of the United Colonies' army, he asked every gentleman present to remember his avowal of his own sense of unfitness; and his letters to his wife and family prove his sincerity.
2. His sublime perseverance. Defeat could not shake, nor disaster quell, his determination. Indeed, they only developed his energy and persistence.
3. Near akin to this we mention his undaunted courage. Cautious, brave, unfearing, unflinching, he could, and did, stand alone at times when every one seemed against him.
4. His patriotism. This was too marked to need mention.
5. Another quality for which his memory is most cherished was his absolute integrity.
6. The crowning element in his character was his faith in God.

Cherish his memory. Imitate his example. Thank God for our nation. Resolve on patriotic devotion to everything which can advance our beloved country.

A STUDY IN HEROES

"Not by might, nor by power, but by my spirit, saith the Lord of hosts." Zech. 4:6.

These sublime words are true, not because Jehovah uttered them, but Jehovah uttered them because they are true. Were it not so, and had they never been spoken, neither Washington nor Lincoln would have become what they were in themselves, and what they became to the land that gave them birth. Perhaps it is not without significance that two of the greatest men the world has ever known were born in the same country, the same month of the year, and grappled successfully with the two greatest crises in that country's history. Nor is it without significance that they were born at opposite ends of the month, the one earlier, the other in the latter half, as they also were representatives of the two extremes of social conditions, Washington being rich, handsome, commanding in personality and position, Lincoln, coming from the ranks of poverty, awkward, ungainly, fighting all his life against fearful odds; yet each attained the same proud eminence, each acquired the same beloved title of "Father"; the one, "Father of his country," the other, our beloved "Father Abraham."

I. The first great lesson to be learned from the study of these noble characters is the truth that God is no respecter of persons when it comes to choosing the right man for the right place. There is an old Chinese proverb to this effect: "God shows what he thinks of money by the kind of people he gives it to." Of course, the inference intended to be drawn from this bit of worldly wisdom is that the Almighty regards with lofty scorn the wealth of this world, because it is distributed in large proportions among the utterly selfish, unthinking, unprincipled men and women of the world, who are lovers of pleasure and of themselves rather than of humanity. But there is much fallacy mixed with the sometimes truth of the old proverb, and many notable cases where its error is overshadowed by the noble integrity of those who have come into great wealth. Washington, although far from being a rich man as the world to-day counts riches, was yet a man of position and wealth for his time. "Born to the purple," he abandoned his home of ease and luxury for the vicissitudes of camp life, choosing, like one of old, to share with his fellow countrymen the suffering and hardships of a Valley Forge if thereby he might lead them on to the victories and liberty awaiting them as a free and independent nation, and thereby and forever winning the love and undying gratitude of a people destined to become the most glorious nation in the whole earth.

There is also a Scotch saying: "When God would make use of a man, he always opens the door"; signifying that no matter what apparent obstacles may intervene, they must all give way before God's ultimate purpose to use the man he deems necessary to the hour; and so we behold an Abraham Lincoln born in the ranks of poverty, awkward, ungainly in appearance, homely as to features, acquiring an education in the face of appalling difficulties, slowly, laboriously, but steadily rising to the grand heights to which destiny had called him, until he, too, has reached the summit, where he stands crowned with the grateful love and homage, not only of his own countrymen, but of the whole race whose shackles he has broken, bidding them go forth free men in the name of him who hath made of one blood all nations of the earth. Has it ever occurred to you that neither of these two great heroes of our land could have successfully filled the place of the other?

II. Each of these in his turn rising to meet the great crises in our nation's history did so because of what he himself was and of what he had to contribute to the nation's need at his own time. A Lincoln in the place of Washington in the beginning of our national history would have proved a failure, though even then slavery existed as an institution, and Washington himself had slaves; though possessed of all the noble characteristics of exalted manhood, he would have been but poorly equipped to meet the exigencies and solve the problems of the martyred Lincoln's time. But the same spirit of the living God animated each and led each in his own way and time on to glorious victory.—"My Spirit saith the Lord of Hosts."

III. Can we not read a third lesson in this brief study of our nation's heroes—that only as that Spirit dominates the life of an individual or of a nation can either rise to the grand opportunities that some time or other is sure to demand of us the best we have to give?

IV. Still further, do we not learn from the history of the nations that the Judge of all the earth does right, chooses right, makes never a mistake, but does all things well? May we not safely entrust all our interests, personal and national, unto Him whose name is Love.

WASHINGTON

"Thy gentleness hath made me great." Psa. 18:35.

I. His enduring fame, shown: 1. By observance of the day. 2. By Gladstone's opinion. 3. By great monument at Washington.

II. Elements of personality on which his fame rests: 1. Natural ability great. 2. Goodness, without which no true greatness. 3. Capacity for growth—with Braddock, as general, and as president. 4. Powers of endurance—Valley Forge. 5. Symmetry; character matches form. 6. Unselfishness—compare with Napoleon.

III. Greatness of fame: 1. Father of his country. 2. "First in war," etc. Compare with Grant the soldier, Sumner the statesman, Garfield the beloved, Lincoln the martyr. Last alone equals him.

WASHINGTON AS A NATIONAL ASSET

"And I will make of thee a great nation, and I will bless thee, and make thy name great; and thou shalt be a blessing." Gen. 12:2.

A text as true of Washington as of Abram.

Great men have ever been a nation's chief asset.

I. Washington is the gold ore from which our American nation is made. What he was and did and represents is of the nature of this republic.

II. In memory of Washington is the coin current of our country, of which a new issue is uttered on his every natal day, by so much enriching the national life.

III. The luster that Washington has lent to this land of ours in the world has given America a worth of international quality and extent.

Let our wealth become increasingly what George Washington meant us to be, until in moral values America is the world's banker.

PART XI: PALM SUNDAY TEXTS AND THEMES

The Triumphal Entry: Mark 11:1. I. The occasion of this homage. II. The scene of this homage. III. The offerers of this homage. IV. The actions of this homage.

Religious Excitement: "And they spread their garments in the way." Mark 11:8. I. Has its sphere of usefulness. II. But it is a mistake to regard emotional excitement as the very essence and substance of religion.

The Royal Procession: "The multitudes that went before, and that followed, cried, saying, Hosanna to the son of David," etc. Matt. 21:9.

Entire Consecration: "The Lord hath need." Matt. 21:3. The Lord hath need of you. I. Your prayers. II. Your praises. III. Your talents.

The King Comes to His Capital: John 12:12-16. I. The King's person. II. The King's credentials. Came by divine appointment. Came as predicted. Came in humility and righteousness—indisputable tokens of his claim. III. The King's welcome. The multitudes. Their homage. Their acclaim, "Hosanna." IV. The King's attendants. Disciples, etc. V. The King's enemies. Pharisees, etc. The certainty that the world will ultimately be won to Christ.

Christ as King: "The scepter shall not depart from Judah, nor a law-giver from between his feet, until Shiloh come; and unto him shall the gathering of the people be." Gen. 49:10.

The Royal Christ: "Yet have I set my king upon my holy hill of Zion." Psa. 62:2.

His Final Authority: "Gird thy sword upon thy thigh, O most mighty." Psa. 45:3.

The Kingdom Set Up: "In the days of those kings shall the God of heaven set up a kingdom." Dan. 2:44.

A True Inscription: "And the writing was, Jesus of Nazareth the King of the Jews." John 19:19.

The Prince of Life: "And killed the Prince of Life, whom God hath raised from the dead." Acts 3:15.

Behold Thy King: "Behold thy king cometh unto thee, meek, and sitting upon an ass, and a colt the foal of an ass." Matt. 21:5.

The Glory of the King: "Now unto the King eternal, immortal, invisible, the only wise God, be honor and glory for ever and ever. Amen." 1 Tim. 1:17.

Who is This That Cometh from Edom? "Who is this that cometh from Edom, with dyed garments from Bozrah?" Isa. 63:1.

The Commencement of Christ's Coronation Procession: Mark 10:46-52.

The Throne and the Rainbow: Rev. 4:3.

A Lesson in Obedience: Matt. 21:1-17.

Palm Sunday as a Decision Day: Matt. 21:11.

Christ's Entrance into Jerusalem: "Much people that were come to the feast, when they heard that Jesus was coming to Jerusalem," etc. John 12:12, 13.

Christ's Lamentation over Jerusalem: "He beheld the city and wept over it." Luke 19:4.

Christ's Popularity: "Hosanna; blessed is he that cometh in the name of the Lord." Mark 11:9.

Temple-Cleansing: "When he had looked around." Mark 11:11.

Preparation for Christ: "Ye shall find a colt." Mark 11:2.

Three Contrasts: Matt. 21:12.

Christ's Entrance into Jerusalem: "Much people that were come to the feast, when they heard that Jesus was coming to Jerusalem," etc. John 12:12, 13.

Palm Sunday Lessons: "In this place is one greater than the temple." Matt. 12:6.

The Enthroned Christ: "When the Son of man shall come in his glory." Matt. 25:31.

Times of Visitation: "Because thou knewest not the time of thy visitation." Luke 19:44. I. In the period of youth. II. Special influences in connection with services in the sanctuary. III. Visits to the heart by the Holy Spirit. At home, in quiet chamber, out under the stars—God's visit. IV. Providential events which may be regarded as a time of visitation.

PART XII: PALM SUNDAY SERMON OUTLINES

THE KINGSHIP OF CHRIST

"He hath on his vesture and on his thigh a name written, King of Kings and Lord of Lords." Rev. 19:16.

Palm Sunday is the day of kingship—the kingship of Christ. Isaiah gives us the promise of a coming Christ. John the Baptist proclaims an approaching Christ. Paul preaches the gospel of a Christ crucified. John gives us the vision of Christ enthroned.

I. Who is this royal conqueror? As we see him in the manger at Bethlehem, or as a child in the temple, or at his baptism at the Jordan, or on the cross, he seems not particularly kingly.

II. Where is his throne? Where lies his kingdom? We must remember the greatest kings have been uncrowned, and their kingdoms have been invisible.

III. Were they disappointed, were they misled, were they false prophets—those who predicted that when Jesus came, he should come as a king? There are psalmists who declared concerning the Messiah, "A scepter of righteousness is the scepter of thy kingdom." David knew how small a thing is political kingship. And he knew by so much as he had spiritual elevation how incomparably greater is royalty of intellect and character. John says that the kingly Christ shall serve as well as save.

IV. Phases of his royalty. There may be more appealing phases of the life of Christ, but nothing is more admirable than his self-control. Self-control and courage may be merely passive, but goodness must be active. It is constructive in its nature. Benevolence is a flowing stream. Kingship is a matter of power and there is no power so like omnipotence as the power of goodness at work.—REV. CHARLES CARROLL ALBERTSON, D.D.

THE TRIUMPHAL ENTRY

"Hosanna to the son of David: Blessed is he that cometh in the name of the Lord; Hosanna in the highest." Matt. 21:9.

Several ideas were expressed in this action.

I. Disciples must prepare the way for Jesus. He cannot go through the world on a triumphant march unless we go with him and before him and make a path for him. Human influences may open the way along which the Spirit of Christ gets into human hearts and into the world.

II. This service costs sacrifice. Garments must be cast down to make the way along which Christ walks. Things that are good and precious to us, our possessions, time and talents, our garments, the very necessities of life, life itself, must be cast down. Nothing is too costly to become a part of this path. The feet of Jesus should not touch the common dust, but should press upon our most precious things.

III. And this path should be a path of beauty. The highway of salvation along which Jesus walks should not seem to be a hard and dusty road, but it should be so carpeted that the world will see it is a way of pleasantness and a path of peace.

IV. The most prominent feature of this procession was its enthusiasm. These people were not afraid to shout. They believed in Jesus with all their might and expressed their devotion in oriental outbursts of joy. They were not ashamed of their King, and when the city was stirred and shaken with excitement and the question of the hour was, "Who is this?" they boldly answered, "This is the prophet, Jesus, from Nazareth of Galilee." It took some courage to say that up in Jerusalem. The people grew wild in their enthusiasm and the hills near and far caught up and flung back their glad hosannas. This is a spirit that is evaporating out of our religious life and that we need to keep and intensify.—REV. JAMES H. SNOWDEN, D.D.

THE LORD HATH NEED OF YOU

"The Lord hath need of him." Mark 11:3.

I. The Lord hath need of you.

1. Of your prayers.
2. Of your praises.
3. Of your talents.
4. He may need your most cherished thing to which your heart holds most fast.

II. The natural heart's reply to this claim.
1. Unbelief denies the claim.
2. Weakness hesitates until the opportunity is past.
3. Stimulation seems to do, but does not.
4. Selfishness hugs her own.—J. V.

THE TRIUMPHAL ENTRY

John 12: 12-26.

I. Jesus Christ is the true King, and is riding triumphantly through the ages.

II. As these people cast their garments before Jesus as he rode in triumph, so we should cast our talents, our money, our time, all that we have, before him, and do all that we can to aid his cause, and hasten his success. It is a great privilege to have part in his triumph.

III. Enthusiasm is a good thing for every one, for any cause that is worthy of enthusiasm. A noble enthusiasm uplifts the soul. Christianity is not dull, lifeless, insipid. There never has been anything on God's earth so adapted to kindle all the enthusiasm of the soul, and to make it an enduring flame.

IV. It should be the desire of every heart to have a more personal, intimate acquaintance with Jesus.

V. We become acquainted with Jesus, by loving him, by working with him for his cause, by becoming like him in character, by studying his life and words.

VI. We should welcome every chance to make others acquainted with our Master.—F. N. P.

POPULAR ATTRACTIONS

Mark 11: 1-11.
Here is a multitude:
I. Attracted by marvelous intelligence.

II. Following the example of the few.
III. Rendering regal honor to the son of a carpenter.
IV. Looking for material aggrandizement.
V. In a little while exchanging "Hosanna" for "Crucify Him."—F. W.

SONGS OR SILENCE?

"Behold thy King cometh unto thee." Matt. 21:5.

I. Jesus was the King of the Jews. His Hebrew lineage was royal, without flaw or break. He was announced to the shepherds, by the heavenly hosts, as a king. He was heralded to the Hebrew nation as king, by the prophet from the wilderness. He claimed to be a king. He had all the personal graciousness and power of a king.

II. Here is the great climax. The prophecies of centuries come to a head. The King, long promised and looked for, has come, and is now riding into the royal city. How will he be received?

III. There is no doubt about the reception by the multitudes. They break branches from the trees, and strew the roadway for his coming. Then one man pulls off his garment and adds it to the green, and another, till the King's colt is walking over a carpet of nature's beauty and man's woven love combined. Then they begin singing, "Hosanna. Blessed be the King!"

A great crowd comes out of the city to meet and greet Jesus. They likewise carpet the road, and pick up the song. And the two crowds sing back and forth, answering each other, joyous antiphonal music, a truly Hebrew and a truly royal scene. This is the answer of the common crowd to the King's claim.

IV. But—but, as they come to the city, an ominous silence greets him. The leaders look. They know what it all means. These leaders are the nation, technically, officially and practically. They understand perfectly the meaning of his action of so riding into the nation's capital. And they understand the crowd's action, too; and more, they understand Jesus' acceptance of the crowd's homage. And this was clear.

But, their own resolution was as set, in a rigid coldness.

Their silence was their answer, their rejection as positive and absolute as rejection could be. It really began in the silent contemptuous rejection of John's testimony to their official deputation at the beginning (John 1: 19-28). They would not accept this Jesus. The King is rejected by the nation.—S. D. GORDON, D.D.

THE CONQUERING KING

Rev. 19: 11-16. Scripture Lesson, Psa. 2 and Daniel 2: 44-49.

Introduction. The ideas and ideals of Jesus are winning to-day. In spite of present appearances they will continue to win. The vision of this text was given to assure us of that in dark days.

1. This is a vision of a present reality. These pictures of the book of Revelation are to give us glimpses of the events of the present age. Each portrays some particular aspect of it.

2. The central figure of this vision is Jesus of Nazareth, glorified. Verses 11 to 13 are the description that identifies him. Faithful and true are attributes. The Word of God. Strange appellation that no man but himself perfectly comprehends, his vesture dipped in blood signifying his destroying his enemies. Riding upon a white horse signifying his conquering progress.

3. The title upon his armor and his garments, "King of kings and Lord of lords." In this he assumes his right to govern and indicates his relations to the governments of the earth as well as individuals.

4. The forces of his conflict are "the sword of his mouth" which is the teaching he gave to men. We see to-day how men will and do fight for those ideals of democracy and individual worth and freedom that are the direct product of his teachings. Those forces of the redeemed which accompany him in white robes are the heavenly staff who witness the triumph of heaven's King.

5. The vision shows him engaged in the conflict of the ages. This is the aspect of the King toward his enemies. It is he that is on the side of righteousness. This conflict will continue so long as the high priests of paganism proclaim from

the temples of earth, "Odin who is greater than Javeh," and it will be the bloody conflict of national warfare as long as any ruler responds, "Amen." It was of this that he spoke when he said, "I came not to send peace but a sword."

Conclusion. From looking at this vision there leaps to our minds the words of the second psalm, "Kiss the Son lest he be angry and ye perish from the way when his wrath is kindled. Blessed are all they that put their trust in him."—REV. WILLIAM PARSONS, D.D.

LESSONS FOR TO-DAY FROM CHRIST'S TRIUMPHAL ENTRY

1. Christ, though disguised and poor, is yet King of this world.
2. But he is a Prince of peace, and his victories are by the weapons of peace.
3. Whatever the Lord has need of we should gladly give to his service.
4. The Lord has need of the humblest of his creatures.
5. Christ inspires the religious feelings with gladness.
6. Christ encourages the expression of religious feeling.
7. Even in the midst of the triumph, there are sins and sorrows to weep over.
8. Christ is yet to come triumphant over all.
9. The triumph is to be by the arts of peace, not of war.

GARMENT GIVERS

"And they spread their garments before him." Mark 11:8.

Have you not sometimes wished that you had been there to see our Lord as he rode into Jerusalem on that long ago day, while his followers out of love and loyalty "spread their garments before him"?

In another way you may see him this year, as "along the King's highway" he goes forth with our missionaries to enter heathen cities and homes across the sea.

And you may show your love and loyalty to him by spreading at his dear feet some of your garments (or the value of them). Will you?

One garment—not because you must, but because you want to do it for this work in the Orient so dear to the heart of our Lord—will you give it?

It might be a hat, small or large, gay or somber, costing—oh, just what you pay for yours. For his dear sake will you give the worth of that?

Long ago Sir Walter Raleigh spread his handsome cloak before his queen to protect her feet from the mud of the street. What about the coat you will buy this season? Could you send the worth of it to protect our queens, brave missionaries, girls who "for the sake of the Name" fare forth to walk mid the filth and slime of heathenism?

The second coat, the second blouse, the second suit! How their worth would protect these queens—from the wild animals as we wall their compounds, from poisonous insects as we screen their houses, from sun rays as we build their verandas, or from disease as we remove unsanitary conditions!

Is it too much to hope for the worth of some sets of furs ($50 or $100)? The second set would warm your heart as the first could not begin to warm your shoulders!

If not coats of fur, what about the pretty shoes that have been your pride and delight. The second pair "spread before him" would entitle you to that old compliment, "How beautiful . . . are the feet of him that publisheth peace!"

Then the gloves—oh, the gloves—short, long, silk, kid, washable, wearable, "givable"! Why not hundreds and hundreds to spread before our King?

Still he rides on, pausing now and then "to sit over against the treasury" and to note the women and girls who share with him the best garment they can afford. Still he says:

> "I gave, I gave my life for thee,
> What hast thou given to me?"

*

PART XIII: GOOD FRIDAY TEXTS AND THEMES

The Word of Forgiveness: "Father, forgive them, for they know not what they do." Luke 23:34.

The Word of Salvation: "To-day shalt thou be with me in paradise." Luke 23:43.

The Word of Love: "Woman, behold thy son . . . behold thy mother." John 19:26.

The Word of Atonement: "My God, my God, why hast thou forsaken me." Matt. 27:46.

The Word of Physical Suffering: "I thirst." John 19:28.

The Word of Triumph: "It is finished." John 19:30.

The Word of Reunion: "Father, into thy hands I commend my spirit." Luke 23:46.

First word from the cross—the word of charity: "Father, forgive them."

Second word from the cross—the word of mercy: "To-day shalt thou be with me in Paradise."

Third word from the cross—the word of filial piety: "Behold thy Son! . . . Behold thy mother!"

Fourth word from the cross—the word of agony: "I thirst."

Fifth word from the cross—the word of humanity: "My God, my God, why hast thou forsaken me?"

Sixth word from the cross—the word of perfection: "It is finished."

Seventh word from the cross—the word of Sonship: "Father, into thy hands I commend my spirit."

The Word of Intercession: "Father, forgive them; for they know not what they do." Luke 23:34.

The Word of Pardon: "To-day shalt thou be with me in Paradise." Luke 23:43.

The Word of Care: "Woman, behold thy son! . . . Behold thy mother!" John 19:26, 27.

The Word of Loneliness: "My God, my God, why hast thou forsaken me?" Mark 15:34; Matt. 27:46.

GOOD FRIDAY TEXTS AND THEMES

The Word of Need: "I thirst." John 19:28.
The Word of Victory: "It is finished." John 19:30.
The Word of Trust: "Father, into thy hands I commend my spirit." Luke 23:46.
Lessons from the Crucifixion: "And they crucified him." Matt. 27:35.
Watchers by the Cross: Luke 23:34-38.
Jesus on the Cross: "And the people stood beholding." Luke 23:35.
The Meaning of the Cross: "I, if I be lifted up, will draw all men unto me." Luke 23:21.
The Solemn Spectacle: "The people stood beholding." Luke 23:35.
The Voice of the Cross: "There they crucified him." Luke 23:33.
The Crucifixion: "There they crucified him, and the malefactors, one on the right hand and the other on the left." Luke 23:33.
The First Good Friday: "Who his own self bare our sins in his own body on the tree," etc. 1 Peter 2:24.
The Atonement: "Be ready always to give an answer to every man that asketh you a reason of the hope that is in you, with meekness and fear." 1 Peter 3:15.
Groups at the Cross and Why They Were There: "And they crucified him, and parted his garments, casting lots; that it might be fulfilled," etc. Matt. 27:35-43.
Man's Unbelief: "They cried, saying, Crucify him! Crucify him!" Luke 23:21.
The Title on the Cross: John 19:10.
The Man of Sorrows: "A man of sorrows, and acquainted with grief." Isa. 53:3.
The Meaning of Christ's Agony: "I, if I be lifted up, will draw all men unto me." John 12:32.

PART XIV: GOOD FRIDAY SERMON OUTLINES

THE CROSS OF CHRIST

"There they crucified him, and with him two others, on either side one, and Jesus in the midst. And Pilate wrote a title also," etc. John 19: 17-22.

I. Under the cross.
   1. The weary pilgrim—Jesus. Exhausted by the agony. Suffering through scourging. Burdened with the weight. Degraded by the tablet.
   2. The varied attendance—robbers, soldiers, etc.

II. Upon the cross. Jesus. Jesus in the midst. On either side a crucified robber proclaiming him the worst of the three. The nails. The pain. A spectacle of woe. Priests and people mocked his misery.

III. Above the cross. The title, verse 19.
   1. Its conspicuous position—seen by all.
   2. Its threefold language—to be read by all.
   3. Its providential use—to attest to all.
      a. Christ's true humanity, "Jesus of Nazareth."
      b. His Messianic dignity, "King of the Jews."
      c. Israel's sin. Had crucified their Sovereign.
      d. The world's hope. He was the Saviour of men.

IV. Beneath the cross. Gambling for the Saviour's clothes, soldiers fulfilled prophecy. Verses 23, 24.
   1. Heartless cruelty.
   2. Moral insensibility.
   3. Appalling criminality.
   4. Unconscious instrumentality.

V. Near the cross. The Galilean women; the post of love. Verse 25.
   1. Their names. The Marys and Salome.
   2. Their positions. By the cross. Indicating courage—

not afraid of the soldiers. Their fidelity, in contrast with the male disciples, who forsook him and fled. Their affection. Their sympathy—intending to console him, as they doubtless did.

3. Their privilege—a gracious opportunity of hearing his last words.

The heroism of the women was inspired by faith and love.
The startling contrasts of life—the soldiers and the women.
The power which lies in the cross to reveal human hearts.—T. WHITELAW, D.D.

WATCHERS BY THE CROSS

Luke 23: 34-38.
I. The friendly watchers, who were learning lessons that would bless all their future life.
II. The unfriendly watchers, who were ill-treating him who was dying to save them from sin and death.

THE WATCHERS AROUND THE CROSS

"And sitting down they watched him there." Matt. 27: 36.
The varied types of watchers around the cross.
I. The careless watch of the soldiers.
II. The jealous watch of the enemies.
III. The anxious watch of the women.
IV. The wondering watch of the angels on high.

THE GROUP AROUND THE CROSS

"And sitting down they watched him there." Matt. 27: 36.
The scene at the crucifixion. What Jesus saw from the cross. Compare Tissot's painting.
1. The Roman soldiers. The careless, indifferent, unseeing.
2. The faithful disciples. Sympathetic, seeing, loving friends.
3. The curious watchers. The pleasure-seekers and intellectually curious.

4. The persecutors, Scribes and Pharisees. Their taunts are testimonies to him.

"What is our attitude beneath the cross?"

"Beneath the Cross of Jesus
I fain would take my stand."

BEHOLD THE MAN!

"Behold the man!" John 19:5.

I. The feelings with which these words were and may be uttered.
  1. Pity.
  2. Mockery.
  3. Faith.
  4. Admiration.

II. Let us by faith behold the Christ.
  1. Behold the Man of dignity.
  2. Behold the Man of humility.
  3. Behold the Man of purity.
  4. Behold the Man of suffering.
  5. Behold the Man of glory.

LESSONS FROM THE CRUCIFIXION

"And they crucified him." Matt. 27:35.

1. The deed transforms the place. Calvary, the place of execution, has become the center of the world's history and the world's salvation. "The great central event in all history is the death of our Lord and Saviour, Jesus Christ. The centuries circle round the cross."

2. The cost of salvation smites all indifference to religion. If Christ was willing to die that we might be saved, what ought not we to do?

3. Those that watch Christ may find in him a King, a Redeemer, an Example, or, if they themselves are bad, only a subject for mockery and insult. Which company shall we join?

4. The cross expresses God's feelings toward sin, his readiness to forgive sin, the terrible evil and danger of sin that

costs such a sacrifice for deliverance from it. No one would suffer so much to save others from a slight evil or little danger.

5. The cross declares, in "letters that can be read from the stars," God's love to man. God did not put punishment upon an innocent person. The atonement on the cross was a voluntary sacrifice. When the Greeks were besieging Troy, and met with ill success, the priest Calchas told them that the only way to appease the offended goddess, and gain the victory, was to sacrifice to Diana, Iphigenia, the beautiful daughter of Agamemnon. And these brave men of old are said to have taken her by strategy and force, and brought this innocent girl to the altar to slay her. This sacrifice (though she was rescued) was mean and unjust beyond words to express. But when any persons have offered themselves, as Horatius and his comrades at the bridge of Rome, or the nobles of Calais to Edward the Sixth, the sacrifice has been the height of heroism. The sacrifice expressed the highest love possible.

6. The cross furnishes every possible motive for turning from sin, touching the heart with love, showing our danger, giving us hope of forgiveness and life, teaching the law of duty, which prefers death to failure or neglect. It shows the value of our souls, the value of salvation, and the worth of eternal life in heaven.—P.

THE SEVEN WORDS FROM THE CROSS

We may well believe that all of our Lord's words as he hung upon the cross have been preserved. In a very wonderful way the seven utterances that have come down to us represent the seven most important phases of Christ's character and work.

The Word of Forgiveness
First word: "Father, forgive them; for they know not what they do." Luke 23:34.
The Word of Forgiveness. This was probably spoken as the cross, with Christ nailed to it, "was lifted up and planted in the ground, with a rough shock of indescribable agony." "He hastened to apply the first outgushing of that redeeming

blood." His coming to earth was that he might prove God's readiness to forgive men, and now he includes in that readiness even his murderers, the harsh soldiers, Annas, Caiaphas, Herod, Pilate, and us, too, when by our sins we "crucify the Son of God afresh."

The Word of Salvation.
Second word: "To-day shalt thou be with me in Paradise." Luke 23:43.
The Word of Salvation, spoken about noon. One of the robbers, moved by Christ's bearing and his words of tender forgiveness, and perhaps having some previous knowledge of him, rebuked the railing of the other robber, and begged for Christ's help into eternal happiness. How ready was Christ to grant it! He had come for that one thing, to seek and save the lost.

The Word of Love.
Third Word: "Woman, behold thy son . . . behold thy mother." John 19:26.
The Word of Love. Joseph, judging from the silence of the record, had died long before, and Mary was a widow. Some have held that Christ addressed Mary respectfully but vaguely as "Woman," "Lady," because had he called her "Mother," she would have been exposed to the rough taunts of the brutal soldiers. Others see in the words, "And from that hour the disciple took her unto his own home," an indication of Christ's desire that Mary should at once be led away by John, and spared the further agony of watching him. "John's devotion to his dying Lord—alone of the disciples exposed to the peril of the cross—is thus abundantly recompensed. As John's was the greatest personal love it was honored with the largest earthly requital."

The Word of Atonement.
Fourth word: "My God, my God, why hast thou forsaken me?" Matt. 27:46.
The Word of Atonement, wherein the Son of God entered the deepest pit of human woe, the sense of abandonment and utter loss, and thus became completely at one with our human-

ity. It was spoken toward the end of that mysterious darkness that seized the country from noon till three o'clock. "The Son of God felt as if he had been deserted by his Father. It was the darkening of his human soul, not the hiding of God's countenance." "The divine horror of that moment is unfathomable by human soul. It was blackness of darkness. And yet he would believe. Yet he would hold fast. God was his God yet. My God—and in the cry came forth victory."

The Word of Physical Suffering.
Fifth word: "I thirst." John 19:28.
The Word of Physical Suffering, as the fourth was the word of spiritual suffering. Christ's thirst must have been torturing, his body exposed, almost uncovered, to the fierce noonday heat of Palestine. There is no agony like that of unassuaged thirst; it is the one cry of the wounded as they lie untended on the battlefield: "Water! Water!" "He thirsts that we may not thirst, that we may receive from him that gift of the water of life which shall cause us never to thirst any more."
The Scripture fulfilled in this cry is Psa. 22:15; 69:21. "Only when all else had been attended to ('Knowing that all things are finished') did Christ attend to his own physical sensations. They filled a sponge, because a cup was impracticable, and put it around a stalk of hyssop, and thus applied the restorative to his mouth. All that was requisite was a reed two or three feet long, as the crucified was only slightly elevated." "He had refused the stupefying draught, which would have clouded his faculties; he accepts what will revive them for the effort of a willing surrender of his life."

The Word of Triumph.
Sixth word: "It is finished." John 19:30.
The Word of Triumph. This is one word in the Greek, and it has been called "the greatest single word ever uttered." "No other man, since the world began, could have said that word as Jesus said it. He had lived a perfect, complete human life, in which there were no mistakes, no omissions, no shortcomings. The atonement was complete, because it was the

offering of a perfect life." "In one sense nothing he did was ended. But the atoning sacrifice had been offered once for all. Our Lord saw a long wake of light crossing the past and stretching forward to the future."

The Word of Reunion.
Seventh word: "Father, into thy hands I commend my spirit." Luke 23:46.

The Word of Reunion, spoken at 3 p.m., the time of the evening sacrifice. "The last act of our Lord in thus commending his spirit to the Father was only a summing up of what he had been doing all his life. He had been offering this sacrifice of himself all the years." "The thought of the Father penetrated and possessed our Lord's whole life. What wonder that he turned to the Father at the last with perfect confidence?"

THE THREE CROSSES AT CALVARY

"And when they came to the place which is called Calvary, there they crucified him," etc. Luke 23:33.

I. The motive of the rulers in crucifying Christ between two malefactors: To make his death seem as odious as possible; to brand him as a great criminal.

II. The unforeseen result of their malice: The Cross became a tribunal. The scene at the Day of Judgment was foreshadowed. The Judge in the center; on one side a penitent, on the other an impenitent sinner. A malefactor became a witness to Christ's mighty, redeeming love.

Lessons:
1. The same cross attracts and repels.
2. The most hopeless may obtain mercy.
3. You may be near the means of salvation, but be lost.

THE SCENE OF OUR SAVIOUR'S EXECUTION

"The place called Calvary." Luke 23:33.

A magic spell and power rest over some scenes and places. The home where our youthful affections were first brought into genial exercise we remember with hallowed feelings. Places of historic interest, too, there are. There are localities also towards which we cherish a deep religious regard. Scenes of the Bible are especially interesting to every saint of God, but no part of sacred history is so suggestive of pious thought and heavenly consolation as that which relates to our blessed Lord. In the scene to which we are introduced by the words before us we behold him in the consummation of his earthly career. We see events which astonished heaven, aroused hell and confounded earth. Let us draw near, then, to this divinely honored place; the place where, be it said with reverence, we see Deity in conflict; "The place called Calvary."

I. It was the place of unparalleled suffering. No alleviating circumstances were to soften his anguish, but the full burden of the world's transgressions rested upon him. None but God could save the world, for none but God could endure the wrath due to the world. What, then, must the meek, expiring Lamb have endured. The darkened heavens and the rended earth gave tokens of sympathy with the suffering Saviour.

II. It was the place of singular phenomena. "And it was about the sixth hour," etc., verses 44, 45. That this was not any solar eclipse is evident from the period at which it occurred, it being at the time of full moon; from the length of the duration of this darkness, no total eclipse having been known to exist more than four minutes, and no partial eclipse more than two hours, and also from the testimony of ancient authors on the point. From Calvary, then, issued the most singular phenomena, for here was the cause of all the extraordinary events. Earth and sky put on their mourning habiliments and creation groaned a requiem to its dying Lord.

III. The place of the most momentous of all achievements. Here did God, even the Triune God, make known his most marvelous work—his acts, his mighty acts. Here, we behold the mightiest moral transactions within the range of human and not improbably within the range of angelic experience. On the brow of Calvary was the price laid down for a lost world; the uttermost farthing of the debt was paid; man's utmost hopes were more than realized; the "promised seed" there "bruised serpent's head." But this suggests another thought, viz.:

IV. That Calvary was the place of glorious triumph. Hear the Conqueror as he proclaims his blessed triumph! "I have trodden the wine-press alone," etc. Isaiah 63:3-6. He met stern justice and silenced her demand. He chained death in his own den, and all insignia of his dread power did he destroy. He arched over the chasm which intervened between earth and heaven and opened the way to glory.

V. The place of pardoning mercy. In the very agonies of death he absolved the thief and took him to the courts above as a spoil of victory—a trophy of redeeming love.

VI. The place of deep devotion and of ardent affection. All were not mockers and scoffers who drew nigh to see the Man of Griefs expire. "Now there stood by the cross," etc.—John 19:25-27. Be it yours to cherish the same faithful affection towards the Saviour and to receive from him similar tokens of love and care. Whosoever shall do the will of my Father which is in heaven, the same is my brother and sister and mother.—J. F.

PART XV: EASTER TEXTS AND THEMES

The Invitation of a Risen Host: "Jesus saith unto them, Come and dine. And none of the disciples durst ask him, Who art thou? knowing that it was the Lord." John 21:12.

The Resurrection a Necessity: "And said unto them, Thus it is written, and thus it behooved Christ to suffer and to rise from the dead the third day." Luke 24:46.

The Earnest and the Harvest: "For as in Adam all die, even so in Christ shall all be made alive. But every man in his own order. Christ the first fruits; afterward they that are Christ's at his coming." Cor. 15:22, 23.

The Resurrection an Attestation of the Divinity of Christ: "And declared to be the son of God with power, according to the Spirit of holiness, by the resurrection from the dead." Rom. 1:4.

Old Testament Intimations of the Resurrection of Jesus: "He, seeing this before, spake of the resurrection of Christ, that his soul was not left in hell, neither did his flesh see corruption." Acts 2:31.

The Touch of Sympathy: "And he came and touched the bier: and they that bore him stood still. And he said, Young man, I say unto thee, arise." Luke 7:14.

The Light in the Tomb: "Now is Christ risen from the dead." 1 Cor. 15:20.

Resurrection Power: "His power is to usward . . . the mighty power which is wrought in Christ when he raised him from the dead." Eph. 1:19, 20.

The Call—the Answer: "He is not here, for he is risen, as he said." Matt. 28:6. Many epitaphs written on tombstones strike us as being singularly artificial in phrasing, but the Rev. Thomas Spurgeon tells us in a sermon of one epitaph in a little mound which bears just these words: "Freddy"—as if some one called—and underneath, "Yes, Father."

He Will Give Them Back: "Refrain thy voice from weeping, and thine eyes from tears. Thy children shall come again to their own border." Jer. 31:15-17.

The Redeemer Liveth: "I know that my Redeemer liveth." Job 19:25.

Christ in Us: "Reckon ye also yourselves to be dead to sin, but alive unto God through Jesus Christ our Lord." Rom. 6:11.

Mourning the Dead: "I would not have you to be ignorant, brethren, concerning them which are asleep." I Thess. 4:13.

The First Easter Sermon: "Mary Magdalene came and told the disciples that she had seen the Lord." John 20:18.

Christ the First-Fruits: "Now is Christ risen from the dead and become the first-fruits of them that slept." 1 Cor. 15:20.

The Conquest of the Grave: "O grave, where is thy victory?" 1 Cor. 15:55.

Making Appointments in the Hereafter: "To-day shalt thou be with me in paradise." Luke 23:43.

Death Not a Divine Mistake: "Lord, if thou hadst been here, my brother had not died." John 11:21.

"God's Amen": "Now is Christ risen from the dead." 1 Cor. 15:20. The Resurrection is God's "Amen" to Christ's "It is finished."

Job's Confidence: Job 19:23-29.
The Blessed Life: Titus 2:11-15.
Christ the Life: John 1:4.
The Stone Rolled Away: Matt. 28:2.
The Bearing of the Age-Long Life: Rev. 21:1-8.
The Easter Message: Rom. 6:4.
A Long Look Ahead: 1 Cor. 15:35-58.

Resurrection from a Legal Point of View: "But he said unto them, Except I shall see in his hands the print of the nails, and put my hand into his side, I will not believe." John 20:25.

Immortal Life: "And they shall see his face." Rev. 22:4.

The Resurrection a Fact, a Force, a Prophecy: 1 Cor. 15:35-58.

The Garden and the Sepulcher: "In the garden was a sepulcher." John 19:41.

Why I Believe in the Immortality of the Soul: "And my

your spirit and soul and body be preserved entire, without blame at the coming of our Lord Jesus Christ." 1 Thess. 5:23.

The Easter Pilgrim: "These all died in faith, not having received the promises, but having seen them and greeted them from afar and having confessed that they were strangers and pilgrims on the earth." Heb. 11:13.

The Natural Immortality of the Soul: "If a man die, shall he live again? All the days of my warfare would I wait, till my release should come." Job 14:14.

The Joy of Easter: "And they departed quickly from the tomb with fear and great joy." Matt. 28:8.

The Resurrection Body: "But some will say, How are the dead raised up, and with what body do they come." 1 Cor. 15:35.

Is Death Merely Good-by? "O death, where is thy sting? O grave, where is thy victory?" 1 Cor. 15:35.

Witnesses that Convince: "This Jesus did God raise up, whereof we are all witnesses." Acts 2:32.

Easter Banishes Fear: "I declare unto you the gospel, wherein ye stand." 1 Cor. 15:1.

PART XVI: EASTER SERMON OUTLINES

THE FIRST EASTER SERMON

"Mary Magdalene came and told the disciples that she had seen the Lord." John 20:18.

Mary Magdalene preached the first Easter sermon, and this was her text: "I have seen the Lord."

1. That was not only an appropriate text, but also a central and substantial one, because it enabled the preacher to speak from personal experience and observation, and that concerning the very event on which the hope of the world hinged. But for the fact that she had seen the Lord, there would have been no Easter, and her sermon would have been a funeral discourse; that is to say, but for the fact of the resurrection and the appearance of the Lord to her, she would have spoken of his death and burial. But in lieu of death there was life, and instead of a dead teacher there was the living Christ. That made a world of difference—an eternity of difference, in fact.

2. This first Easter sermon was preached on the first day of the week, and by the one who was first at the tomb with the "other Mary." These first things come first in the development of the Easter story, which grows in interest and power as the years go by.

3. The point of this first Easter sermon, the pith of Mary Magdalene's preaching, so far as we are now concerned, is to be found in the spiritual translation of the text. Have we seen the Lord? Has he called our names, and have we responded, "Master"? Has he presented to us his hands and his side, and were we glad when we saw him? Yea, us hath he quickened, who were dead in trespasses and in sins, and hath raised us up together. "We have seen the Lord."

ENDLESS POWER FOR ENDLESS LIVING

"The power of an endless life." Heb. 7:16.

1. There is power over gloom for all who live in the risen Christ: "In him is no darkness at all."
2. Power over temptation is Easter's gift to mankind; the Conqueror of death was also the conqueror of temptation.
3. Power over weakness is a fruit of the resurrection; whom the all-powerful Saviour strengthens is strengthened indeed.
4. Power over injustice is a fruit of Christ's rising again; if Jesus bore injustice uncomplainingly, then conquered it, we too may follow in his train.
5. Power over remorse comes from Christ's rising again; remorse never visits the person who, trusting in Christ's victorious might, never falls a prey to sin.
6. The resurrection means power over sin; Christ, proved divine, by his power over death, is able to deliver us all from sin and from its end, which is eternal death.
7. Power for understanding comes to all men who cling to the risen Christ. What is impossible to understand here—suffering, sorrow, distress, weakness, privation and our multitude of apparently unmerited ills—"some day we'll understand."
8. Power for service, satisfying and worthwhile service, is ours because with Christ we live an endless life. What we do now for him is only a moment's beginning for service that is to continue, with constantly increasing power, until "the end of the ages."
9. Power for endless joy, perfect joy and unashamed joy is God's Easter gift to all who will accept it. And the token of our acceptance is simply obedience.
10. Power over poverty and privation is a gift that comes from the risen Master; he was rich, yet for our sakes became poor and by so doing he won eternal riches for us all.
11. Power for growing and complete sanctification (purity, sinlessness, godliness)—this is what will come to all God's children who accept the Easter fact as fact and the risen Master as Master.
12. Power for a broad vision comes to all who accept

Christ as the risen Lord. Whoever lives eternally will view things from an eternal standpoint, not with a temporary vision that counts the small delights of to-day as all-important. It is hard to live with Christ and be petty minded.—REV. P. P. F.

THE RISEN CHRIST

"Thanks be to God, which giveth us the victory through our Lord Jesus Christ." 1 Cor. 15:57.
  I. He has conquered Physical Death.
    1. He arose from the dead.
    2. He raised others from the dead.
    3. He promises to raise all from the dead on the last day. This comforts mourning hearts.
  II. He has conquered Spiritual Death.
    1. God is life. To be estranged from him is to be in death. This is the natural condition of man.
    2. Through his word and the Holy Sacraments Jesus calls men out of death to life. The believers live in Christ.
  III. He has conquered Eternal Death.
    1. Eternal death—exclusion from the gracious presence and the beatific vision of God.
    2. Jesus by his sufferings and death bore the eternal punishment for our sins and merited for us eternal life.
    3. Natural death does not end all; there is a life of bliss beyond.

THE EMPTY GRAVE

"Come and see the place where the Lord lay." Matt. 28:6.

The angel here addresses the visitors to the tomb. To prove the certainty of his resurrection he refers to their senses. We notice:

  I. The Resurrection of Christ was foretold.

David declared, "Neither wilt thou suffer Thine Holy One to see corruption."

Christ distinctly predicted and asserted his crucifixion, his death, and his resurrection from the grave.

II. The testimony of those to whom Christ appeared after his resurrection.
   1. The enemies of Christ both believed and testified his resurrection. The conduct of the scribes and Pharisees clearly indicates that, in their own hearts, they feared Christ would rise again. They sought to overthrow the true statement of their own guards by falsehood. The Roman soldiers knew that Christ had risen.
   2. The friends of Jesus bore witness of his resurrection. (a) The angel positively announced to the women: "He is not here, he is risen." (b) On their way to tell the disciples the glad tidings, Jesus met them. They knew his voice, they recognized him as their crucified Lord. (c) He appeared to the eleven when assembled with closed doors. (d) To Thomas. (e) To more than five hundred brethren at once.

MARY'S JOY IN HER RISEN LORD

"Jesus saith unto her, Mary," etc. John 20: 16, 17.

That was a memorable morning because on it Jesus broke the bands of death and appeared to a living, anxious, seeking woman.

I. Mary was attached to Christ. Luke 8: 23. But test of love is seen in sacrifice. To be with Jesus when men applaud was pleasant; but after one sold him, another denied him, and all the rest "forsook him, and fled," Mary was faithful.

II. Mary was the first to see Christ after his resurrection. When Christ appeared she did not know him. He is often nearer than we think.

III. Mary was the first to preach a risen Christ. Thou hast joy, then share it with others. Thou hast seen Jesus, then go tell others.

THE RISEN CHRIST

"Fear not ye; he is not here; he is risen; come see the place where the Lord lay." Matt. 28: 6.

It is with Christ's risen life that faith connects us.

I. The security of the risen life. Faith knits us to him.

II. The power of the risen life. It was the Risen One who spake. "All power is given unto me." We have his power.

III. The love of the risen life. Resurrection is a new and higher state of being. The instrument is now more perfectly tuned; is capable of sweeter sounds.

IV. The sympathies of the risen life. Resurrection does not throw a gulf between us and the Risen One. It is the filling up of the gulf. It is the shepherd bringing himself nearer his flock.

V. The affinities of the risen life. We are risen "with him."

VI. The joys of the risen life. In the tomb the Man of Sorrows left his sorrows. We share his joy.

VII. The hopes of the risen life. We are begotten unto a lively hope by the resurrection of Christ from the dead.

THE RESURRECTION A FACT

"Now is Christ risen from the dead and become the firstfruits of them that slept." 1 Cor. 15:20.

I. The resurrection of Jesus Christ from the dead is a historical fact. As such it is proved like any other historical fact—by the testimony of competent witnesses and by the witness of related facts and results.

II. The resurrection of Jesus Christ from the dead is more than a historical fact. It is a spiritual force in the lives of men. Through fellowship with the risen Christ, men rise from a death in sin to a life in holiness. "Now is Christ risen from the dead." "Ye are risen with Christ." In Christ the believer is a risen man.

III. The resurrection of Christ is more than a historical fact and more than a spiritual force. It is prophecy and hope and assurance of future life. "Because I live, ye shall live also." Men have ever nursed and nurtured the thought of life beyond the grave. It is a sort of instinct of humanity. The thought is as old as the heart-beat and as natural.—Rev. John F. Carson, D.D.

AND PETER

"Go tell his disciples and Peter." Mark 16:7.

I. Tell Peter, although he has sinned so grievously. It was heartless, repeated, public, willful.

II. Tell Peter, for he has wept. God's anger against his children ceases with the commencement of their penitence.

III. Tell Peter, for he has suffered. His thoughts were God's chastening rod.

IV. Tell Peter, he is dear to Christ. Sin can grieve Christ, cause him to withdraw, wound and disfigure us; but it cannot alter his love.

V. Tell Peter, for he is your brother. They have sinned. Have not we denied our Lord?

THE LESSON OF EASTER

Easter gives vitality to life. Without the fact of Easter life would be dull, flat, and meaningless; there would be no more value to human life than there is to brute life, simply living on a better physical plane, and with less real enjoyment, for the natural, universal dream of humanity is toward the idea that Easter reveals immortality brought to light. That which was the eternal "dream" of man, from the earliest known times, that which was the longing of man became a reality when Jesus Christ arose from the dead.

I. The imperishable life. The outstanding fact of Easter is immortality.

II. The abundant life. If we are only physical, our very "abundance" of things is a mockery. To know, to think, to feel, to long, to dream, is the abundant life only as we consider it in connection with Jesus. We need him to make it "full." And for that he came. "I am come that they might have life, and might have it abundantly."

III. The expanding life. It is not only full, abundant, but there is a development of life, which the resurrection assures, which is possible only in Jesus Christ. "But we all, with unveiled face, beholding as in a mirror the glory of the Lord, are transformed into the same image from glory to glory."

IV. The triumphant life. Everything about us tells us a

story of defeated life. The air is full of farewells to the dying, and mournings for the dead. The outer man is perishing—perishing every day. If that is all there is of us; if what we call spiritual life is only a chemical combination of matter, we not only die, but completely perish. But listen to the triumphant cry of Paul: "The inward man is renewed day by day."

V. The final great lesson of Easter is the proper sense of values. "The things that are seen are temporal." It does not say that the things that are seen are unreal; he accepts their reality, but denies their permanence. Grip the truth. Are we living in the things that are seen? Are we building upon the things that are not seen, yet are eternal?—REV. W. H. GEISTWEIT, D.D.

THE FIRST GOSPEL SERMON

"And he saith unto them, Be not affrighted: Ye seek Jesus of Nazareth, which was crucified: he is risen; he is not here: behold the place where they laid him," etc. Mark 16:6, 7.

Here we have the first gospel sermon preached after the gospel had been finished on the cross, and sealed by the fact of the resurrection. Not a sentence that dropped from the speaker's lips by accident; nor are its words mere words that came uppermost, as though some other words might have done as well. They hold the germ of which the preaching of all true evangelists is but the expansion.

I. The first title under which Christ was proclaimed by a messenger from heaven after his crucifixion.
　1. Jesus. The name given at the annunciation. Now it is fulfilled. He has saved his people from their sins. Henceforth this name shall be above every name. All through our life in time let us sing with Bernard, "This name is sweetness in the mouth, music in the ear, joy in the heart," and all through our life in eternity let us expect to penetrate deeper and deeper into the soul of its beauty, and glory, and meaning.
　2. Jesus of Nazareth. A lowly title, despised by men.
　3. Jesus of Nazareth, which was crucified. Words used among men to express contempt, an angel is proud to

use; and the last phrase of degradation which his enemies flung at him on earth was the first title under which he is proclaimed by a flaming prophet from heaven.

II. The first notice of Christ's resurrection. Christ's resurrection is:
1. A mystery.
2. A miracle.
3. A victory over death.
4. A fulfillment of his promise.

—Rev. C. Stanford, D.D.

EASTER TALK TO CHILDREN

"He is not here, but is risen." Luke 24:6.

Look at this queer gray thing (showing a cocoon), and listen to a true story about it.

Last fall there was a fuzzy brown caterpillar climbing up an apple tree. Up, up it went till it could stretch itself out on a green leaf. Then it was tired and wanted to cover up and go to sleep. What do you suppose it did for covers? It spun out a long gray, silky thread—I never can tell you how he did it—God makes a fuzzy worm to do things you and I cannot do or even understand.

So it spun out a long gray, silky thread, and wrapped it round and round the stout apple leaf till it drew up at the sides and made a cradle—a cradle with himself inside! There, snug and dry and warm, the little caterpillar went to sleep.

Frosty days came. Most of the leaves fell off the trees, but the stout apple leaf held on. You stopped playing hide-and-seek and went to school. You had Thanksgiving and Christmas and stormy days, and still the apple-leaf cradle was swinging on the tree with the caterpillar fast asleep inside.

Now the sunshiny days are here. You are throwing off caps and mittens and running out to play. And soon there will come a-knocking on the inside of the cradle. People knock on doors to get in, but here is something trying to get out! Pretty soon a hole will come in the end, and out will come—not a fuzzy brown caterpillar, but a shiny yellow butterfly with wings like silk.

Boys and girls, listen! Some day you and I will go to sleep down here—people will say we are dead, and they will put our bodies down in the ground to stay while our souls go to God; but the God who can change an ugly caterpillar into a beautiful butterfly can give our souls new, glorious bodies that can never die. He says he will do it for "those who keep his commandments." Remember this story when you see a gray cradle swinging in a tree.

THE POWER OF HIS RESURRECTION

"That I may know him and the power of his resurrection." Phil. 3: 10.

It is doubtful if Paul ever saw Jesus in the flesh. He speaks of the desire to know him, the purpose and the expectation. Paul thought of Jesus as still alive, and has excellent reason for this belief. Jesus had appeared to him and he came into the Christian church as one born out of due time. This saying is not so strange, this purpose not so unusual, as the desire to know the power of his resurrection.

I. How can one who is alive know the power of any resurrection? Ah, we forget that Paul was even now dead. He had cut himself off from the old life, with all its ideas and ideals, quite as completely as if he had died and had been buried. The old self was dead.

II. But Paul is not the man to be content with mere negation. He would make his death to self and sin a birth to life that is life indeed. Even as Jesus' universal ministry began only after his death, Paul looks for an experience in his Christian life that shall be continual evidence of Christ's resurrection in him. This, as we see it, is the obvious meaning of the words, "that I may know the power of his resurrection."

This is not the sole meaning, but it is the first meaning. Paul looks for proof of his new life in Christ in a certain daily experience. He will be satisfied with nothing less than demonstrable evidence that the life he now lives, he lives by the death of the Son of God.—REV. CHARLES CARROLL ALBERTSON, D.D.

ROLLING AWAY THE STONE

"Thanks be unto God which giveth us the victory, through our Lord Jesus Christ." 1 Cor. 15:57.

Victories are much more delightful than defeats, as summits are finer viewpoints than valleys. Our Lord turned his defeat on Calvary to a glorious triumph; in dying, he conquered death.

I. Unbelief died when Christ arose; they saw him, touched him, ate with him, prayed together and then at last beheld him ascend to his heavenly glory, to prepare for their coming in a little while. No wonder they preached Christ and the resurrection ever after!

II. Millions have seen him by faith since that day—though not an actual vision as Paul enjoyed, yet the spiritual view is just as vivid and real. Christ comes to human souls as he did to the disciples when the doors were locked, and no one knew of his approach; he comes in to dwell with us forever, to pardon sin, to cleanse the heart, to give victory over the world.

III. Millions have been rolling away the stone in the pathway of human progress that the world might march on in the glorious resurrection of peace.—REV. E. W. CASWELL, D.D.

EASTER GLADNESS IN SEEING THE LORD

"Then were the disciples glad when they saw the Lord." John 20:20.

And well they might be; for they felt as orphans deserted and desolate when their Master was gone. Their sorrow had been deep, but now it was turned into joy.

I. They were glad on account of the gratification of their natural attachment. They could once more gaze upon that well known and beloved face, so radiant with love.

II. They were glad because they recognized him as Lord of all, as the Supreme God, as God manifest in the flesh, and now felt, after a night of doubt and gloom that his Omnipotent care was over them.

III. They were glad because his resurrection proved the completion of his atoning work.

IV. The disciples were glad when they saw the Lord because his resurrection was a pledge of their own future resurrection and of their eventful participation in that glory which he was speedily to take possession of in their name. "In my Father's house are many mansions; if it were not so I would have told you; and if I go, I will come again, and take you to myself, that where I am, there ye may be also."

V. We, too, are glad when we have seen the Lord, not with our bodily eye but with eye of faith, for then we have an evidence that we are his, and that, in due time, we shall enter into his glory. And if these spiritual visions cheer us now, fill us with holy joy, what will be the vision and portion of his glory in the heavenly world; when freed from sorrow and from sin we shall see him as he is, and bathe our very souls in the sunshine of his love.

THE SPIRITUAL PARABLE OF CHRIST'S CRUCIFIXION, RESURRECTION, ASCENSION AND RETURN

"Dead with him," "Risen with him," "Hid with him," "Appear with him." Col. 2:20; 3:1, 3, 4.

I. Introduction. New Testament use of "With Christ," "In Christ," "Through Christ," etc. The keynote of Paul's conception of the Christian life; used about one hundred times. In Ephesians alone the phrases are connected with grace, peace, spiritual blessing, adoption, choosing, redemption, forgiveness, acceptation, union, inheritance, sealing, wisdom, revelation. Especially found in connection with the death, resurrection, ascension, and return of Christ in a parabolic or figurative sense. Rom. 6:4, 6-11; Gal. 2:19-21; Eph. 4:9-13. The text is a striking illustration of this parabolic use; the words "dead," "risen," "hid," "appear," picture four phases of the individual Christian life.

II. Discussion. (Be careful to distinguish the parabolic from the literal meaning.)

    1. "Dead with Christ." Christ died on the cross a sacrifice for sin. He nailed everything earthly to it. He entered the tomb dead, separated from the world. Separation from the world the phase of Christian life

figured here. "Reckoned as dead," "crucified with him," is our attitude toward the old nature. A tomb door between us and sin. This the negative phase of Christian life.

2. "Risen with Christ." Christ rose from the dead to a new life, the full eternal life. In a real living sense we shall rise with him to immortal hope and share in his glorified life. But the thought here figures the positive side of Christian life. "Dead to sin," but also "alive to righteousness." A risen life. A rising life; "on stepping stones of our dead selves."

—H. H. BARSTOW, D.D.

THE POWER OF CHRIST'S RESURRECTION

"That I may know him, and the power of his resurrection." Phil. 3:10.

The power of Christ's resurrection has cast a mysterious spell over about 600,000,000 of living people of the present day, so that they love him, and are exemplifying him, in all the various parts of the world. This power is universally recognized everywhere by foes as well as by friends of Christ.

The fruits of this marvelous power of Christ's resurrection may be clearly seen from three angles:

I. It is a personal transforming power. 1. It is seen in the new life in Christ. Faith in Christ is its basis (Rom. 4:25). 2. It is seen in the spiritual knowledge. The best evidences are seen in boots, not books. There is no greater force than the back of the certain, "I know," for Christianity can be attested by personal experience.

II. This marvel is seen in that it is a world-transforming power. 1. See the battle in array. The early problem was a billion pagans against twelve disciples of Jesus. This seems to us of to-day almost absurd, but the triumph was assured. 2. The internal enemy, too, was conquered by the real thing. Heresy, many times, is worse than paganism, as it is more insidious in its workings, and more difficult to deal with. It is a civil war, the worst kind of war. But Christianity conquered here.

III. The power of Christ's resurrection is seen in that it

transforms death. 1. It transforms the angel of gloom into an angel of light. It makes one to sense the Light of the World illumining "the valley of the shadow of death." With a real consciousness of Jesus' Real Presence, there can be no death, as ordinarily understood. 2. In Christ, in him alone, there is a glorious triumph. Paul in the presence of the martyr's block rejoiced in the "Crown of righteousness" (2 Tim. 4:7, 8). Jerome, of Prague, had no fear of physical pain, while Christ was near. At the martyr's stake, three Quakers in more recent times in England, in their last moments, could clap their hands in holy triumph, because they felt the power of Christ's resurrection!

Thus to-day we may realize the tears, to-morrow we shall know the triumph, to-day we may know earth's sorrow, to-morrow we shall know the joy; to-day we view the mounded graves, to-morrow we shall view the triumphal glory, and this all because of "the power of Christ's resurrection!"

THE RISEN CHRIST

"Fear not ye; he is not here; he is risen; come see the place where the Lord lay." Matt. 28:6.

He is risen! He has tasted death, but he has not seen corruption; for he is the Holy One of God, and upon holiness corruption cannot fasten. It is with this risen life that faith connects us, from the moment that we believe in him who died and rose again. Let us note, then, such things as these:

I. The security of the risen life. The faith that knits us to him makes us partakers of his resurrection.

II. The power of the risen life. It was as the Risen One has spake: "All power is given unto me," etc. In that power we are made more than conquerors.

III. The love of the risen life. The resurrection was a newer and higher stage of being and with the perfection of life there comes a perfection of love.

IV. The affinities of the risen life. The resurrection breaks no bonds save those of mortality.

V. The joys of the risen life. In the tomb the Man of sorrows left all his sorrows, as he left all our sins. Then they were buried with him. At this resurrection his full joy began. But the fullness of that risen joy is also in reserve for us.

VI. The hopes of the risen life. "We are begotten again unto a lively hope by the resurrection of Christ from the dead."

PART XVII: LORD'S SUPPER TEXTS AND THEMES

A Joyful Approach: "I went with them to the house of God, with the voice of joy and praise, with a multitude that kept holyday." Psa. 42:4.

A Message First: "I will not eat until I have told mine errand." Gen. 24:33.

Climbing Round by Round: "Behold a ladder set up on the earth, and the top of it reached to heaven," etc. Gen. 28:12.

Consecration: "But first gave their own selves to the Lord." 2 Cor. 8:5.

Love for the Unseen Saviour: "Whom having not seen ye love." 1 Peter 1:8.

A Visit to Calvary: "And sitting down they watched him there." Matt. 28:36.

Song of the Pilgrims: Psa. 84.

Minds Stirred to Remembrance: "I stir up your pure minds by way of remembrance." 2 Peter 3:1.

A Dying Wish Respected: "This do in remembrance of me." Luke 22:19.

Living to Christ: "For to me to live is Christ." Phil. 1:21.

The Duty of Christians to Study Christ: "Wherefore, consider the Apostle and High Priest of our profession, Christ Jesus." Heb. 3:1.

A Personal Question: "What mean ye by this service?" Ex. 12:2.

Duty and Obligations of Christians to Keep the Communion Feast: "Therefore let us keep the feast." 1 Cor. 5:8.

Good to Draw Near to God: "It is good for me to draw near to God." Psa. 73:28.

Beautiful with Sandals: "How beautiful are thy feet with shoes, O prince's daughter." Song of Sol. 7:7.

The Great Festal Gathering: Rev. 5:11, 12.

At the Last Supper: "Now when even was come," etc. Matt. 26:20-22.

Spiritual Progress: "Grow in grace." 2 Pet. 3:18.

The Great Resolve: "We will walk in the name of the Lord our God for ever and ever." Micah 4:5.

The Lord's Supper a Covenant: "And Moses took half of the blood," etc. Ex. 24:6-8.

Sacraments Connecting Heaven and Earth: "Thou art near, O Lord." Psa. 119:151.

The Remembrance of Christ's Earthly Life and of His Death: "This do in remembrance of me." Luke 22:19.

Eucharist, a Memento of Christ's Life in Glory: "Thou hast ascended on high," etc. Psa. 67:18, 19.

Advantages of the Perpetual Remembrance of Christ: "This do in remembrance of me." Luke 22:19.

The Eucharist a Renewal of the Covenant: "This cup is the new testament in my blood, which is shed for you." Luke 22:20.

The Presence of Christ in the Supper: "And he took bread, and gave thanks, and brake it, and gave unto them, saying, This is my body which is given for you." Luke 22:19.

Partakers of Christ: "For we are made partakers of Christ, if we hold the beginning of our confidence steadfast to the end." Heb. 3:14.

The Bread of Life: "For the bread of God is he which cometh down from heaven, and giveth life unto the world." John 6:33.

Grace Given in the Lord's Supper: "Are not Abana and Pharpar, rivers of Damascus, better than all the waters of Israel? May I not wash in them and be clean?" 2 Kings 5:12.

Communion in the Lord's Supper: "That which we have seen and heard declare we unto you, that ye also may have fellowship with us; and truly our fellowship is with the Father, and with his Son, Jesus Christ." 1 John 1:3.

The Worthy Communicant: "But let a man examine himself, and so let him eat of that bread, and drink of that cup." 1 Cor. 11:28.

The Action: "This do ye." 1 Cor. 11:25.

The Paschal Lamb: "Christ our Passover." 1 Cor. 5:7.

The Bread of Life: John 6:33.

The Bequest of Jesus: "Peace I leave with you, my peace I give unto you." John 14:27.

A Last Wish: "This do in remembrance of me." Luke 22:19.

The Gospel Festival: "A feast of fat things, a feast of wine on the lees, of fat things full of marrow, of wine on the lees well refined." Isa. 25:6.

Neglect of the Lord's Supper: "And they would not come." Matt. 22:3. "I will sup with him." Rev. 3:20.

The New Passover Feast: "And they made ready the Passover." Luke 22:13.

The Surroundings of the Supper: "After the same manner also." 1 Cor. 11:25.

On the Threshold: "He brought me to the banqueting house." Song of Solomon 2:4.

Eternal Life in Christ: "The gift of God is eternal life through Jesus Christ, our Lord." Rom. 6:33.

Invited to the Feast: "Come, for all things are now ready." Luke 14:17.

The King's Guests: "When the king came in to see the guests." Matt. 22:11.

Afterthoughts: "So when they had dined." John 21:15.

Good to Draw Near to God: "It is good for me to draw near to God." Psa. 73:28.

The Mount of Privilege: The transfiguration. Mark 9:1-14.

After the Mountain-top, What? Work awaiting at its base. Mark 9:14-27.

Duty and Obligation of Christians to Keep the Communion Feast: "Therefore let us keep the feast." 1 Cor. 5:8.

A Personal Question: "What mean ye by this service?" Ex. 12:2.

Fulfilling Our Vows: Jacob building the promised altar. Gen. 35:1-7.

Encouragement for the Timid: "As for me I will come into thy house in the multitude of thy mercy," etc. Psa. 5:7.

Invited Closer—A Day of Communion: "Master, where dwellest thou? ... Come and see." John 1:38, 39.

Being with Jesus Shows: "They took knowledge of them that they had been with Jesus." Acts 4:13.

Love's Question: "Lovest thou me?" John 21:16.
Meditation Kindling Love: "My meditation of him shall be sweet." Psa. 104:34.
Practical Religion: "Faith without works is dead." Jas. 11:20.
Rest in the Midst of Toil: "Come ye yourselves apart and rest a while." Mark 6:31.
Let Us Draw Near: "Having, therefore, boldness . . . let us draw near with a true heart," etc. Heb. 10:19-25.
Communion Continued: "But they constrained him, saying, Abide with us," etc. Luke 24:29.

PART XVIII: LORD'S SUPPER SERMON OUTLINES

STIRRING TO REMEMBRANCE

"I stir up your pure minds by way of remembrance." 2 Peter 3:1.

The power and use of memory. God uses this faculty in building up Christian character. In our coming Communion we remember especially the facts and the purpose of Christ's life and death.

I. The Gospel has a history to be remembered.
 1. Bring to remembrance Christ's sufferings.
 2. Bring to remembrance our sins.
 3. Bring to remembrance God's love.

II. The Lord's Supper has a purpose to be remembered.
 1. It is a commemoration of Christ.
 2. It is a communion with Christ.
 3. It should bring consecration to Christ.—H.

CHRIST EXPECTED AT THE FEAST

"What think ye, that he will not come to the feast?" John 11:56.

I. What is there to cause us to fear that he will not be at the feast?
 1. Our sins against him.
 2. Our neglect of doing commanded duty.
 3. Our lack of love for him.

II. On the other hand what is there to encourage the hope that he will be at the feast?
 1. His character.
 2. His disposition to forgive.
 3. His love.—H.

THE DUTY AND OBLIGATION TO KEEP THE FEAST

"Therefore, let us keep the feast." 1 Cor. 5:8.

I. First, let us keep the feast because the obligations rests on Christ's dying command.

"Keep my commandments." "Ye are my friends if ye do whatsoever I command you." "This do in remembrance of me."

II. Let us keep the feast as a public confession of Christ. It offers a blessed opportunity of testifying in the presence of fellow disciples and of the world that we are not ashamed of Christ. "I will pay my vows now, in the presence of all his people."

III. Let us keep the feast because in not doing so we would incur spiritual loss. It is a blessed means of grace, and the loss is great when neglected. It is called a "feast" because it refreshes and strengthens the soul.—H.

COMMUNION

"This do in remembrance of me." 1 Cor. 11:24.

These words were uttered by our Lord in the most solemn and yet the sweetest service that he had with his disciples. Jesus had borne many things and had faced all manner of trials and sufferings, but could not bear to be forgotten. He wants to be remembered.

I. In what he wants to be remembered.
    1. Not so much in his deeds of kindness.
    2. Not so much in his social endeavor.
    3. Not in his miracles.
    4. But in his death and what it meant to all.

II. The spirit in which he wants to be remembered.
    1. The spirit of love.
    2. The spirit of obedience.
    3. The spirit of progress and conquest.

III. What he gave us to remember him by.
    1. Bread. The staff of life. Broken bread. Broken body. Life-giving.

2. Wine, the blood of the grape. The poured-out wine, the spilled blood of Christ, the life-giving blood.

These two emblems of life he gave that his disciples should remember his death till he came again.

EMPTY PLACES AT THE LORD'S TABLE

"David's place was empty." 1 Sam. 20: 25.
I. Some absent who might be expected to be present.
   1. Children of good parents.
   2. Hearers of the word.
   3. Those who have proved the vanity of the world for themselves.
II. Some apparently absent who are really present.
   1. The timorous and fearful.
   2. Those whose love is greater than their hope.
III. Some present who ought to be absent.
   1. Hypocrites.
   2. Schemers.
IV. Some absent on the most frivolous excuses.
   1. Nothing worth hearing.
   2. Inconsistencies of other people.

INVITED NEARER: A COMMUNION MEDITATION

"Master, where dwellest thou? He saith unto them, Come and see." John 1: 38, 39.

In the sacramental service we receive an invitation to nearness with Christ. It is a gracious invitation to partake of nearer and more confidential communion with our Master.

I. About to accept his invitation let us begin with confession to him of our sins. "With my burden I begin; Lord remove this load of sin." Let us tell him of our waywardness, our coldness of heart, of our neglect of his word, of prayer, of fellowship. Keep nothing back. "He will abundantly pardon."

II. So near to Christ we will confide to him our troubles and sorrows, too. In this sacramental service the burdened and the afflicted are especially invited near and are assured of Christ's sympathy and comfort. "Come unto me all ye that labor and are heavy laden, and I will give you rest," "Cast your care on him, for he careth for you"—literally, "bears you upon his heart." Draw near, and tell him your troubles.

III. This is a precious invitation to those just beginning to follow Christ. Such were John and Andrew. Such is the case with many in this church to-day. You are asking, "Master, where dwellest thou?" You want to know him better. He invites you to the nearest and sweetest relationship: "Come, and see." "Come, tarry with me a while; listen to my words: learn my spirit; know my desires; become intimate with me and the things of my kingdom." It is so he speaks to you—you who are just entering upon his service. Recite to him your fears; tell him of your longings and aspirations; make known to him your resolutions, and ask him to help you keep them.

IV. Some of the blessedness of being brought near. "I sat down under his shadow with great delight and his fruit was sweet to my taste. He brought me into his banqueting house and his banner over me was love."

1. Nearness. It is blessed just to be near him.
2. Rest. It means getting a rest that will refresh for going on to new endeavor.
3. Protection. Shade from the burning sun of temptation, affliction, etc.
4. Sweet fruit. Such as pardon, peace, power, assurance, joy, hope; indeed, sweet foretastes of heaven.—H.

PREPARATORY SERVICE

"There make ready." Matt. 26:17.
For us, where make ready? In our hearts! In our hearts!
I. What the communion is.
 1. The feast.
 2. The provision.
 3. The design.
II. The necessity of preparation. Often unprofitable for lack of it.
III. What is a good preparation?

It is preparation that brings us into sympathy with Christ. We are to try to get his feelings.
1. About sin.
2. About salvation.
3. About spiritual growth, strength, consecration.
—Rev. W. R. Taylor, D.D.

LOVE MADE THE SUPPER

"There they made him a supper." John 12:2.

That haunting "they"! Who is "they," this beautiful "they"? It eludes us like the voice of the vesper sparrow. It hints of the beautiful poetry of love.

This supper was a neighborhood affair. In point of personal accuracy it was Simon who gave it. I think he paid the bills; but the neighbors took a hand at this sweet dinner at Simon's desire. They who loved him made him a festival.

I. Simon the leper; the supper was at his house. Toward him Christ walked despite the warning, raucous voice of leper Simon, "Unclean, unclean, beware." Toward the voice came the holy feet and outstretched was the holy hand to touch the untouchable leper and not to be rendered unclean thereby but to cleanse the leper. It was Christ, and his touch means cleansing.

And then Simon the leper came home all unawares, and wife and children wept aloud, and sang aloud and kissed aloud, "Welcome home." And Simon made his Saviour a supper! Likely enough, and rightly enough. A beautiful supper.

II. But next door in lovely Bethany beneath the olive trees dwell the grown-up orphans, Martha and Mary and Lazarus. And to these Christ had come also. He had touched their hand of death and Lazarus sprang up a living man. Small wonder Simon knew that they must be at the supper. And Simon sat at the table and Jesus beside him, and Lazarus sat at the table, but not to eat but just to look and adore. And Martha, to be sure. Martha served. We should have known that without the telling. And John's Zebedee was there to see it all and to love to rehearse it all in this endearing phrase "and they made him a supper."

III. There never was any supper like this. A supper of

love. And who is absent? Are we all here? It looks somehow as if somebody was away. Why, Mary is not here! Why is Mary away? Has she forgotten "The Resurrection and the Life"? Martha is among those that serve, but where is ———. When coming running with a little alabaster box, with her eyes shining love and her black tresses loose like a flying veil, is Mary, and stops not till she reaches the feet, the blessed naked feet of God, "and anointed the feet of Jesus and wiped his feet with her hair; and the house was filled with the odor of the ointment." Love made him a supper!

IV. And then his Love made them and us all the Lord's Supper, where we all kneel to partake, and he girds himself and serves us and breaks upon our heads and hearts the alabaster box of his love, until all the world is filled with the odor of the ointment.—W. A. Q.

THE VALUE OF SPIRITUAL DREAMING

"And he dreamed, and behold a ladder set up on the earth, and the top of it reached to heaven." Gen. 28:12.

I. Here was restlessness due to distance from God. Jacob had sinned against his brother, his father and his God. He knew it, and he had a restless slumber. He dreaded punishment. He wanted communion with God. He dreamed of it.

II. The meaning of the ladder symbol. It was the New Testament in the Old. It was the sign of communication between earth and heaven, between God and man.

A ladder suggests perilous emergency. A ladder suggests possible salvation. A ladder suggests immediate use.

III. This occurrence may well suggest to us that the Christian's career is upward. The ladder was on earth, but it reached to heaven. It ended at the throne. We are to mount toward the throne of God. It is our duty to advance. Our ascent may be gradual, but it ought to be steady, continuous. "Grow." Aspire. Climb.

IV. The value of spiritual dreaming. See that you make your life after the pattern shown you in the mount. God gives you visions, ideals. Work toward them. Let this sacramental season be to you a new start toward heaven.—H.

COMMUNION CONTINUED

"They constrained him, saying, Abide with us; for it is toward evening, and the day is far spent; and he went in to tarry with them." Luke 24: 29.

Like these disciples on their walk to Emmaus, when we have the Saviour's company a little while, we will not be contented until we have more of it. Some liquors men drink increase thirst. Never is the Christian tired of Christ's company. Love's logic is always ready with a plea, "Abide with us, for it is toward evening."

The suggestion also comes that if we would keep Christ with us we must constrain him. Christ will not intrude where he is not wanted. The question then becomes one as to how we can keep him with us.

I. First, allow no rivals in your heart. Christ will never tarry in a divided heart. Be sure of that. He must be all to us or nothing. "Ye cannot serve God and mammon." Let us be watchful that we love him with an undivided love and serve him with unvarying delight.

II. Retain no darling sin. Charles Spurgeon once said, "A little evil will spoil our peace, just as a small stone in one's shoe will spoil his walking." Many people lose Christ's presence through the indulgence of what they call little sins.

III. Make your heart a fit temple for Christ's indwelling. Out with the money changers, and unholy traffic. Give no place to the things that defile the body or degrade the soul. Keep the heart clean, and the mind pure. Make your heart not a place for harsh and warring sounds, but make it indeed a house of prayer. If it is made a fit place for Christ's presence, he will come and make his residence in the temple of your soul.—H.

THE LORD'S SUPPER

1 Cor. 11: 25, 26.

I. Divinely Commanded. "This do ye."
II. A Commemorative Event. "In remembrance of me."
III. A Proclamation to the world of the glorious fact. "Ye do show the Lord's death."
IV. A continued obligation. "Till he come."

THE FRIENDSHIP OF JESUS

"Ye are my friends, if ye do whatsoever I command you. Henceforth I call you not servants," etc. John 15:14, 15.

Friendship is indispensable. Consider a few of the characteristics of a true friend.

1. He is always accessible. You will never find "No admission" written upon his door. For you, at least, his latch string is always out, his heart and his home is always open.
2. The true friend is sympathetic. Your sorrow makes him sad; your joy gives a keener note to his rejoicing.
3. A true friend always construes you favorably. His judgments are never harsh. He looks upon your good qualities and puts his emphasis on them.
4. A true friend will make sacrifices on your behalf.
5. But perhaps the most conspicuous element of all is his constancy. A true friend remains the same no matter how the wind may blow.
6. Now, in outlining these qualities of the ideal friend, you observe I have simply been describing our blessed Saviour. My only purpose has been that you might see him, and whom else do we want to see at such a service as this. Take these qualities upon which I have touched and see how beautifully they apply to him.
   1. He is always accessible.
   2. And as for his sympathy, it is too wonderful, too boundless, too infinite, for our poor minds to grasp.
   3. He always sees what is best in us and appeals to that.
   4. His sacrifice—infinite unselfishness!
   5. His constancy. The same yesterday, to-day and forever.—Rev. Robert F. Coyle, D.D.

THE SCENE OF CALVARY

"The place which is called Calvary." Luke 23:33.
1. It was the scene of strange prodigies.
2. It was the scene of unequalled suffering.
3. It was the scene of all-sufficient sacrifice.
4. It was the scene of glorious triumph.
5. It was the scene of peerless example.

LESSONS FROM THE NAMES OF THE ORDINANCE

"For I have received of the Lord that which also I delivered unto you." 1 Cor. 11:23.
1. The Lord's Supper.
2. The Communion.
3. The Eucharist.
4. The Sacrament.
5. The Feast.

LESSONS FROM THE NATURE OF THE ORDINANCE

I. The Sacramental emblems.
   1. The bread, the emblem of Christ's body or human nature.
   2. The cup, the emblem of his blood or sacrifice for sin.
II. The sacramental actions.
   1. On the part of Christ, who blessed the elements, and gave them with his own hand to the disciples, after breaking the one and pouring out the other.
   2. On the part of the disciples, who received the bread and wine, and partook of them.
III. The sacramental words.
   1. This is my body—the Incarnation.
   2. This is my body which is broken—the Passion.
   3. This is my body, which is broken for you—the Atonement.
   4. This cup is the new testament in my blood—the Covenant of Grace.
   5. This cup is the new testament in my blood, which was shed for many for the remission of sins—Justification.
   6. Take, eat. Drink ye all of it—Faith.

LESSONS FROM THE DESIGN OF THE ORDINANCE

1 Cor. 11:23.
1. It is commemorating.

2. It is confessing.
3. It is communicating.
4. It is covenanting.
5. It is sealing.

MEDITATION

"While I was musing the fire burned." Psa. 39:3.
I. Proper subjects of meditation.
  1. The character of God.
  2. His providential dealings.
  3. The plan of salvation.
  4. Our relation to God.
  5. Our future.
II. The benefits of meditation.
  1. The acquisition of religious power.
  2. The production of religious pleasure.
  3. The realization of religious hopes.

—Rev. W. W. Wythe.

"COME AND DINE"

"Then Jesus said unto them, Children, have ye any meat? They answered, No. Jesus saith unto them, Come and dine." John 21:5, 12.

Our Lord did not need the great draft of fishes they had caught, by casting the net on the right side of the ship; he had bread and fish already on the fire.

I. Where the faithful toiler is, Christ is always present. He is One among the lowly, ready to feed the hungry.

II. After the meal is over, he has meat to give them they know not of. He says, "I am the living bread of life; he that eateth of me shall live by me. He that drinketh of the water I shall give him, shall never thirst." Therefore partake until the soul is fully satisfied. Christ's peace is medicine to lessen pain; his love, food for the famished.

III. He commissions his disciples to go forth and invite the world to come and dine, saying, "Go out into the highways and hedges and compel them to come in to my supper." Bread may run short in famine and war, but he has an inexhaustible supply. He can feed thousands as well as one. The upper room, the Transfiguration Mount and the seaside were eating-places for all the people who followed him.

IV. When he breaks the bread, every place is a sacrament, every scene of fellowship is a Holy Communion supper with him. Bodily food is an emblem of the spiritual manna which comes down from heaven. He helps in business life as well as in soul prosperity. He tells where to cast the net for multitudes of fishes or for a lost world. Ask him, the great Guide; he knows the way, and how, when and where. Obey his command, launch out in the deep waters of his love, you who are standing on the shore fearful of the waves. He will not suffer you to sink down; his hands hold, his fullness fills. Come and dine with the King of kings, the Lord of glory; his table is full and free and forever waiting your coming.—REV. E. W. CASWELL.

COMMUNION ADDRESS

"This do in remembrance of me." Luke 22:19.

There is a retrospective view of the Lord's Supper, a looking backward. There is an introspective view, a looking within one's self, and there is a prospective view, a looking forward to the coming of Christ again.

I. Retrospective. Looking backward, communion brings us face to face with Christ on the cross. Looking backward still more we see through a long line of changing scenes the passover down there in Egypt. The plan was that when the destroying angel saw the blood he would pass over that home. From that day the Hebrews have recognized the feast of the passover. How significant that Jesus Christ should institute this feast of the Lord's Supper at a time when the feast of the passover was being observed. While they were celebrating the slaying of a lamb that saved life, he was dying, a lamb slain to take away the sin of the world.

In looking backward we see our Saviour on the cross, breaking his body and shedding his blood and in this sacrament we remember his death.

II. Introspective. Let a man examine himself. Look into self and decide whether the heart is right or not. This is not a class feast. It is for every one who is a child of the King. It is not for me to say who shall partake. It is not for the church to say, and I thank God that it is not for any man to set bounds on the Lord's supper. You look into your own heart. By the light of God's love look in. By the help of God's Word look into your heart. Are you right with God? You say, "I am not right." But shall that keep you away from the feast? No; that is the very reason why you need to come. This feast needs to be one of confession of sin. Do you feel your need of Christ? Let us all bow down and quietly pray that with the help of Jesus we may look into our own hearts and be made right with him.

III. Prospective. "For as often as ye eat this bread and drink this cup, ye do show forth the Lord's death till he come." Jesus bids us look up. He bids us look forward. There is not a note of retrograde in all the Gospel of Christ. The Master said, "I will not leave you comfortless, I will come unto you." He has gone to prepare a place for us. Then we are to show forth his death till he comes. We will do that by eating this bread and drinking this cup. This is a feast for our spiritual needs. Bread taken into our bodies causes them to grow and sustain life. Blood is emblematic of life. So these elements in a pictorial way are to feed our spiritual lives and cause them to develop.

Also let us look forward to a better life—a greater degree of consecration—a more full-faith life and a more faithful life—a more useful life in service—a more interested life in doing the things for which he broke his body and shed his blood. Show forth this sacrifice till he come. He is coming again—yes, coming to get a full report of your life's service. He wants you to be his living sacrifice so that the world may know of his death. Let us not fail him in this.—REV. J. S. HODGES.

SELF-EXAMINATION

"Commune with your own heart." Psa. 4:4.
  I. The subjects of self-examination.
   1. Our sins.
   2. Our conversion.

3. Our principles.
   4. Our pleasures.
   5. Our prayers.
II. The manner in which it should be conducted.
   1. Seriously.
   2. With reference to the Bible as a standard.
   3. With prayer for divine guidance.
III. Its advantages.
   1. Self-knowledge will direct us in the use of the means of grace.
   2. Self-knowledge will assist us in the performance of religious duties. Make Communion blessed.
   3. Self-knowledge will guard us against temptation.

COMMUNION A MEDITATION

"Meditate upon these things." 1 Tim. 4:15.
I. The nature of meditation.
   1. It is not mere thinking.
   2. It is not mere study.
   3. It is set and sustained thought for a practical purpose.
II. The seasons of meditation.
   1. Periods of solitude.
   2. Times of sleeplessness.
   3. Seasons of sickness.
   4. The Sabbath.
III. Rules for meditation.
   1. Lay up a good store of scriptural truth in the mind beforehand.
   2. Banish every thought that is out of keeping with the exercise.
   3. Apply the whole force and energy of the soul.
   4. Lift up the heart to God in prayer.
   5. Let not the exercise be unduly protracted.

PART XIX: ARBOR DAY TEXTS AND THEMES

Trees as Good Citizens.
Trees as Friends and Protectors of All Wild Life.
The Forest as Nature's Workshop.
Nature's Praise: Psa. 35:13.
The City with Trees: "In the midst of the street of it, and on either side of the river was the tree of life." Rev. 22:2.
The Unfading Leaf: "His leaf shall not wither." Psa. 1:3.
Firmly Rooted: "And he shall be like a tree planted." Psa. 1:3.
God's Planting: "The trees of the Lord are full of sap; the cedars of Lebanon, which he hath planted." Psa. 104:16.
The Good-News of Out-of-Doors: "And the Lord took the man and put him in the garden of Eden to dress it and to keep it." Gen. 2:15.
Trees by a River: Psa. 1:1-6.
Forest Texts: 2 Kings 19:33; Psa. 50:10; Jer. 10:3; Jer. 46:23.
Lessons from the Forests and Fields: Psa. 104:1-35.
Perpetual Arbor Day: Mark 4:14.
Plant a Tree: Rev. 22:2.
Trees Teaching God's Care: Num. 24:5-9.
Grafted On: Rom. 11:16-24.
Rest Under the Trees: "Rest yourselves under the tree." Gen. 18:4.
Wisdom Like a Tree: "She is a tree of life to those that lay hold upon her." Prov. 3:18.
Some Lessons from Springtide: "For, lo, the winter is past," etc. Song of Solomon 2:11-13.
A Seed-Time Lesson: Matt. 13:3, 23. I. The Sower. The Lord Jesus. II. The Seed. The Word of God. III. The soils. The hearts of sinners.

The Trees Teaching: I. Pulled down. Conviction. 1 Kings 5: 6-9. II. Planted. Conversion. Matt. 15: 13. III. Pruned. Education. John 15: 2. IV. Plucked up. Exposure. Jude 12.

A Spring-Time Lesson: "He that ploweth ought to plow in hope." 1 Cor. 9: 10.

Trees Teaching Praise: 1 Chron. 16: 29-34.

Trees Teaching Probation: Matt. 3: 5-10.

A Tree Telling the Sin of Hypocrisy: Mark 11: 12-14.

A Green Tree: Psa. 37: 23-36.

Nature Praising God: "Then shall the trees of the wood rejoice before the Lord." Psa. 96: 12.

Trees Entering into Man's Joy: Isa. 55: 12, 13.

Trees Teaching Us to Express Gratitude to God: Psa. 96: 12, 13.

Wisdom a Tree of Life: Prov. 3: 18.

Lessons from Fruitfulness and Non-Fruitfulness of Trees: Matt. 7: 17-20.

What Do the Trees Teach Us About God? Isa. 41: 19, 20. Gen. 1: 11, 12.

How Do the Trees Seem to Enter into Man's Joy? Isa. 55: 12, 13.

Whom Does Isaiah Call "Trees of Righteousness"? Isa. 61: 3.

To What Does the Wise Man Compare Wisdom? Prov. 3: 13, 18.

To What Does the Prophet Compare a Man Who Trusts in God? Jer. 17: 7, 8.

To What Wrong Use Had Man Put the Trees of the Wood? Isa. 44: 14-17.

To What Does Jesus Liken the Kingdom of God? Matt. 13: 3, 32.

How is the Reward of Christian Faithfulness Symbolized in the Revelation? Rev. 2: 7; 22: 1, 14.

PART XX: ARBOR DAY SERMON OUTLINES

MEN AND TREES: ARBOR DAY TALK

Men in the Bible are in many places compared to trees. There are good trees and corrupt ones, good men and bad men. "A good tree cannot bring forth evil fruit, neither can a corrupt tree bring forth good fruit." So with men: "By their fruits ye shall know them."

The godly man is "like the tree planted by the rivers of water, that bringeth forth his fruit in season . . . whatsoever he doeth shall prosper." Stephen was spoken of as being a good man, and was full of faith and the Holy Ghost. A good man is one who not only has the indwelling presence of the Holy Ghost but also the fruits of the Spirit.

The Tree of life bears twelve manner of fruit and yields her fruit every month, an ever green and ever bearing tree. "The fruit of the righteous is a tree of life." The righteous flourish like the palm tree. The palm is tropical, and tropical fruit grows the year round; just so those who have the fruits of the Spirit, have their "fruit unto holiness" and are always "abounding in the works of the Lord." They do not wither, but grow like the cedars of Lebanon.

Some of the joys are love, peace, long-suffering, gentleness, goodness, faith, meekness, temperance, virtue, knowledge, godliness; here are at least twelve manner of fruits, and those who are established in the Christian graces, who have been purged from dead works to serve the living God are like "the trees of the Lord," "full of sap," being filled with the fruits of righteousness. "The same bringeth forth much fruit."
—L. B. W.

GIDEON UNDER THE OAK, OR A HERO COMMISSIONED

Judges 6:11.
The Bible, an arboretum. Full of trees.
Its trees are eloquent. Shadow great events.
The oak was supposed to be abode of spirits, v. 12.
1. Gideon is hospitable to divine guests, v. 19.
2. The call comes to a busy man, v. 11.
3. Our hero is God-armed, v. 14.
4. Gideon is assured by Divine Fire, v. 21.

Conclusion: The Divine arrest in human life. Appropriate the strength of the oak.—REV. S. B. DUNN, D.D.

PERPETUAL ARBOR DAY

Mark 4:14.
Describe the Arbor-Day movement, the spoliation of forest lands, and the need of replanting. Draw then the parallel between planting seeds of trees and planting the gospel: (a) in new countries, and (b) by personal work.
1. Planting seeds of kindness.
2. Preparing the soil, by helpful service, in other hearts.
3. What seeds am I planting?
4. The inevitable growth of influences that we scatter.
5. Each man "like a tree." Psa. 1.
6. Sowing seeds in young people's minds.

THE SEED WE ARE SOWING

"Whatsoever a man soweth, that shall he also reap." Gal. 6:7.

This is seedtime. We look around us and we see the farmers sowing the various kinds of seeds; and the women are sowing their garden and flower seed. But they are very careful to select the best seed.

As it is now time for planting seed in the ground, it is also time for planting it in the heart, for we are sowing seed of some kind every day. Just as the seed planted in the ground must be good seed, and carefully tended, so the seeds in our hearts must be good. Our thoughts should be pure, for they are the seed, and our deeds are the fruits.

1. We are planting and cultivating all the time. We leave impressions on those with whom we come in contact, and influence them for better or worse. "Sow an act and you reap a habit; sow a habit and you reap a destiny." Since this is true, how necessary that we nourish only pure thoughts and form ennobling habits.

A sunny smile, a cheerful answer, a loving deed, a little song and a sympathetic word will all be precious seed that will grow to lovely flowers for Jesus. So let us sow such seed bountifully.

Many good Christians have sown the good seed, but have laid down their work and passed over the river to take up a nobler work. Some one must take their place. "Whose place will you take?"

There was once a boy who had a remarkable dream. He thought that the richest man in town came to him and said: "I am tired of my house and grounds; come and take care of them and I will give them to you." Next came an honored judge and said: "I want you to take my place; I am weary of being in court day after day. I will give you my seat on the bench if you will do my work." Then came a doctor and wanted him to take his place. And last came a drunkard and said: "I am wanted to fill a drunkard's grave. I have come to see if you will take my place in these saloons and on these streets." I wonder whose place that boy took.

Years ago a man, interested in bee culture, drove along the roads, in a certain section of Illinois, and scattered sweet clover seed as he went. He threw out small quantities of seed, first on one side of the road and then on the other. The seed grew, the plant spread, and now, in midsummer, the roads for miles and miles are lined with the sweet clover. Most farmers say the plant is a nuisance, and that it is spreading to their fields. A few people see some good in it, especially the bee men and those who permit their cattle to graze by the roadside. But the sweet clover is there, and it is there to stay, all because some man scattered a small amount of seed here and there as he passed along.

2. Well, how about the seed that we purpose sowing on

life's land? What kind of seed are we preparing to sow? We do not have special reference to the work done in the open, for that is usually well guarded, but we refer to personal influence.—REV. JOHN LEMLEY, D.D.

TREES OF THE LORD

"The trees of the Lord are full of sap; the cedars of Lebanon, which he hath planted." Psa. 104:16.

Even a careless reader of the Bible must be impressed by the fact that trees figure prominently in the Scriptures, standing for various truths and preaching many a beautiful homily. They are the chief feature in the Garden of Eden, and only disappear with the fading out of the last vision of the Apocalypse. Under their grateful shade the forefathers of the race find rest in primitive simplicity. They give names to cities, Jericho being the City of Fragrance, and Tappuah (Josh. 15:34), Apple-town; while the chief natural feature in the vicinity of Jerusalem was and is the Mount of Olives. Nor should the twentieth century after Christ, carefully setting aside its forest reserve, forget that in earliest legislation of the chosen people were laws especially protecting these beautiful and beneficent gifts of God, even amid the devastations of war, from ruthless destruction. Had those laws been faithfully observed, Palestine might still be a land of brooks and orchards, its hills covered with flocks, its valleys rich with corn.

I. The tree figures in the Bible as a favorite symbol of a godly man. The man filled with the spirit of the Almighty seemed to the poet prophet a veritable "Tree of Righteousness" (Isa. 61:3), an oak of Mamre or a cedar of Lebanon, able to resist a stormy wind and furious tempest. Such a man is no bowing bulrush, no clinging vine. He is swept but not swayed, arboreal in his vigor and forever resilient. Like some giant cottonwood planted by irrigating streams, for such is the symbolism of the First Psalm, his life is fed by hidden streams; and amid the burning noons of the Assyrian summer his leaf remains bright with the freshness of abundant life.

II. For the glory of a tree is not in its simple strength, but in that union of strength, beauty and utility which no other floral product possesses to anything like the same degree. Its charm is not that of some red aguille of the Alps jutting heavenward in threatening grandeur. Its strength is not even that of a marble pillar, dull and cold. But its power is robed in flowing lines, its mighty limbs enveloped in graceful vestments. It would be difficult for us to say which charms us most, the pyramidal fir, the plumy elm or the swaying willow.

III. But beyond the question of their strength, and above all thoughts of beauty, the trees of the Lord are rich in their beneficence. Our republic has wakened slowly to the value of its forests, awakened after the ruthless ax in a single state has reduced four million acres to a desert. We have been consuming our trees for all purposes at the rate of forty million cubic feet a year. Yet upon them we depend for the even flow of our rivers, for the graceful repose accorded to our flocks, as well as for the fruits with which we close our most epicurean feasts. Few persons realize the extent to which tree-fruits enter into the food of the nation. We read that the Arab knows few wants which the date-palm does not through one or the other of its products supply. We know that the South Sea Islander finds in the breadfruit tree all his table needs. Of late years we have found in the banana condiment and nutrition combined. But we have scarcely begun to realize the source of wealth which is to be found in a plantation of oranges, of peaches, apples, prunes, or pears.

IV. That man who is a Tree of Righteousness is not simply strong as an oak and spiritually beautiful as an elm is physically perfect, but he is a blessing to the world in which God planted him. He becomes a shade to the weary and the fruit of his abundant life supplies food to the exhausted toiler. He may at first appear like his Great Master to be little more than a branch from the stem of some greater name in the past, but the world will find him at last like those aged and luxuriant olives planted in the holy courts of the sacred temple upon Moriah's heights "bringing forth fruit in old age," and to the last hour of a well-prolonged life a benediction. And when at last the world misses his presence and mourns his loss there is for him the joyful and well assured hope that "if he be cut down," he will spring forth again, and the tender branch of his divinely implanted life will grow again in the paradise of God.

A SERMON FOR BOYS AND GIRLS

"He shall be like a tree." Psa. 1:3.

You have had "Arbor Day." You have planted a tree or have helped. At least you have looked on to see others plant trees. You have recited poetry about the trees. You all love trees. The Bible says much about trees. Much of the country of the Bible was dry, and a tree was a delight. We read of the palm trees of the desert; the cedars of Lebanon; the oaks of Bashan; the fir and the box, and the bay, and the sycamore and the pine. We all delight in trees. Arbor Day is good. The text says a godly man is like a tree. Why? Let us see.

I. Because he amounts to something. He is not even a weed, not even a flower, not grass, not a bush nor a shrub. All these have their teaching, but they have little character as compared with a tree. You can look up to a tree and admire it. The Bible sometimes calls them "trees of God," mighty ones. So a man when he becomes a Christian has sins forgiven him; his nature is changed. He begins to grow for the ages. He is no shrub. "He shall be like a tree," and that is something that abides. When you look at a great oak next summer think what a noble thing a Christian is as God plans.

II. We like a tree because it stays. You know where to find it. It can be depended upon. You plant a good tree and its roots fix themselves in the soil, deeply and widely. It abides. It could not be true in any other way. So a godly man has deep roots. He must stay somewhere. He cannot fulfill his mission and grow in character without the stability which makes him like a tree. It is a good deal to say of any man: "You can always tell where to find him." When you are tempted then to move, to give up your work, to flit away to this and to that as fancy may take you, remember the tree. Whenever an uneasy spirit takes hold of you, remember the tree. The tree commands your respect because it stays. It is what it is and does the work it does because it is content to stay. Its roots run deep and find out hidden springs because it stays. Many do not stay long enough to find out the good that is hidden for them. Most Christians of this restless age need to learn the parable of the tree. Churches need it. Ministers need it. Children need it.

III. The tree spoken of in this text is a planted tree. It is not a wild tree that springs up and grows anywhere. It has been transplanted with care, and put into a place most favorable for its good. So is the godly man. God has taken hold of him. In most cases it was when he was little. Perhaps he found him where the wild beasts would tread him down; perhaps there was no good soil; perhaps there was no moisture; perhaps where all the storms of the desert could blow upon him. He has taken pains to plant him carefully in the right spot.

There are two things about this planting. The first we shall find in the Ninety-second Psalm, thirteenth verse: "Those that be planted in the house of the Lord shall flourish in the courts of our God." So the Christian, if he is going to be like a tree in character, must be planted in the church. That is the place for him. There he will flourish and bear fruit.

But the second thing is spoken of in the first Psalm. "He shall be like a tree planted by the rivers of water." Wherever you find trees in a dry country you may be sure there is underground water. Look and you will find a spring. Just as at Elim, where the children of Israel encamped, there were "three-score and ten palm trees and twelve wells of water." What does the water mean? Always God's truth.—REV. ADDISON BLANCHARD.

A MESSAGE FROM SPRINGTIME

"He hath made everything beautiful in its time." Eccl. 3:11.

Test this statement of the Wise Man and see how true it is.

I. In nature everything is beautiful. There is no other white that compares with the whiteness of the snow. There is no blue so deep and marvelous as the blue of the sky. There is no crimson like the crimson of the sunset. Painters cannot portray nature. They try, but their best efforts only convince us how far short human art is of the divine.

He hath made everything beautiful. If it is not so it is

because sin has marred it. Wherever on earth you find ugliness and filth and hate, there you know man has been, for God has made everything beautiful.

II. More than this, he has made everything beautiful through and through. Recently we saw a house that was being torn down. The front of it was very handsome. It was as perfect as the workmen could make it. But away in the back, where human eyes did not often rest upon it, it was cheap and flimsy. This is a characteristic of everything that is human-made. It will not bear too close a scrutiny.

But the things that God has made are thoroughly beautiful. The inside of the flower which you cannot see is as lovely as that which your eyes rest upon. The more closely you examine the snow-flake under the glass the more wonderful it is. It was this that led the world's greatest botanist to cry out, as he saw the flower that was revealed by his microscope, "I have seen the glory of God pass by."

"But," you say, "I know of many things that are not beautiful. There is a rainy day for example, or a sorrowing heart. These things are not beautiful and no one can convince me that they are."

III. But look carefully at the words of the text. "He hath made everything beautiful in its time." A rainy day is not beautiful in your time. But you are impatient. Wait its time. Wait till the clouds break, and the sun shines through, and the bow spans the heavens, and the vegetation, bright and green, smiles in your face.

Sorrow is not beautiful in your time. But tarry a little. James M. Barrie, in his "Margaret Ogilvie," tells us how his mother came to have her sweet face. It was long before when he was a little child. There came one day to the door of their home a neighbor with the tidings that her son, her eldest, had been fatally hurt. She went at once and for days she watched beside him and then the end came. Every one knew how terrible had been the blow to her as she came back and took up the tasks of life again. Those who saw her then, said Barrie, understood where she got her sweet face, and that gentle voice that was never raised in anger, and that sympathetic heart that brought the neighbors first to her when they were in trouble. God had made her beautiful in the time when sorrow had done its refining work.

There is nothing that God ever made or ordered that did not have in it a beauty and glory if we bide his time.—REV. STUART NYE HUTCHINSON, D.D.

A SPRING-TIME LESSON

"He that ploweth ought to plow in hope." 1 Cor. 9:10.

Paul is speaking about apostolic liberty and the right of the worker to expect some reward for his work.

I. Toil that is devoid of anticipation becomes drudgery; to plow in hope—that is the secret of efficient labor. The toiler's hope is the idea of creating, or putting something into the world that was not there before. This gives work a sanctity; this lifts the mind above the slavery of daily routine.

Have you ever seen a Vermont farmer take a piece of worthless-looking land, that can be hired for a few dollars an acre, drive his plow through its rocky soil, harrow it, fertilize it, and seed it and then after the sun and the rain have had a chance at it, harvest a crop that is worth forty dollars an acre? He has created something to enrich the life of man. Have you seen a village carpenter take a tree and, by honest toil, convert it into chairs or the foundation of a house? There is something intangibly sacred in the expression of his face as he stands off and surveys the creative product of his hands.

> "Toiling, rejoicing, sorrowing,
>   Onward through life he goes;
> Each morning sees some task begun,
>   Each evening sees its close;
> Something attempted, something done,
>   Has earned a night's repose."

II. The field may seem small and mean, but to make it yield even so little is to plow in hope.—C. S. C.

PART XXI: ASCENSION DAY TEXTS AND THEMES

"When he ascended up on high, he led captivity captive, and gave gifts unto men." Eph. 4:8.

"So then after the Lord had spoken unto them, he was received up into heaven, and sat on the right hand of God." Mark 16:19.

"And it came to pass while he blessed them, he was parted from them, and carried up into heaven." Luke 24:51.

"He was taken up and a cloud received him out of their sight." Acts 1:9.

The Last Beatitude of the Ascended Christ: "Blessed are they that do his commandments, that they may have right to the tree of life, and may enter in through the gates into the city." Rev. 22:14.

After His Ascension: "And ye also shall bear witness of me, because ye have been with me from the beginning." John 15:27.

The Glorification of the Lord: "He was received up into heaven, and sat on the right hand of God." Mark 14:19. The glorification was: 1. As Prophet. 2. As Priest. 3. As King.

PART XXII: ASCENSION DAY SERMON OUTLINES

LESSONS FROM THE ASCENSION

"And it came to pass while he blessed them he was parted from them, and carried up into heaven." Luke 14: 51.

I. Since our Lord is ascended we are never to think of him as dead.

II. Since our Lord is thus alive we are to be sure that all the great offices pertaining to his exaltation are in active exercise.
    1. He stands in heaven to-day the living Head of his redeemed church.
    2. He stands in heaven to-day our priestly advocate.
    3. He stands in heaven to-day as the controller of all things in God's providential government.

III. Since our Lord has ascended we are never to think of him as distant.

> "Closer he is than breathing,
> And nearer than hands and feet."

IV. Since our Lord has ascended we are never to think of him as different.

HEAVEN'S ASCENSION DAY MESSAGE

"Ye men of Galilee, why stand ye looking into heaven? This Jesus, who was received up from you into heaven shall so come in like manner as ye beheld him going into heaven." Acts 1: 11.

I. A rebuke to inactive curiosity—"Not for you to know times or seasons."

II. A reminder of human limitation—"Many things to say . . . ye cannot bear them now. . . ." John 16: 12.

III. An intimation for faith to be exercised in service—"Ye shall be my witnesses."

IV. As assurance of a similar return—"In like manner as ye beheld him going to heaven."—C. R. S.

AN ASCENDED YET EVER-PRESENT LORD

"Lo, I am with you alway, even unto the end of the world." Matt. 28:20.

These are the final words of a gospel, but the inaugural words of a ministry. They seem to mark the close of a dispensation, yet they open a perspective to the "end of the world." They mark the end of a temporal relationship, but the beginning of an eternal one.

I. This seems not impossible when the unique speaker is taken into account—Emmanuel, glorified and risen.

II. The only condition of fulfillment devolves upon the human chosen ones who receive and obey.

III. The resultant comfort is especially adapted to human longings.
1. In temptations. "Temptations lose their power when thou art nigh."
2. Sorrow or adversity: "Though I walk through the valley of the shadow of death, I will fear no evil, for thou art with me."—C. R. S.

CAPTIVITY LED CAPTIVE

"Wherefore he saith, when he ascended up on high, he led captivity captive, and gave gifts unto men," etc. Eph. 4:8-10.

The first step in the exaltation of Christ was his resurrection from the dead. The second step was his ascension into heaven. This is the topic set forth in the words of the text, which we proceed to consider in the fourfold view in which it is here presented.

I. The manner in which he ascended. "When he ascended up on high he led captivity captive, and gave gifts unto men." The character under which he is here spoken of is that of a mighty conqueror. His ascension was his public entrance into the eternal city. As it was usual for conquerors to distribute presents among their followers, so it is here said of our victorious Lord that he "gave gifts unto men."

II. The state from which he ascended. "Now, that he ascended, what is it," etc. This may include,
   1. His incarnation.
   2. His assumption of our nature in its humblest condition.
   3. His death and burial.

III. The place to which he ascended. It was "far above all heavens." In his humiliation he became low indeed; but what his humiliation was in its unparalleled depth, that his exaltation was in its matchless and inconceivable height. Was he tender and loving on earth? He is "the same also" in heaven.

IV. The design for which he ascended. "That he might fill all things." The expression includes two particulars:
   1. That he might fill all things with his influence.
   2. That he might direct and overrule all things by his wisdom and power.

CARRIED UP INTO HEAVEN

"And he led them out as far as Bethany; and he lifted up his hands and blessed them. And it came to pass, while he blessed them, he was parted from them and carried up into heaven." Luke 24: 50, 51.

The ascension of Christ occurred forty days after his resurrection. During this time he manifested himself to his disciples to convince them of the certainty of his resurrection, as well as to give directions in carrying on the work of evangelizing the world.

I. The place of his ascension. "He led them out as far as to Bethany." There was a great deal of propriety in selecting this place. Near Bethany was the Mount of Olives, to which the Saviour often retired for prayer. The garden of Gethsemane, where his sufferings began, was also close by. Near the spot where his sufferings began, there also his glory was to commence.

II. The circumstances that attended his ascension.
   1. "He lifted up his hands and blessed them." His last

act upon earth was blessing his disciples. How well did such a conclusion suit the rest of his life. The disciples never forgot the uplifted hands of their Master.
2. "A cloud received him out of their sight." No whirlwinds, no thunders, no chariot of fire. The Saviour of the world was gently received up in a cloud; in harmony with the peaceful spirit of the Gospel and its Author.
3. Angels were also present. They were present at the creation of the world; at the birth of our Lord; at his resurrection, and now again at his ascension.

III. The purposes of his ascension.
1. By it, was shown that the object of coming into the world was fulfilled.
2. By it, Christ again came into possession of the glory of which he had divested himself.
3. That he might act, in the presence of God, as our interceding High Priest.
4. That he might exercise, in heaven, the office of King.
5. To send the Holy Ghost.

CHRIST'S ASCENSION

"While they beheld, he was taken up; and a cloud received him out of their sight." Acts 1:9.

The account of the ascension of Christ is the connecting link between gospel history and Christian church history, between the work of Jesus during his early life and his continued work ever since. It contains the finish of the most important episode of history, the earthly sojourn of God incarnate. It contains the beginning of that sojourn's most transcendent result, the mediatorial and yet-to-be triumphant reign of Jesus.

I. Christ's life in the world is divided into action and doctrine, the things he did and the things he taught. Luke had written to his friend Theophilus before. But he wants him to know that the "former treatise" was only about beginnings. The things spoken of were the things Jesus "began to do and teach." His present writing he wishes him to understand as a second volume of the acts of Jesus and a further record of the teachings of Jesus. Well we know to-day that "began" does not stop with any written record. The fountain has become the source of an ever-flowing river of grace giving the world an ever-widening stream of blessing. The gist of the gospel is that Jesus lives to-day and personally directs his followers.

II. The continued acts of Christ are "through the Holy Ghost." He had told his disciples that it was really expedient that he should go away, in order that his greater work through the Holy Ghost might begin. Whatever was done, therefore, after Christ's death and resurrection, after he had finished his great work of atonement, was to be regarded in a particular sense as under the influence of the Holy Ghost. Even his parting instructions and commission to the apostles were to be regarded as coming within the department of the peculiar activity of the Holy Spirit. Under these instructions and accompanied by this Spirit the apostles were to go forth and by his aid to convert the world.

III. While he was speaking the farewell moment arrived. Lifting up his hands in blessing and "while they beheld"—that they might have clear proof of his ascension, assurance that there was no deception—he began to rise from the earth and ascend higher and higher until "a cloud received him out of their sight." It is impossible to add to that simple account. It may have been some glorious cloud like that symbol of God, the "fiery, cloudy pillar," or Elijah's "storm chariot," or the bright halo of the transfiguration. But no attempt is made to cause the event to seem dramatic. Seen from the earth side, how quietly done! But seen from the heaven side, what a spectacle it must have been: "Lift up your heads, O ye gates; even lift them up, ye everlasting doors; and the King of glory shall come in!"

IV. Even gazing into heaven must not be too prolonged or fixed. At the expostulation of the angels the apostles withdrew their wistful eyes and returned obediently to Jerusalem, no doubt comforting themselves with the thought of his return. They went back not knowing exactly what to do; but content to wait until he should tell them. They go to the upper room, where they had eaten their last passover supper with the Lord. They found the other disciples there. With them they "waited." They waited by prayer, by conference together, by doing necessary duties. The waiting was not sleeping with folded hands. It was alert and obedient. We know the blessing they received. Mere gazing up to heaven will do nothing for us; but prayer in the upper chamber will do everything. Now we are to work and wait knowing that our Saviour is exalted at God's right hand and is controlling all things in his kingdom for the good of mankind and his own ultimate glory.—H.

THE ASCENDED LORD

Luke 24: 50, 51.
I. Ascended—there is enlargement of the blessings that come through him.
II. Ascended—let our hearts follow him there.
III. Ascended—we shall follow him there.
IV. Ascended—let us be faithful to him until we ascend.

In the sacrament (sacramentum, oath) we renew our oath of allegiance to him.

THE ASCENSION OF THE LORD JESUS CHRIST

Luke 24: 50-53.
The ascension of our Lord Jesus Christ is of greater importance than is usually realized. Here we have the Son of God—the Son of Man—the Saviour of the world departing. If his incarnation was so much of an event and his active ministry so notable, here is where it stopped as far as his personal appearance is concerned.

1. But consider the ascension from the standpoint of a Farewell and you will realize a weighty hour—what a moment in the life of the men who saw him—felt him, etc. The world ignoring him could not help but see and feel his wonderful influence while he was about ministering—yet ignoring him. So the world could not help but take notice of his death: "Earth was dark and trembled." Its inhabitants sore afraid, etc. "Surely this must have been the Son of God," some cried. And now I can well reason that if the world

was so set in commotion at his coming and at the time of his dying, that surely his departure was of no small moment.

2. The ascension is not only a farewell, but consider it from the standpoint of an attainment—a victory—a fulfillment and, thank God, an accomplishment.

Here was demonstrated the truth of his words, "I go to prepare a place for you." Then as well as now many people disregarded the fact that there is a Heaven. Here Heaven opened, etc.

Here broke out upon them the Light of the Son of Man. Here he was recognized as God's Son—as a Deity—"And they worshiped him." The uplifted arms were the arms and hands that labored and suffered, blessed and helped, appeared over them as never before to give his most wonderful blessing—well may they bow their heads, for God is going into his own; into his power; into his victory; into his Heaven. Well may his people go back to Jerusalem and go "with great joy." Heaven has not only come down to earth, but there is now a connection between earth and Heaven. For soon the Holy Spirit will come. (It would not come otherwise.) Soon the Light of a new Hope—the truth of a new Life will fill the hearts of men with a Holy Spirit.—REV. R. H. MUELDER.

PART XXIII: MOTHER'S DAY TEXTS AND THEMES

The Possibilities of Motherhood: "The price of a virtuous woman is far above rubies," etc. Prov. 31:10-31.

Our Debt to Motherhood: "Render, therefore, to all their dues, . . . honor to whom honor," etc. Rom. 13:7.

The Wise Son: "My son, hear the instruction of thy father, and forsake not the law of thy mother." Prov. 15:20.

An Utter Folly: "A foolish man despiseth his mother." Prov. 1:18.

Love to Parents: "Let me, I pray thee, kiss my father and my mother, and then I will follow thee." 1 Kings 19:20.

The Law of Thy Mother: "My son, keep thy father's commandments, and forsake not the law of thy mother." Prov. 6:20.

A Divine Command: "For God commanded saying, Honor thy father and mother." Matt. 15:4.

Family Devotion: "Behold, I and the children whom the Lord hath given me." Isa. 8:18.

Jesus' Mother: "Is not his mother called Mary?" Matt. 13:55.

A Mother's Thoughts: "But his mother kept these sayings and pondered them in her heart." Luke 2:51.

The Mother's Cross: "His mother stood by the cross." John 19:25.

A Christian Mother: "Salute Rufus and his mother." Rom. 16:13.

A Mother's Care: "And he delivered him to his mother." Luke 7:15.

A Mother's Hurt: "A foolish son is the heaviness of his mother." Prov. 10:1.

The Blessing Omitted: "There is a generation that curseth their father, and doth not bless their mother." Prov. 30:11.

A Good Mother: "When I call to remembrance the unfeigned faith that is in thee, which dwelt first in thy grandmother Lois, and thy mother Eunice; and I am persuaded in thee also." 2 Tim. 1: 5.

A Mother's Comfort: "As one whom his mother comforteth, so will I comfort thee." Isa. 66: 13.

Our Mothers—An Appreciation: "When Jesus, therefore, saw his mother," etc. John 19: 26, 27.

God and Motherhood: "For God commanded saying, Honor thy father and mother." Matt. 15: 4.

A Holy Family: "Behold I and the children whom the Lord hath given me." Isa. 8: 18.

A Mother's Wages: "Take this child and nurse it for me and I will give thee thy wages." Ex. 2: 9.

The Nobility of Motherhood: "The price of a virtuous woman is far above rubies," etc. Prov. 31: 10-13.

Honoring Father and Mother: Ex. 20: 12; Prov. 30: 11.

The Encircling Love and Loyalty of Mother: "And the man called his wife's name Eve; because she was the mother of all living." Gen. 3: 20.

The Power of Purity: "Keep thyself pure." 1 Tim. 5: 22.

The Blessing of Purity: "Blessed are the pure in heart for they shall see God." Matt. 5: 8.

The Mother Love: "Can a woman forget her child?" Isa. 49: 15.

An Anxious Mother: "Then came to him the mother of the sons of Zebedee." Matt. 20: 20.

The High Mission of the Mother: "Behold King Solomon with his crown wherewith his mother crowned him." Sol. Song 3: 11.

Pure in Thought and Speech: "The words of the pure are pleasant words." Prov. 15: 26.

Purity of Imagination: "Whatsoever things are pure . . . think on these things." Phil. 4: 8.

Promises to Children: "Honor thy father and thy mother; that thy days may be long upon the land which the Lord thy God giveth thee." Ex. 20: 12.

The Wise Son: "My son, hear the instruction of thy father, and forsake not the law of thy mother." Prov. 1: 8.

Thy Father and Thy Mother: "The father of the righteous shall greatly rejoice; and he that begetteth a wise child shall have joy of him. Thy father and thy mother shall be glad, and she that bare thee shall rejoice." Prov. 23:24, 25.

Love to Parents: "Let me, I pray thee, kiss my father and my mother, and then I will follow thee." 1 Kings 19:20.

A Divine Command: "For God commanded saying, Honor thy father and mother." Matt. 15:4.

Family Devotion: "Behold, I and the children whom the Lord hath given me." Isa. 8:18.

The Father's Family: "That ye may be the children of your Father which is in heaven." Matt. 5:45.

The Hand that Rocks the Cradle: "Moreover his mother made him a little robe, and brought it to him from year to year, when she came up with her husband to offer the yearly sacrifice." 1 Sam. 2:19.

Grieving Mother: "A foolish son is the heaviness of his mother." Prov. 10:1.

A Mother's Way: "But his mother kept these sayings and pondered them in her heart." Luke 2:51.

The Mother Influence: "When I call to remembrance the unfeigned faith that is in thee, which dwelt first in thy grandmother Lois, and thy mother Eunice; and I am persuaded that in thee also." 2 Tim. 1:5.

Type of Best Consolation: "As one whom his mother comforteth, so will I comfort thee." Isa. 66:13.

Sign of Degeneracy: "There is a generation that curseth their father, and doth not bless their mother." Prov. 30:11.

God's Jealousy for Parents: "The eye that mocketh at his father, and despiseth to obey his mother, the ravens of the valley shall pick it out, and the young eagles shall eat it." Prov. 30:17.

PART XXIV: MOTHER'S DAY SERMON OUTLINES

THE HIGH MISSION OF THE MOTHER

"Behold King Solomon with his crown wherewith his mother crowned him." Sol. Song 3:11.

No wonder the noblest men have uttered the sweetest words of tongue or pen about her who is dearest of all loved ones. Even they could express but little of the beautiful devotion of motherhood. For from her did we not learn our childlike faith in God? Did she not teach us to be good and do good, dedicating us from infancy to the service and love of the heavenly Father? Thinking about the angel-mother is almost enough to transfigure the soul into the likeness she bore of her blessed Master.

A friend asked a rich Roman matron to see her most precious jewels; she immediately gathered her children around her and said, "These are my jewels." Every mother knows that these may be stars in her crown of rejoicing forever. Her children have a beginning in parenthood, but no ending in God's endless years.

It is thus parents can help adorn their children with the beautiful crown of character, and these redeemed ones become their own crown in the presence of the Lord at his coming. Faithfulness in the family brings its own reward in pearls of purity, gems of peace and diamonds of gracefulness that will never cease to shine.—REV. E. W. CASWELL.

MOTHER

"Forsake not the law of thy mother." Prov. 6:20.

Between Easter and Children's Day, how beautiful to observe a Mothers' Memorial Day; the white carnation, the memory flower, is an emblem of the purity and fragrance in the lives of holy motherhood. Jesus, Home and Mother are words that touch the heart of the world deeper than any others. If it is an angel mother, she makes heaven more inviting; if still in the earthly home, she is the guide and unchangeable friend, moving about in sweet ministries and loving service.

A friend said to S. S. Prentice, "I congratulate the mother who has such a son." He replied, "Rather congratulate the son on having such a mother." Richter says, "To a man who has had a noble mother, all women are sacred for her sake." The mother, more than any other, affects the moral and spiritual part of the children's character. She is their constant companion and teacher in formative years. The child is ever imitating and assimilating the mother nature. It is only in after life that men gaze backward and behold how a mother's hand and heart of love molded their young lives and shaped their destiny.

No child can fully realize the intensity of a mother's anxiety as she bids good-by to the son or daughter going out of the old home to enter school or business life. She realizes that she will not be able to give counsel as in their younger days; she does not need to promise to remember them in her prayers. She cannot help praying—every breath is prayer. Oh, that the youth of America may be true to their mothers and their mothers' God.—REV. E. W. CASWELL, D.D.

OUR DEBT TO MOTHERHOOD

"Render, therefore, to all their dues. . . . Honor to whom honor (is due)." Rom. 13:7.

Let us render honor to whom honor is due. First of all, let us honor our mothers. To them most of us owe more than to any other human beings. They were the first persons with whom we had to do in this world and for a long time were the most important persons in our lives. If we honor our mothers we are likely to honor where it is due.

I. First, let us honor our mothers, for to them we owe our lives. At no small cost to themselves, they have given us our lives. This is obvious, but it is also obvious that we are in danger of forgetting it in these days of advanced thought. This service, the perpetuation of the race, would seem to be the basic service, the service upon which all development and progress depend.

To what woman do you and I look to-day as the best and noblest of her kind? To what woman do we look with supreme gratitude and reverence? Is it to Deborah, the Hebrew heroine, who led the forces of Israel to victory when men skulked in their tents? Is it Joan of Arc, the stainless maid of France, or to Queen Elizabeth, most masterful of monarchs; to "George Eliot," peer of any man that has written an English novel? Is it to Julia Ward Howe, who has given us the finest battle song ever written, or to Frances Willard, whose fire-filled personality has done more than any man has ever done to undermine the power of the liquor traffic? You may look at some of these, or to some other woman distinguished for her public services. For my part, I look to one closer than any of these.

But who is the most famous of all women to-day? What woman has appeared most largely in art? What woman, rightly or wrongly, has been the greatest influence in religion? There can be no doubt that it is she who in the spirit of prophecy exclaimed, "All generations shall call me blessed!" And all generations have called Mary blessed, and all generations to come will call Mary blessed, because in the fullness of time it was she who gave birth to the child Jesus, and because in the humble house at Nazareth, as a faithful mother under God's guidance, she shaped the disposition and character of the Saviour of the world.

II. Second, let us honor our mothers, for to them we owe the most important part of our education. From the standpoint of education the first six to nine years are the most important in the life of a child. Then obedience is likely to be learned, if it is ever learned; then a habit of prayer is formed, if it is ever formed; then gentleness of speech and consideration for the rights and feelings of other people are learned, if they are ever learned. Then the disposition is formed, and the foundations of character are laid. Then the bent of the life is received.

What climax in all literature is so satisfactory and delightful as when, at the bidding of Pharaoh's daughter, the swift-footed Miriam ran to procure a nurse for little Moses, who had been found among the bulrushes and brought back—and brought back to his mother!

III. Third, let us honor our mothers, for to them we owe our homes. It is the mother most of all that makes the home. A great service this to the human race. There is no sound in the English language that strikes upon the heart strings like the word "home." In the home the worry of life is forgotten. There the waste of life is repaired; there the hurts of life are healed; there the pleasures of human companionship and sympathy are enjoyed in their purest form; there each one has a place which no other can fill or take away. And it is the mother who creates and dominates the home.

IV. Fourth, let us honor our mothers most of all for the love which they have given us. Love is what humanity needs more than anything else. There is no need to prove that. There is nothing that so sustains and restrains, encourages and strengthens us as the consciousness of being loved. Surely the passage concerning love in the thirteenth chapter of 1 Corinthians is the picture of a Christian mother's love: "Love suffereth long and is kind, doth not behave itself unseemly, seeketh not her own, is not easily provoked, thinketh no evil. Beareth all things, believeth all things, hopeth all things, endureth all things. Love never faileth."

And this mother love is like God's love. He loves us not because we are lovable, but because it is his nature to love, and because we are his children. Study the love of God as it is portrayed in a hundred ways in Scripture, and I think you will confess that there is no human love so much like God's love as is the love of a mother for her children.

"So God created man in his own image; in the image of God created he him; male and female created he them." God's fatherhood then is richer in its nature than any human fatherhood. In it are the attributes of both fatherhood and motherhood. Deeper even than a mother's love is the love of God for his children. There is no passage in the Bible more surprising and satisfactory than a part of the forty-ninth chapter of Isaiah: "Can a woman forget her nursing child, that she should not have compassion on the son of her womb? Yes, they may forget, yet will I not forget thee. Behold, I have graven thee upon the palms of my hands!" How, then, shall we render honor to our mothers for all their benefits to us, especially for this love, which is second only to divine love? There are two ways of honoring our mothers, and of these the second way is the better, but the first ought not to be neglected: First, we can express our affection for them in some definite and unmistakable way. They will go right on serving and loving us, whether we express our appreciation or not, but for that very reason let us make them sure their love is returned. Second, we can highly resolve that with God's help we will be the men and women that our mothers want us to be. Then they will be satisfied, for their happiness has always been centered, not in themselves, but in their children.—REV. EDWARD J. RUSSELL, D.D.

THE ENCIRCLING LOVE AND LOYALTY OF MOTHER

"And the man called his wife's name Eve; because she was the mother of all living." Gen. 3:20.

Barrie once described a lady by saying, "She had a mother's face."

I. It is a magic name—Mother. No word in Anglo-Saxon has such power of suggestion; none is so packed with divine emotion. It is not strange that the name is associated with the Bible.

II. Your own mother may have been a humble working-woman in a cottage; while now you may be a learned man, dwelling in a palace. It matters not—her power and influence remain. Why did Lincoln say, "All that I am and all that I hope to be, I owe to my angel mother"? Why do we remember the songs she sang? Why are her words still ringing in our ears, as clearly as if they had been spoken but yesterday? Why do we compare all womankind to that early model?

> "There's a simple rural cottage that looks out
>   across the sea;
> There's a rose-bush by the doorway, and a
>   crooked apple tree;

> By the rose-bush, little Mater (so we called
> her) always sat;
> She called the spot her heaven, so I like to
> think of that."

III. It is because she possessed the eternal qualities of the lasting universe—love and goodness. She embodied elements that never die. When others scorned and abandoned us, she remained loyal. She covered our mistakes with a golden cloud of sympathy. She hid our failings in the folds of her long-suffering garments. She taught us that to be truly great is to be simply kind.

IV. He who has known such unfailing affection finds it easier to understand what Jesus meant when he said, "Greater love hath no man than this, that a man lay down his life for his friends."—C. S. C.

THE MOTHER LOVE

"Can a woman forget her child? . . . Yet will I not forget thee." Isa. 49:15.

The best of human beings fail to be true at times, but mother love is more constant than any other human, earthly affection. There is never a prison where she would not knock for the liberation of her child; her love does not change because of misfortune or unfaithfulness.

A degenerate mother in the toils of Satan's power might forget, but there is One who remembers always to love the objects of his affection. He will never leave and never forget. "As one whom his mother comforteth, so will I comfort you." A mother would give her drunken son the last crust of bread in the house. If expostulated with, she would say, "How can I help it? I am his mother. I would give him all and then die for him, for I was willing to give my life for him at his birth." Though all other friends forsake her child, though the law may seize him and the gallows slay him, her pitying affection will never give him up, and on his grave she will refuse to be comforted, because he is not.

"If I were drowned in the deepest sea,
　Mother o' mine, mother o' mine;
I know whose prayers would come down to me,
　Mother o' mine, mother o' mine."
　　　　　　　　—Rev. E. W. Caswell.

OUR MOTHERS—AN APPRECIATION

"When Jesus, therefore saw his mother," etc. John 19:26, 27.

This is one of the "side lights" on the life of the Son of man which prompts every man to a deeper appreciation of his own mother. It is well that America should set apart a day for a fuller appreciation—not of the abstract principle, "motherhood"—but of the concrete reality "mother."

I. Appreciate the Confidence in Us. Mary "pondered," and every other mother does likewise. This confidence encourages, when youthful inexperience fails. Benjamin West said, "My mother's kiss of approval made me a painter." It stimulates patience, enabling mothers to trust when others desert; e.g., Mary at cross. It leads to sacrifice. How many influential men owe their education and power to the self-denial of their mothers!

II. Appreciate the Fact that Mother's Touch is Toward the Higher Life. Fathers may teach the handling of the plow or the counting of money; but gentler hands and words have added the nobler touch which have made the Ruskins, Lincolns, and Gladstones. This is the touch that turns a life Godward.

III. Recognize a Stepping Stone Toward Heaven. Not that this love should obscure the heavenly love (as a great and ancient church has caused it to do), but that this enduring, uplifting influence should lead us to know the love that "passeth knowledge"; and which "cometh down from above."

PART XXV: MEMORIAL DAY TEXTS AND THEMES

The End of War: Psa. 46:9.

Promises of Peace: Psa. 29:11.

The Devastation of War: Joel 1:13-20.

A New Memorial Day: "What mean ye by this service?" Ex. 12:26.

A Nation's Tribute to Its Heroic Dead: "This day shall be unto you for a memorial." Ex. 12:14.

America the Wonderland: "Thou shalt bless the Lord, thy God, for the good land which he hath given thee." Deut. 8:10.

The International Court: "He shall judge among the nations." Isa. 2:4.

The Unification of the Nation: "One law shall be to him that is home born, and unto the stranger that sojourneth among you." Ex. 12:49.

The Wounds of the War and the Red Cross: "He healeth the broken in heart, and bindeth up their wounds." Psa. 147:3.

The Patriotism of Jesus: "O Jerusalem, Jerusalem . . . how often would I . . . and ye would not!" Matt. 23:37.

A Memorial of Liberty: "What mean ye by these stones?" Josh. 4:21.

The Christian a Soldier: 2 Tim. 2:3, 14.

The Great Service: "Nebuchadnezzar, king of Babylon, caused his army to serve a great service," etc. Ezek. 29:18-20.

Brave Leaders and Brave Men: "Amasiah, the son of Aichri, who willingly offered himself unto the Lord, and with him two hundred thousand mighty men of valor." 2 Chron. 17:16.

The Transfiguration of Trouble: "I was in the isle that is called Patmos. . . . I was in the spirit on the Lord's Day." Rev. 1:9, 10.

Our Sure Foundation: "We have our hope set on the living God." 1 Tim. 4:10.

Reveille: "Awake thou that sleepest, and arise from the dead, and Christ shall give thee light." Eph. 5:14.

Spicery for Our Dead: "And, behold, a company of Ishmaelites came from Gilead with their camels bearing spicery and balm and myrrh, going to carry it down to Egypt." Gen. 27:25.

Death for Others: "For none of us liveth to himself, and no man dieth to himself." Rom. 14:7.

Life Given: "These all died in faith, not having received the promises, but having seen them afar off." Heb. 11:13.

The History of Liberty: "Their line is gone out through all the earth," etc. Psa. 19:4.

A People for God's Possessing: "But ye are a chosen generation, a royal priesthood," etc. 1 Pet. 2:9.

God's Gift to America: "Then thou spakest in vision to thy holy one," etc. Psa. 89:19.

Loss in Life's Battles: "Pride goeth before destruction," etc. Prov. 16:18.

The Men Who Win: "Know ye not that which run in a race run all, but one receiveth the prize?" 1 Cor. 9:24.

Heroes Are Immortal: "As dying, and behold we live." 2 Cor. 6:9.

Decoration Day and Its Lessons: "And he said unto me, Son of man, can these bones live?" Ezek. 37:3.

War Not Glorious: "Who smote great nations, and slew mighty kings." Psa. 135:10.

National Dangers: "Thou shalt no more be termed forsaken; neither shall thy land any more be termed desolate," etc. Isa. 62:4.

Flowers for Memorial Day: "What shall I render unto the Lord for all his benefits?" Psa. 116:12. Praise is comely. Flowers of gratitude are sweet-smelling savor. A banquet of patriotic graces; freedom, religious liberty, self-sacrificing love and brotherly kindness.

The Day of Memory: "What mean ye by this service?" Ex. 12:26.

The Veteran as an Oracle: 2 Sam. 16:23.

A Memorial of Liberty: "What mean ye by this service?" Ex. 12:26.

The Christian a Soldier: 2 Tim. 2:3, 14.

The Christian Warfare: "I have fought a good fight." 2 Tim. 4:7.

A Sermon of the Sword: "The sword of the Spirit which is the word of God." Eph. 6:17.

The Great Service: "Nebuchadnezzar, king of Babylon, caused his army to serve a great service," etc. Ezek. 29:18-20.

PART XXVI: MEMORIAL DAY SERMON OUTLINES

THE MEMORIAL OF LIBERTY

"What mean these stones?" Josh. 4:21.

Israel marked the great events of her history with monuments. This heap of stones at Gilgal was to memorize to their children the end of the wilderness journeying and the Jordan passage into the Promised Land. It is the patriotic duty of Americans to teach their children the meaning of their Memorial Day.

I. It means that in a supreme crisis the American stood the test. The world then learned what kind of character belongs to Americans. (1) They stood for principles. (2) They exhibited unparalleled courage. (3) They showed the strength of their love for liberty.

II. It means that democracy and brotherhood rest upon tremendous sacrifices.

III. It means that for the birth and vast extension of democracy you cleared the way. Preserving the American institutions and liberty, you made possible an America which might lead mankind up the path to brotherhood, equality, true freedom.

IV. It means to this generation that we must conserve the fruits of your victory by new victories. We possess the land. A right appreciation of "these stones" as your memorial will only be realized by going on in the path you pointed out. So your work and ours shall bring nearer the kingdom of God.

GESTURES OF PROGRESS, PERSONAL AND NATIONAL

Phil. 3: 13, 14.

In coming time and in perspective of history, landmarks of American life will be: the war of Independence, the war for the Union, and the war for Democracy.

I. A Leaving Behind. War of Independence.
II. A Reaching Forth. Civil War.
III. A Pressing Forward. Present World War.

The same gestures must be made personally.—Rev. S. B. Dunn, D.D.

FORGET-ME-NOTS GATHERED FROM GOD'S ACRE

Battlefield of Waterloo in springtime is carpeted with forget-me-nots.

I. The Faith They Died In.
II. The Promise They Saw.
III. The Perfection They Shared.

Cherished memory of our soldier dead.—Rev. S. B. Dunn, D.D.

FLOWERS FOR MEMORIAL DAY

"What shall I render unto the Lord for all his benefits?" Psa. 116:12.

Praise is comely. Flowers of gratitude are a sweet-smelling savor.

Tradition has it that after the last battle fought in behalf of the Stuarts there sprang up to mark the spot on Culloden Moor a singular little blue flower, unknown in that region before. The natives called it the "flower of Culloden," because it sprang from the soil made sacred and rich with the blood of their kin. Seeds sleeping for ages sprung into life and beauty when they received their baptism of blood.

Culloden flowers are always the choicest because of the cost of production. They of all others grow from soil fertilized with sacrifices and dyed with blood. What are they? How do they look?

1. Freedom.
2. The Mayflower: Religious liberty.
3. The Lily of the Valley: Pure and white springing from the blood-stained ground at the foot of the Cross.
4. A Bouquet of Patriotic Graces: Self-sacrificing love and brotherly kindness.—C. A. T.

THE ORIFLAMME OF GOD

Text: "Thou hast given a banner to them that fear thee, that it might be displayed because of the truth." Psa. 60: 4.

We have great reason to praise God to-day. He has led us safely through the horrors of war, and has blessed and guided us until crushed and trampled nations seek our protection. In their shell-torn and weakened condition, they want the oriflamme of our nation to wave over them, for it is the oriflamme of this nation that means liberty, freedom, and security. There is, however, a great oriflamme of which we speak, to-day; the oriflamme of our Lord Jesus Christ. All writers insist that although there is some reference to the kingdom of David in this text, that the banner here mentioned refers to the Messiah, and that it is the banner of his presence, of his love, and of his person, that will guide those who fear him. We are sure that this is the case, for in him we find the clew to all history and the solution of all prophecy; and whether we are to interpret life or history, he is the banner and ensign that is lifted up before the army of the church.

I. The banner or flag in war is always used to rally and to encourage the soldiers. It was with some meaning, when on that historical morning the soldiers of the young Republic thought their forces may have been defeated, that they strained their eyes to catch a glimpse of Old Glory waving in the fog of battle smoke, and expressed their feelings in the words:

> "Oh, say, can you see,
> By the dawn's early light,
> What so proudly we hailed
> At the twilight's last gleaming."

So Christ is our banner whom we must follow, who must inspire and encourage us, or we will be lost in defeat amid the battle of life. Look to Christ. Is he at the mast-head of our life, or in these times of stress has he become a mere figure-head?

II. The banner is always displayed as the center of activity, and that must be the reason Christ was given. Christianity is not a soothing syrup, nor the church a spiritual rest-room. The Christian life is an impelling force, and the church supposed to be the power-house and workshop of Jesus Christ. In ancient warfare, when the leader wanted to rally his soldiers, the army banner was lifted, and the division ensigns were left behind as all soldiers gathered around the one oriflamme. In the war and walk of life this is ever needful, and whether the division under which we fight and live is business, society, or home life, if we heed only the one division standard, and fight not for the great Oriflamme, Jesus Christ, we shall go down in defeat as the soldier who fights only for the division standard, and forgets the oriflamme of the nation.

III. Again, in time of war, the oriflamme of the nation is a great guide-star. If the standard-bearer fell, great effort was made to hoist the flag again before it met the ground. So it seems in these times, when men seem to have forgotten God, great effort should be made to display the Christ on the battle-field of life and activity, that the divisions of business, society, home, may not be defeated, but march on hand in hand with God and to victory, with higher hopes and brighter blessings.

IV. This oriflamme of God was to be displayed because of the truth, and the one to-day who fails to see the reality of the Christian life is blind, for, because of his reality and truth, his life is the only solution to the manifold problems before us to-day.—Rev. J. Calvin Leonard, D.D.

SPICERY FOR OUR DEAD

"And, behold, a company of Ishmaelites came from Gilead with their camels bearing spicery and balm and myrrh, going to carry it down to Egypt." Gen. 37: 25.

On this Memorial Day a great company bring sweetest things for our precious dead.

I. By their devotion they supply us with "spicery and balm and myrrh," such as few nations can boast.

II. Our American soil is the Gilead where such things have always grown, and abound to-day.

III. The aromatic gifts we bring to-day are our gratitude and our love for the brave men who died for the flag we fly and plant in their memory. Every cemetery we visit is our "Egypt."

IV. Our nation's chief article of commerce, the main source of our real wealth, are those moral qualities that our veteran dead exemplify.—Rev. S. B. Dunn, D.D.

WAR DEPRECATED

"Rebuke the company of spearmen, the multitude of the bulls, with the calves of the people, till every one submit himself with pieces of silver; scatter thou the people that delight in war." Psa. 68: 30.

The war-spirit is to be prayed down. The Christianity of the nation is at war with war.

I. "The company of spearmen," by their arms, may provoke the war-spirit, and so call forth rebuke.

II. War is essentially brutal, smacking of "bulls" and "calves."

III. Better buy off the enemy, when possible, "with pieces of silver," as England did in the "Alabama" case, than resort to the arbitrament of the sword.

IV. "The people that delight in war" are best "scattered" by being kept out of office.

Our Civil War is most piously commemorated by recalling its horrors and cherishing ideals of peace.—Rev. S. B. Dunn, D.D.

THE REIGN OF THE DOVE

"And the dove came in to him in the evening; and lo, in her mouth was an olive-leaf plucked off; so Noah knew that the waters were abating from off the earth." Gen. 8: 11.

The dynasty of the war eagle shall yet usher in the reign of the peace dove, whose scepter is the olive branch.

"Let us have peace!" is the lesson of Decoration Day.

I. The reign of the dove is foretold. Micah 4: 3, 4.

II. The reign of the dove is furthered by the tender of the olive leaf. The dove-mouth! The leaf carried!

III. The reign of the dove will know no deluge. No deluge of blood. No deluge of devastation. But a sky with a rainbow, and a new earth wherein dwells righteousness.

The dove reigns in "God's acre"; let it reign above ground. That day shall be radiant as our flag and redolent as our flowers.

BRINGING BACK THE KING

"And Absalom, whom we anointed over us, is dead in battle. Now therefore why speak ye not a word of bringing the king back?" 2 Sam. 19:20.

The Absalom rebellion had collapsed and national unity was marked by bringing back the king.

I. The royal path to peace was paved with the dead. "Dead in battle." How many an Absalom fell in that awful Civil War of ours!

II. A new spirit it was, that proposed the bringing back of the king. "Whom we anointed over us." The royal North is met by a loyal South.

III. The spectacle seen now is that of a united nation. "The speech of all Israel," v. 11. "The heart of one man," v. 14.

IV. The pledge of national warfare lay implicit in this act of bringing back the king. Capping "the powers that be" is the King of kings whose reign and rule must be acknowledged by our Republic.—Rev. S. B. Dunn, D.D.

THE VETERAN AS AN ORACLE

"And the counsel of Ahithophel, which he counseled in those days, was as if a man had inquired at the oracle of God." 2 Sam. 16:23.

The veteran, as much so as was Ahithophel, is an oracle whose voice to-day has many things to teach and counsel.

I. From memories of war he counsels peace. This day breathes love and concord.

II. By his own example of devotion he counsels patriotism. This day fires the breast with love of country and the desire to live for it.

III. In the victory God gave his arms he counsels faith in Providence. The God of our fathers is with us yet.

IV. With other enemies to be met he counsels the martial spirit. The war is still on, and the Christian veteran is needed above ground.—Rev. S. B. Dunn, D.D.

OUR MEMORIAL DAY

"And the Jews ordained and took upon them, and upon their seed," etc. Esther 9: 27, 28.

In these words we have an account of the founding of the Jewish National Memorial Day. It was not so much a religious as a national memorial day. It celebrated a day of victory and triumph; and they made it memorable by annual observance. Purim means "lot." It was a day when God decided the lot in favor of the Jewish nation. We are told what great care was taken that their national deliverance might be kept in remembrance. The people took upon themselves a national memorial day. It was not definitely commanded—they took it upon themselves—but it was a day when they recognized the hand of God in their deliverance; and it has been faithfully kept throughout all their generations from that day until this.

But let us not forget that we have a double reason for keeping our Memorial Day. The Jews had a bloodless victory; but ours was purchased at the price of precious lives, even those of our own brothers and sons and husbands and fathers.

I. First, then, let us think of it as a Memory Day. There are those who think it unkind to recall the memory of the dead or even to speak to the bereaved of their losses. There are some who think that the only way to console is by diverting the thoughts from all memory of that which occasioned pain. There is no more mistaken treatment for the human heart than to prescribe oblivion for its cure. The very memory of the loved ones blesses us and makes us more gentle and tender toward the living. Every memorial observance shows nobility and tenderness and genuineness of heart. It is neither manly nor womanly, nor human, to be either hardhearted or forgetful. Then, can you doubt that the heart of our nation is softened, and that sympathy, sensibility and true greatness are promoted by our observance of a national Memorial Day?

II. In recalling the past we find, secondly, that our Memorial Day is a day with very important lessons.

1. It teaches Christian patriotism. Love of country is not only a natural sentiment in every true heart, but it is right in the sight of God. No man can ignore his relation to his country and not sin against God.
2. Again, our Memorial Day teaches the value of peace. It shows war at best a necessary evil, to be justified only by a righteous cause. It shows the cost of war. What it cost us in dollars and cents may some day be wiped out and forgotten; but that it cost us hundreds of thousands of precious lives will never be forgotten while Memorial Day continues to be observed. At a great price we obtained this freedom. It was the price of blood—the blood of a nation's heroes whose memory we so gladly honor. Our nation will not soon forget the value of peace purchased at such a cost. Memorial Day is a constant reminder of the terrible price paid.
3. The day also brings lessons of gratitude and hope. Memory is the mother of gratitude. So when we recall our national blessings, how much cause we have for gratitude to God! We can truly say: "The Lord hath done great things for us, whereof we are glad!" "The Lord of Hosts is with us, the God of Jacob is our refuge."—H.

THE DAY OF MEMORY

"What mean you by this service?" Ex. 12:26.

The thirtieth day of May has long been set apart as Memorial Day, a day when every loyal citizen of these United States commemorates the deeds of valor, self-sacrifice, and heroism, and love of those brave men who have given their lives for their country; a day when a tribute is paid to their memory in song and stirring address; a day when, to the sober strain of the funeral march, the comrades of those who have gone before, journey to the cities of the dead to pay them the respect they merit; a day when our youth gather the choicest blossoms to adorn the graves of the nation's heroes, and on many a tide-swept strand scatter wreaths and garlands on the waves as a tribute to those who found a last resting place under the waters of the great ocean.

I. It is fitting that Memorial Day should be thus kept, and that honor and respect should be shown to our silent heroes who fought valiantly for the right, and who sought to establish justice and equity.

Under a banner which represents these purposes, a mighty army marched forth. Their tread was strong and manly. Full many had but fairly begun the journey of life, and marching onward, some found nameless graves, while others, halting by the wayside, dropped wearily from the ranks. These ranks have been growing weaker and shorter ever since and the buoyancy of the step is gone, but the same spirit burns in their hearts to-day, and dominates their purposes, and to no other class of American citizens is the thirtieth of May so dear as to the veterans of the war of 1861.

II. All honor to the living who shared in the glories of that period of strife!

Speaking of that great mass of soldiers who gave their lives that the nation might live, and who fell at Gettysburg, Abraham Lincoln pleaded: "That from these honored dead we take increased devotion; that we here highly resolve that these dead shall not have died in vain; that the nation shall, under God, have a new birth of freedom, and that government of the people, by the people, for the people, shall not perish from the earth."

How bright were those honors to await those dead! Their memory is precious. Their hands shall plant the rose and myrtle on the graves where they lie, and when time and the elements destroy them, the love which prompted the gift shall endure, still paying sincere tribute to them, and others shall rise to guard sacredly their last earthly resting places. That grand army is dead but in name; that patriotic host still influences our thought, thrills our souls, and stirs anew our noblest impulses; just as the setting sun leaves a glow of light to guide the weary toiler home, so the light of their brave lives and deeds may guide us to deep and loving remembrance, and devotion to the cause of right and justice.

It is said that "the grave buries the dead dust, but the character makes the world." Worldly rank, wealth, honors, are all perishable and faulty; but zeal for the right, loyalty to God and fellow-man have immortality which no sword point can pierce, nor cannon ball shatter. "Thus living we act, dead we speak," and that in no uncertain manner.

III. Tall monuments, artificially chiseled with rarest skill, cannot honor our dead soldiers as much as the loyal, patriotic impulse planted in the hearts of our boys and girls to-day by the record of their deeds, impulses which, if properly nourished, shall engender loyalty, patriotism, and love for the flag which makes free,—

"That flag of the heroes who left us their glory,
Borne through their battlefield's thunder and flame,
Blazoned in song and illumined in story,
Wave o'er us all who inherit their fame."

IV. The strife is over; the battles all ended. The scroll of the century that was marked by the strife is rolled together. We join in giving

"Love and tears for the Blue,
Tears and love for the Gray."

The history so glad and so glorious which chronicles the stern struggle in which right and liberty were won by such an awful baptism of fire and blood, is written in the grave of every veteran. Their work is done. In the words of Ridpath, the historian, "Peace to the memories of the fathers! Green be the graves where sleep the warriors, patriots, sages! Calm be the resting place of all the brave and true! Gentle be the summer rains where armies have met in battle! Forgotten be the animosities and heart burnings of the strife!

"Sacred be the trust committed to our care, and bright the visions of the coming ages!"—REV. H. H. HUTCHINS.

THE INCOMPARABLE DAY

"And there was no day like that before it, or after it, that the Lord hearkened to the voice of a man, for the Lord fought for Israel." Josh. 10:14.

I. It was a great thing for our nation that we had that incomparable experience of trial and victory in the Civil War; so great that the Spanish War, with its resulting expansion, seems but a little thing.

II. The main element of that greatness was that we got down so low that we had to cry mightily to God, and he gave us the grand uplift of his hearing and help.

III. God's mighty help is always ready, and each of us may have an incomparable and heroic day when the sun and moon shall stand still for us because God hearkens to the voice of man.—F. N.

NEW ISSUES CALL FOR NEW COURAGE

"The Egyptians whom we have seen to-day, ye shall see them again no more forever. The Lord shall fight for you." Exod. 14:13, 14.

I. The issues of our Civil War are past and can not be recalled, nor can foolish reactionaries reverse their decision. Slavery is dead, and there will be no more rebellion nor "State's rights."

II. New issues will be raised as Israel found new foes along the way to Canaan. They needed Moses' uplifted hands, and Aaron and Hur to help. There are new appeals to new courage.

III. All issues, old or new, require God's help; and we need faith as well as courage to secure the same providential care that helped the earlier heroes.—F. N.

LESSONS OF MEMORIAL DAY

I. Two Grand Armies—one below—worn, still in service, diminishing; the other above—swelling in size, life's warfare accomplished.

II. Two Grand Reviews. One in Washington at the close

of the Civil War. One in heaven, wherein all the glorious tatters and rags, marks of our trials and struggles here on earth, will be acclaimed by an angelic throng.—AUTHOR UNKNOWN.

SHARING THE HERO SPIRIT

"For I know that ye knew what great conflict I have for you." Col. 2:1.

The heroic Christian apostle shows a high form of that "struggle for others" which Drummond declares a large part of human activity. Of this our soldiers show another form. The soldier possibly thinks little about winning other men to his own heroic spirit, yet he does so win them, and it is a victory greater than any over the enemy, and a more valuable service. Memorial Day is a strong help toward this higher result of brave effort.

1. Memorial Day helps us to understand the heroism of our noblest men.
2. To know their spirit will be to come under the influence of high and generous impulses.
3. To know their spirit will make us better appreciate our country in its nobler aspect.
4. The difference between them and us is in the absolute sacrifice which they actually made for patriotism.
5. Patriotism as it dared death was a holy thing. It sanctified the veterans, and to think of it helps to sanctify us.
6. Seeing and feeling the power of this profound emotion, as they show it, is one of the strongest influences to ennoble our lives.
7. Thus our heroes uplift us to a higher plane of living and acting.

THE SUPREME GIFT OF PATRIOTISM

"Who loved me and gave himself for me." Gal. 2:20.

When we gather at an ordinary funeral we may have respect and even love for him who is taken away; but here to-day we come with another thought.

I. These men gave themselves. They did not keep from

danger, nor call in the physician to fight off death with every remedy conceivable. They were pressing forward with a purpose so strong that death did not stay them. "Neither count I my life dear unto myself," said Paul, "so that I might finish my course with joy."

II. They were "volunteers"; to what? To death. What more can a man do for a cause than die for it? This is the supreme proof of earnestness and devotion.

III. They gave themselves for us in these two senses.
  1. Their sacrifice results for our good.
  2. They meant to serve us. They deliberately chose the good of the land, of their children, of all the people, in preference to their own good.

IV. In all this they followed in the footsteps of Christ, and I may therefore use about them a text written about Christ. They help us to understand what Christ did. So they may save us in the highest sense.

THE INSPIRATION OF HEROIC MEMORIES

"But call to remembrance the former days." Heb. 10:32.

The wise-hearted, broad-minded men have not been the merry men; for the higher the enlightenment the more we see to grieve over, even if we plan and hope for better things; and the wisest man earth ever saw was "a man of sorrows." After great sorrows are past, it is wise to learn their lessons, and this might be our work to-day.

I. We call to remembrance the dying pain of the brave men who saved the country from disruption and disgrace.

II. We recall the mothers and wives who gave their husbands and sons to their country.

III. We recall the general spirit of loyal devotion in all our communities, which filled the armies with recruits taking the places made vacant in the ranks.

IV. We recall the tears and praises poured forth as our dead were brought home for burial.

V. We recall the orderly disbanding, and the return of the veterans to the quiet work of peace.

A NEW MEMORIAL DAY

"What mean you by this service?" Ex. 12:26.

Not a new Memorial Day, but a new, an added, meaning to the old Memorial Day is coming. Let such an incident as that of the sounding of taps for the first American soldiers who died in France teach us what is meant.

The first three American soldiers killed in the trenches in France are sleeping in French soil, honored by the American army and the people and army of France. Their final interment was made there. With a guard of French infantrymen, in their picturesque uniforms of red and horizon blue, standing on one side, and a detachment of American soldiers on the other, the flag-draped caskets were lowered into the grave as a bugler blew taps and the batteries at the front fired minute guns. As the minute guns boomed, the French officer commanding the division in this section paid tribute to the fallen Americans. His words, which were punctuated by the roar of the guns and the whistle of shells, touched both the French and Americans. In conclusion, the French officer said:

"In the name of the —th Division, in the name of the French army, and in the name of France, I bid farewell to Private Enright, Private Gresham, and Private Hay, of the American army.

"Of their own free will they had left a prosperous and happy country to come over here. They knew war was continuing in Europe, they knew that the forces fighting for honor, love of justice and civilization were still checked by the long-prepared forces serving the powers of brutal denomination, oppression and barbarity. They knew that efforts were still necessary. They wished to give up their generous hearts and they have not forgotten old historical memories, while others forget more recent ones.

"They ignored nothing of the circumstances and nothing had been concealed from them—neither the length and hardships of war, nor the violence of battle, nor the dreadfulness of new weapons, nor the perfidy of the foe. Nothing stopped them. They accepted the hard and strenuous life; they crossed the ocean at great peril; they took their places on the front by our side, and they have fallen facing the foe in a hard and desperate hand-to-hand fight. Honor to them. Their families, friends and fellow citizens will be proud when they learn of their deaths.

"Men! These graves, the first to be dug in our national soil and only a short distance from the enemy, are as a mark of the mighty land we and our allies firmly cling to in the common task, confirming the will of the people and the army of the United States to fight with us to a finish, ready to sacrifice as long as is necessary until final victory for the most noble of causes, that of the liberty of nations, the weak as well as the mighty. Thus the deaths of these humble soldiers appear to us with extraordinary grandeur.

"We will, therefore, ask that the mortal remains of these young men be left here, left with us forever. We inscribe on the tombs, 'Here lie the first soldiers of the Republic of the United States to fall on the soil of France for liberty and justice.' The passer-by will stop and uncover his head. Travelers and men of heart will go out of their way to come here to pay their tributes.

"Private Enright! Private Gresham! Private Hay! In the name of France, I thank you. God receive your souls. Farewell."

PART XXVII: CHILDREN'S DAY TEXTS AND THEMES

Lessons from the Birds: "Surely in vain the net is spread in the sight of any bird." Prov. 1:17.

The Sky Telegram: "Ask and it shall be given to you." Matt. 7:7.

Flowers and Their Uses: "Consider the lilies, how they grow." Matt. 6:28.

The Benediction of Kindness: "Be ye kind one to another, tender hearted," etc. Eph. 4:32.

Tapping the Wheels: "Take heed unto thyself." 1 Tim. 4:16.

Castles in the Air: 1 Cor. 3:12. Building character-castles strongly and well. Not with mud-brick foundations, as some pyramids had in Egypt. Golden bricks, honor, bravery, truthfulness, thoughtfulness, kindness—all the good thoughts, good words, good deeds of life are pure gold. And these are the only bricks worth using to make your life-castle with.

Honor Bright: "By patient continuance in well doing seek for . . . honor." Rom. 2:7. An honorable boy or girl not made by chance, not by luck, not by fortune, but by always doing well. Patient continuance in well doing. Boys wishing to impress with their promises say: "I will, honor bright." Keep your honor bright by constant use. Practice goodness and truth every day.

Growing: "And the child grew, and waxed strong in spirit," etc. Luke 2:40. "The child grew." And he was neither round-shouldered nor hump-backed. He kept his head back and his chest out, as all boys and girls ought to do. He kept sweet. I think that is one reason why he "waxed strong." He grew all round. Body, mind, and spirit well attended to. Health. Take care of your body. Wisdom. Cultivate your mind. Spirit. Keep the soul on top. Make Jesus your model in all things.

CHILDREN'S DAY TEXTS AND THEMES

On Growing Up: Luke 2:52. How often children talk of what they will do "when they grow up." What being grown up means. How we grow. Begin growing in wisdom now. Begin to practice good ways, kind acts, patient, painstaking work now.

Play-time: Zech. 8:5. God notices boys and girls at play. Play fair. Never play when you ought to be working. Keep your temper. Never let your games become quarrels. Don't excuse your own slips and laugh at your opponent's mistakes. It ought to be the other way around. Do your best to win, but whether winning or losing, "play the game." Never forget the unseen Watcher at the games.

Little Foxes: Song of Sol. 2:15. Have you ever seen a little fox? It is so cunning you want to cuddle it. But for all its charming looks, it is a fox—will soon be at its mischievous work among the vines. The beginnings of sin in childhood are much like "little foxes." Look out.

What Is Your Name? John 1:42. The text tells us how Peter got his name—Petros—rock. Children earning a name. Earning regard. Earning love and respect or dislike and suspicion.

Strayed Sheep: "All we like sheep have gone astray.... And the Lord hath laid on him the iniquity of us all.... He is brought as a lamb to the slaughter." Isa. 53:6.

The Best Book: "The law of thy mouth is better unto me than thousands of gold and silver." Psa. 119:72.

Cooking the Brain: "Awake, ye drunkards, and weep." Joel 1:5.

A Magnet: "And I, if I be lifted up from the earth, will draw all men unto me." John 12:32.

A Beautiful World: "It shall blossom abundantly, and rejoice even with joy and singing." Isa. 35:2.

Face Strings; or, How to Grow Beautiful: "They have made their faces harder than a rock; they have refused to return." Jer. 5:3.

Lighthouses: "Thy word is a lamp to my feet, and a light unto my path." Psa. 119:105.

Railroad Lamps: "Thy word is a lamp unto my feet, and a light unto my path." Psa. 119:105.

Foresight and Hindsight: "A prudent man foreseeth the

evil, and hideth himself; but the simple pass on, and are punished." Prov. 22:3.

Airy Castles: "Now Haman thought in his heart, To whom would the king delight to do honor more than to myself?" Esther 6:6.

The Giant Killer: "These were born unto the giant of Gath; and they fell by the hand of David, and by the hand of his servants." 1 Chron. 20:8.

Religion's Pleasant Ways: "Her ways are ways of pleasantness." Prov. 3:17.

A Sermon on Spring: "The time of the singing of the birds has come." Sol. Song 2:12.

Storms in Life: "A refuge from the storm." Isa. 25:4.

God Is: "The fool hath said in his heart, There is no God." Psa. 53:1.

The Thief in the House: "Whoso is a partner with a thief hateth his own soul." Prov. 29:24.

Children's Church: "I write unto you, little children, because your sins are forgiven you for his sake." 1 John 2:12.

Our Hope: "Fear not; I will help thee." Isa. 41:13.

Little Ships: "And then were also with him other little ships." Mark 4:36. I. Little ships carry precious cargo. II. Little ships need guiding. III. Little ships can be useful. IV. Little ships must be careful. V. Little ships may be lost.

Lessons from Little Things: I. It was only a little coat. 1 Sam. 2:19. II. It was only a little cake. 1 Kings 17:13. III. It was only a little cloud. 1 Kings 18:44. IV. It was only a little coney. Prov. 30:26. V. It was only a little girl. But what good service she rendered! 2 Kings 5:2.

Ways of Knocking: 1 Thess. 5:17. Asking, seeking, knocking are three special features of real prayer. I. The timid knock. Want of faith. James 1:6. II. The runaway knock. Want of patience. Psa. 40:1. III. The late knock. Want of time. Luke 13:25. IV. There are five proper ways of knocking. 1. Knock early. While young. Psa. 5:33. 2. Knock earnestly. With all your heart. James 5:17, 18. 3. Knock distinctly. Matt. 7:7. 4. Knock repeatedly. Importunity. 1 Thess. 5:17. 5. Knock expectantly. Psa. 27:14.

The Garden of the Lord: Isa. 51:3. In the garden of the Lord there are: I. Weeds to be removed, sin, selfishness, disobedience. II. Life to be nourished. III. Flowers to be cultivated. Beauty. IV. Fruits to be gathered. V. Blessings to be enjoyed. Reward.

PART XXVIII: CHILDREN'S DAY SERMON OUTLINES

THE EYES OF YOUR HEART

Ephesians 1:18.

How many eyes has a spider? Don't know? Give it up? Well, it has eight; two at the front of its head, two at each side, and two at the top! So the spider can look all around, like a man in a lighthouse tower. How many eyes has a fly? Oh, two great bunches: hundreds! A bee? Three thousand eyes, they say.

Now, how many have you? Two, you answer? No: more. You have eyes inside, as well as those outside: "The eyes of your understanding," as in the A. V.; "of the heart," R. V. These eyes within are of utmost value; often seeing what is hidden from the outward eyes. "Eye hath not seen, nor ear," etc.; "but God hath revealed them unto us, by his Spirit," that is, to the inner senses. Why? Father and Mother see much more in you than other people see! "I wish he saw me with Grandpa's eyes," said a little girl, when some one was finding fault with her. Yes, love gives the seeing eye, and the understanding heart! That is why God wants you to love him. It opens the inner eyes. Then—

I. God is seen—Everywhere. "Father and Friend. Thy Light. Thy Love," etc.

II. Our Saviour Too—Some "saw no beauty." Others "beheld his glory."

III. The Bible—How David loved it! And what he saw. "Open thou," etc.

IV. The Sabbath—"A delight!" Pearl of Days! Well called Sunday!

V. House of God—Sanctuary, sacred place. Refuge. Children's Home.

VI. Openings for Doing Good—At home, school, everywhere; if sought.

Pray the prayer of the blind man of Jericho—"Lord, that our eyes may be opened!"—Rev. J. Ellis.

THINGS TO WATCH

"Watch." Matt. 26:41.

I. Watch self. This is very important, and you will have all you can well attend to if you keep self in subjection.

II. Watch your eyes so that they will look upon the beautiful and see the wants of the needy.

III. Watch your nose so that it will keep in the right direction, and not go prying around where you have no business to go.

IV. Watch your mouth that nothing unclean enters, or that nothing vicious comes out.

V. Watch your tongue that it speaks no guile nor unkind words, but is used to praise and honor God, and to teach the Gospel.

VI. Watch your hands that they steal not, nor be idle, but use them industriously.

VII. Watch your feet that they do not lead you into saloons nor into any other evil places, but that they walk in the pathway of duty and the highway of holiness.

VIII. Watch your temper that it may be like-minded with Christ. In fact, watch self at all times and in all places, and ask God to help you gain the victory so that you may be a dutiful child, a true citizen, in the full sense of the word.

A BRIGHT PIN

One evening I held a pin in my hand and said, "Now, Mr. Pin, let us hear what you have to tell me about yourself that will help me to talk to the children on Sunday."

I. The Pin replied, "Well, sir! I want you to understand that I am straight, that whenever I have work to do I go at it right away; and all because I am straight. I am welcomed into all kinds of homes and am used for all kinds of purposes. Ladies delight to have me as their constant companion. I dine with princesses, and kings display me in gorgeous scarfs. I am also welcomed in the home of the poor, and save the workers a great amount of labor. Oh! but it is dreadful to think that when I become bent or crooked I am thrown away, and trampled upon! Millions of my brothers and sisters are lost every day because they are crooked! So long as I am straight it is all right." Boys and girls, listen to that: "So long as I am straight I am all right." What about you? Are you straight with father, mother and companions? If you are not, depend upon it, you will become useless.

II. Secondly, says the Pin, "I am sharp." A dentist had a troublesome client who wouldn't open his mouth; so the dentist gave a boy a pin and told him when a certain signal was given to push it into the man. He did, and in less time than you can say "Jack Robinson" the tooth was out. The pin was sharp and went in. Boys and girls need to be sharp. The pin says: "Be straight! Be sharp!"

III. Thirdly, says the Pin, "I am bright." You can't do anything with a rusty pin. Rusty children are not much use. They are always in the way. They get up in the morning and crawl to breakfast, and are too lazy to clean their boots. They are so rusty that if asked to do anything for mother they don't hear. Pins get rusty by being in the wrong place, amidst dirt and dust. Isn't that where boys get rusty?

IV. The pin said that it had two other things, a head and a point. All of us have heads, but some of us never get to a point, but are like a few preachers I know, who go round and round, and never get anywhere, but a pin that is "straight," "sharp," and "bright" always has a point and gets there when required.

V. And then the pin says: "But there is something I haven't that I wish I had—that is some brains. I can only act on the push of another." No brains indeed? Then you are not much after all, and how can I help the children by talking about you? Then it said: "Tell the children that to be what I am, they must use what I have not—brains." So it amounts to this: To be straight, sharp, bright and have a point we must use the brains that are in what a pin has as well as ourselves, the head.—REV. JOHN DUSTAN.

THE BLESSEDNESS OF CHILDLIKENESS

"When Israel was a child then I loved him." Hos. 11:1.

A feeling of sadness steals over us when comparing the man with the former child-character. We say: "Then I loved him."

I. Children are remarkable for their trust. What undoubting faith in our words! What unquestioning confidence in our judgment! When explanations are asked for of things which cannot be understood by children, the answer is enough when we say: "You will know when you are older." "When" we had this childlikeness, "then" God loved us.

II. Children are remarkable for their purity. Apart from hereditary taint, how sweetly pure! Pure as the heavens ere the clouds are born. Pure as the early dew—the untrodden snowflake—the pellucid stream—the unplucked flowers. "Then" how lovely!

III. Children are remarkable for their sincerity. What open-heartedness! What frankness of speech! What absence of hypocrisy! When like this, "then" God and man love us.

IV. Children are remarkable for their simplicity. How free from vanity, and conceit, and pride, and vainglory! A beggar's hand is clasped cordially, if only clean. The servant maid and the high born lady on equal footing. Social distinctions are paper walls. When the early church resembled this character—"believers were added daily" to its ranks; for "then" it was lovely.

V. Children are remarkable for their contentment. No "making haste to be rich"—the penny as satisfying as a sovereign when small wants are met. No sitting up late and rising up early to eat the bread of carefulness. But calm contentment and happy trust in parental provisions.

VI. Children are remarkable for their gladness. The blood is pure—the circulation healthy—the appetite eager—the sleep dreamless—freedom from "torment"—"perfect love casting out fear." When our souls are thus replete with health and gladness "then" God loves us.—J. P.

THE MINISTRY OF CHILDREN

"And a little child shall lead them." Isa. 11:6.

"Take this child away and nurse it for me and I will give thee thy wages." Ex. 2:9.

Quite commonly throughout Christian lands Children's day is celebrated on the second Sunday in June. It is a glad day, full of the odor of flowers, the singing of birds and the sweet sound of the voices of innumerable children. It is also a day full of suggestive instruction for young and old alike. It will be well if in our homes at this time we speak of the children, confer in regard to their interests, pray for God's blessing upon them, and, as older people, open our hearts to the lessons we may learn from them.

God has many ministers besides those that bear that distinctive name. The babbling brook, the deep blue sea, the starry firmament, the many-tinted flowers of the field, the birds of the air, all speak to our hearts about the glory and majesty, the power and the love of God. Children, too, are his "ministers," and it is especially of them we will now think. Children teach us many lessons in many ways and influence us greatly.

I. They purify. There is a sweet fragrance streaming forth from the life of every little child, which makes us older people long to get back to the sweetness, the simplicity, the teachableness, the purity of our days of early youth and childhood. They preach to us, not so much by their lips as by their innocence.

II. They elevate. Children appeal to the highest and best instincts of our nature. They take our thoughts away from things sordid or low, and lift us to high thinking and noble acting.

III. They stir. They arouse our laggard wills and move us to better living. They make us careful of conduct that is likely to be reproduced in them, and stimulate our finer qualities. They inspire us with hope, rouse us to wholesome sacrifice, impel us to industry and set us forward in ways of physical, moral and spiritual well-being.

IV. They instruct. God speaks to us through them. He taught Eli by young Samuel. He used the little boy to in-struck the aged priest. And has not God in like manner often spoken since Eli's day to those of riper years through the lips of children? He has manifested himself through a child's prayers, through a child's piety, through a child's example. He has taken infantile lips and filled them with strange and startling messages from himself.

V. They console. No one can overestimate the amount of blessing children have brought to hearts and homes in the way of taking our minds off our troubles and giving the cheer and consolation of a sweet and clinging love. In no direction is their ministry more marked than in healing the wounds of bereavement and sorrow.

VI. They reconcile. They not only console our sorrow, but they most powerfully reconcile us to life's hardships. How many a mother struggles against hardships and poverty, toils day and night for her little ones, and yet "thinks her lot divine" because she has them to toil for! How many a father, returning home from the labor and cares of the day, has had his heart cheered and strengthened by the prattle of his little children! Thus they remove our thoughts from self. They say so many kind and sympathetic things that we are cheated of weary care and are reconciled to our lot in life.

VII. They gladden. Children are the flowers of life, the poetry of life, the sunshine of life. Their presence is always gladdening. Their loveliness surprises us into a pure and abounding joy. How poor, how dismal, how uninviting the world would appear were there no children in it!

VIII. They soften and make us tender. Their helplessness appeals to us so that we relax our hardness and become tender. No mother's heart is ever just the same after having clasped her own child to her breast. No father can feel the touch of a tiny hand without being softened and made more gentle. The birth of a dear child binds the hearts of parents more closely and tenderly together, and all who come in contact with the little one are made more kindly and affectionate and gentle.

IX. They lead Godward. "A little child shall lead them." How innumerable the instances and how remarkable the ways in which parents and friends have been brought to God through the influence of little children! Let us open our eyes to see what children may become to us, as well as what we ought to be to them; for in a suitable and reverent sense children are the salvation of the race; their ministry the most powerful ministry for good.—H.

MANNERS

The way you do things are your manners. The way you look, the way you speak, the way you act, the way you move, are your manners. What you do with your hat is a part of your manners. I do not mean hanging it up, I mean taking it off or keeping it on. Everybody has to have some way to do things. There are two kinds of manners, good ones and bad ones. Your face looks better when you are having good manners than when you are having bad ones. I have heard of six kinds of bad manners, and one more. I will mention them. Pig manners, one; bear manners, two; donkey manners, three; post manners, four; cock-a-doodle-doo manners, five; cow-in-the-parlor manners, six.

1. Pig Manners. And if you want to know what they are, go and look in the pig pen when their dinner is in their trough. Every piggy hurries to get the most and the best. Every piggy looks out for himself, and does not care for the other ones. Children that have pig manners are the kind that want to be helped first at meal times, and want the best things for themselves, and the biggest pieces. They look out for themselves and do not care about other people getting anything good.

2. Bear Manners. Children that have bear manners are the kind that are gruff and grum, and growly. They have cross looking faces, and sometimes stick their lips out, and snarl, and growl, and are almost always grumbling and growling about something they want to do, or they don't want to do. They talk in this way: "Find my hat." "I want to go out." "Open the door." "I want something to eat," and never think of please or thank you, and they get cross very often, and look cross.

3. Donkey Manners. Children that have donkey manners are the kind that want to do just what they want to do, and

nothing else, no matter how much you ask them and coax them. If you ask them to move they stay still. If you ask them to stay still they move. If you ask them to keep quiet they make a noise. If you ask them to make a noise they keep quiet. If you ask them to go on an errand, they say, "Don't want to," or "I ain't going to," and the worst kind, "I will," and "I won't." When they are playing they never will do what others want to but only what themselves want to.

4. Post Manners. Children that have post manners are the kind that do not answer when they are spoken to, any more than a post would. If a visitor says, "How do you do?" or "Do you like to play tag?" or, "Do you like pictures or butterflies or anything?" they stand still as a post, and do not speak; but maybe if you should ask them if they like candy, they would speak one word, and I guess it would be yes.

5. Cock-a-doodle-doo Manners. Children that have cock-a-doodle-doo manners are the kind that feel big and act so. A rooster struts among the hens as if he felt so big he did not know what to do, and sometimes he seems to feel so big that he has to get upon a fence and clap his wings and crow, cock-a-doodle-doo. Sometimes there will be a lot of fellows playing, and a cock-a-doodle-do fellow will come there, and he will act as if he knew the right way to do everything better than anybody, and he'll give them the rules and he'll strut around like a rooster; and in his house he does the same way to his mother and the other grown-up ones, and the ones that are not grown-up. That kind of a fellow ought to stand up on a fence and clap his wings, no, I mean his elbows, and crow, cock-a-doodle-doo: "I know better than you."

6. Cow-in-the-parlor Manners. Children that have cow-in-the-parlor manners are the kind that are always getting in somebody's way or pushing themselves in between people, or going in front of people, or stepping on somebody's feet, or on the bottoms of ladies' clothes, or leaning against people, or stumbling over things, or bumping against the furniture, or against people, or tipping over their own chairs, or knocking down a vase or a work basket, or a tumbler of water. They are clumsy as a cow in a parlor, and do not mind what they are about any more than a cow in the parlor would mind what she was about.

7. Besides those kinds of manners there is another kind I have heard of called interrupters. Interrupters are the kind that begin to talk while other people are speaking; no matter if 'tis father or their mother, or company, the interrupters do not wait for anybody to stop talking but break right in and say what they want to.

THE MESSAGE OF THE FLOWERS

Matt. 6:28-34; James 1:9-11.

The first passage is taken from the Sermon on the Mount. Christ calls attention to their beauty and reminds his hearers of the fact that God had made them beautiful. He drew a striking contrast between Solomon in all his riches and glory and the flowers in all their natural beauty with which God had clothed them. This passage is rich with instructions for us, and brings to us a practical lesson that should never be overlooked. We should seek first the kingdom of God, and all other necessary things will be added thereto. "A man's life is a greater blessing than his livelihood." "Knowledge and greatness are the perfection of man, not beauty, much less clothes."

The second passage is from the practical man James. He makes a comparison between man and flowers. He shows how frail and destructible is grass and the flowers thereof, and said: "So also shall the rich man fade away in his ways."

I. The flowers speak to us of their Creator. It requires divine power to design and create them. Man cannot make even the seed of a flower, and cause its life to be arrayed in beauty.

II. The flowers tell us something of God's character. They reveal to us the conception of beauty, utility, and adaptability. Just think of the great variety of flowers as to their form, color and beauty. Think of the practical purposes to which they are adapted. Think of the varying conditions of their lives; for example, the lily of the valley, and the blossoms of the snow-capped mountains.

III. They teach us the lessons of God's providence. This is the practical value of the first passage above, and God who gives the flowers life will certainly give them care. And God who gives us being will certainly supply our wants.

IV. They teach us the lesson of frailty. James compares man to the valley grass, and he makes it stronger and more pointed by taking a rich man. He may be more able to stand against some of the adverse conditions of life.

V. Flowers teach us the dependence and union of life. The flowers borrow beauty and fragrance from one another, and when combined give their most pleasing effect. Although there are many species, there are a fewer number of genera, and all of these unite in the common life.

VI. Flowers are the messengers of love and thoughtfulness. A bouquet of flowers is the type of a cluster of thoughts. Its sweetness typifies their kindliness. It is interesting to notice how often Christ uses the flowers in his teaching, and what strong and helpful doctrines he presents by them. It will help you to study the botany of the Bible devotionally.—Rev. W. M. Anderson, D.D.

SIX MINDS

I. Mind your tongue! Don't let it speak hasty, cruel, unkind, or wicked words. Mind!

II. Mind your eyes! Don't permit them to look on wicked books, pictures, or objects. Mind!

III. Mind your ears! Don't suffer them to listen to wicked speeches, songs or words. Mind!

IV. Mind your lips! Don't let tobacco foul them. Don't let strong drink pass them. Don't let the food of the glutton enter between them. Mind!

V. Mind your feet! Don't let them walk in the steps of the wicked. Mind!

VI. Mind your heart! Don't let the love of sin dwell in it. Don't give it to Satan, but ask Jesus to make it his throne. Mind!

THE SWANS' DINNER BELL

There is a pretty story told about the swans in the moat of the palace of the Bishop of Wells, England. The old gate-house, with its gray, ivygrown walls, still stands, and the swans sail up and down the dark waters of the moat, which centuries ago was a defense of the castle.

The peculiar thing about these swans is that they ring a dinner bell whenever they are hungry, and expect to have it answered at once. A long string hangs out of the gate-house window and, as the story is told, when the swans are hungry, the leader swims gravely up to the bell rope, pulls at it, and then waits quietly for the lodge-keeper's wife to bring out her basket of bread.

It is said that fifty years ago the daughter of the bishop who lived there then taught the swans this trick with great patience and care. The swans that have come since then have apparently in turn learned the secret of the bell-rope so that one who is able to perceive the connection between the pulling of the string and the appearing of the bread-basket has always been among them. That the swans communicate their demand for bread to their leader, who is always the one to ring the bell, is evident from the fact that after the black swans were introduced into the moat the ringing became so frequent that the housekeeper had to take the string in to secure herself a little peace. Evidently the newcomers were hearty eaters.

We all have a right to pray: "Give us this day our daily bread." We are taught, "Ask and ye shall receive." Let the swans teach us this Children's Day the lesson of prayer.—H.

CHILDREN'S DAY TALK

There are three sorts of people in the world (little or big), and each sort may be likened to a boat. Which boat most fairly represents your life?

I. First, there are the people who are like row-boats. They have to be pulled wherever they go. Sometimes it is a hard struggle to keep them pointed the right way.

II. Next are the people who are like sail-boats. If the wind blows east, that is their direction. If it blows west, they go that way. Of course, it is possible for them to "beat against the wind," but rarely, if ever, are they found doing it. Their main tendency and purpose incline them to follow every wind of emotion or of popular sentiment.

III. Finally there are folks who are like a steamboat, people who ride against wind or tide, and are not so much dependent upon circumstances. Of course we cannot press the figure too far, but it is fair to say that these generalizations define the attitude of many people to-day. Which boat are you like?

IV. People are like boats in other ways. Some seem made for pleasure, some for carrying freight; others, for carrying passengers. Some are trim and taut, with lines of real beauty, and are well-kept in every way. Some go on long voyages, some on short ones. You will look out over river and sea this summer and some day meditate upon the different kinds of boats and their likeness to human life.—A.

RHODA, A GIRL CHRISTIAN

"And as Peter knocked at the door of the gate, a damsel came to hearken, named Rhoda," etc. Acts. 12:13-16.

Rhoda and Miriam are the only girls of the Bible whose names we know. Rhoda was evidently an earnest Christian, and occupies an important place in the records of the early church. The mention of her name, the memorial of her life, and the fragrance of her service are abiding marks of her testimony for Jesus. Rhoda means a rose, the emblem of beauty, sweetness and fragrance, and these certainly were some of the features of Rhoda's character.

On a girl's tombstone in France there is a rose nicely carved with these words underneath: "She was just like that." And this is the picture the Holy Spirit has drawn of Rhoda in the New Testament. A bright, beautiful blessing, "She being dead yet speaketh."

I. Rhoda was a true Christian. But you ask, How do you know? She was in fellowship with the Church, Acts 2:47. She was interested in the prayer-meeting—prayer, the evidence of life, Acts 9:11. She was glad when Peter was released; Christian love a family mark; grace, life and fellowship, all true marks of a real Christian.

II. Rhoda was a careful Christian. She was placed on guard. No doubt she was set to watch and listen whilst they prayed. There were many enemies about, Acts 12:1.

She used her ears well. She hearkened carefully. She used her tongue wisely. She asked who was there. She was very quick. She recognized Peter's voice. Grace makes us wise. Danger makes us careful. Love makes us quick.

III. Rhoda was a warm-hearted Christian. "She opened not the gate for gladness." Rhoda got a little excited, still there was joy. Her whole soul responded to the fact that prayer was answered and Peter released. There were three good reasons for Rhoda's gladness. Rewarded faith, answered prayer and relieved anxiety. These blessings are always means of great joy and happiness.

IV. Rhoda was an active Christian. "She ran and told how Peter stood before the gate." She had a quick ear, warm heart, nimble feet, and a ready tongue, all alive for Jesus. If we are not like this, let us breathe that oft-repeated prayer in Psalm 119:25, "Quicken thou me according to thy word."

V. Rhoda was a useful Christian. She was most useful to the church then and has been ever since. It was only very humble service, but it has been recognized and recorded. It is a guide and pattern for every follower of Christ. It was wise, hearty, helpful, happy service for the Lord. So every Christian, young or old, with head clear, heart warm, soul glad, faith strong, feet shod, and the tongue touched by the Holy Ghost can do wonders for the Church and the world too.—REV. CHARLES EDWARDS.

A CHILDREN'S SERMON, WITH WHITE MICE AS A TEXT

Of course you have all of you seen pictures of submarines; and maybe when some of you have been at sea you have watched them pass under the water or your quick eyes have picked out a submarine's tower showing just above the waves. It cannot be very nice to be inside one of them. But if you went for a little voyage in one you would find plenty to interest you. Among other things you would almost certainly find some white mice; and I am sure you would wonder why they were there. This would be the reason. In submarines they carry gasoline, which spreads out and loses itself in ordinary air when it has the chance; and to prevent its escaping and perhaps being harmful, it has to be specially cooped up. Even then, unless everybody is careful and all goes well, the gasoline escapes; and the white mice are kept, because as soon as any gasoline escapes they smell it and begin to squeak. And, of course, the moment the sailors hear the squeaking they know something is wrong and they hurry to set everything right.

I am rather sorry to say that some clever person has invented a machine for detecting the escape of gasoline; and so the order has gone forth from the Board of Admiralty that soon no more white mice are to be carried on submarine craft. But for all that it is good to think of white mice warning great sailor men of danger, and so sometimes even helping the crew to save their lives. It shows that whether we are small mice or small children we can always do something to help others. Also it sets me wondering whether all my little hearers have the sense and the courage to cry out whenever anything is really wrong and likely to harm other people. Of course we all call out when we ourselves are hurt, just as white mice squeak if their tails are pinched. But do you call out when anything seems likely to harm others?

1. A lie is always harmful. Do you call out when you hear a lie?
2. Cheating and bullying and using words that are not clean are all of them sins that do more harm than an escape of gasoline.
3. Do you call out when any one plays unfairly or hits some one smaller than himself, or talks filth?
4. Of course you cannot say anything if you are always doing such naughty things yourself. But if you are wise you will refuse to do anything that will harm others; and if you are as wise as white mice in a submarine you will call out the moment there is danger to other folk.—REV. J. G. STEVENSON.

WATCH YOUR STEPS

"If thy children take heed to their way." 1 Kings 2:4.

At the subway stations in New York there is a man whose business it is to repeat, "Watch your step," as passengers are coming and going to trains, for a misstep might mean a serious accident if not death. This man receives a good salary for the performance of the simple but important duty.

Many an accident might be prevented by watching one's step. It is a true saying "that it is the first step that counts." Why? Because many persons have been started on the road to ruin by carelessness in taking the first step. After the first step downward is taken, it is much easier to take the second, third, and so on.

Is not that a good lesson for us all? How important it is that we watch our steps, especially when we are tempted to go to a wrong place or do a wrong thing. Don't make a misstep. Don't take a hasty, thoughtless step. Don't take a wrong step. Watch your steps.

MAKING FACES

"The show of their countenance doth witness against them." Isa. 3:9.

Every day as we walk along the street we meet many people and look into many faces. Some of these faces are hard and unpleasant, others are pleasant and beautiful. At one time not many years ago, each of these faces had the privilege of expressing kindness and beauty. We know that in ten years from now, as to-day, we shall see hard cruel faces as well as noble and kind ones. These faces are going to be made by the boys and girls of to-day.

As the artist makes his picture line by line, so are we just as surely making faces. We can see the artist at work because he works on the outside of his picture. We cannot see our friends or ourselves at work, because it is all done on the inside. The artist works with a brush, but we work with thoughts, words and deeds. Whenever we are tempted to say an unkind word or do an unkind deed to hurt somebody else, then we ourselves receive the greater harm. In time they may forget our cruelty, but it is built into our lives and finds its way to our faces, where it is seen by the world.

In the theater men paint their faces to fit the parts they play. If they are to represent a wicked man they make their faces look wicked. In life, whatever part we play, our faces grow to look the part. We should all desire to have beautiful faces, which stand for character. When the artist paints a picture, he has a model to follow; if the model is ugly he paints an ugly picture, and if the model be beautiful he paints a beautiful picture.

When we say that a boy or girl may be a Christian we mean that they may take for their lives the most beautiful model. We always think of Jesus as having a beautiful face because his life was beautiful. If we follow his life and teaching we cannot have hard, cruel faces for the world to see. God meant all faces to be kind and noble, and therefore he has given us his Son for a model.

We must always remember that what the poet says is true for us:

> "Beautiful thoughts make a beautiful life,
> And a beautiful life makes a beautiful face."
> —Rev. Chester J. Armstrong.

CANDLE SERMON FOR CHILDREN'S DAY

Text: "O satisfy us early with thy mercy; that we may rejoice and be glad all our days." Psa. 90:14.

An evangelist was talking to a meeting of children. He brought out a row of candles on a board; a very long candle was at one end, a very short one at the other. Between the long candle and the short one were candles of various heights. He said that by these candles he wanted to represent the grandfather, father and mother, boys and girls and the baby of a family who never heard of Christ until a missionary came —whom he represented by a lighted candle—and they all gave their hearts to Jesus, and from that day loved and served him. He then asked which candle they thought represented the grandfather, the mother, and so on. They all thought that the tallest candle would be the grandfather, but he told them: "No, that stands for the baby, the youngest member of the family." Presently one little boy said, "I know why; he has the chance to shine the longest for Jesus."

Yes, that is one of the greatest advantages of being a little Christian—of beginning early. You have the privilege of shining for Jesus so long. If any of you have not done so, that is a very special reason why you should give your hearts to Jesus now, while you are young. Then you can shine for him as long as you live, and you can also have the joys of his religion as long as you live. Pray, "O satisfy us early with thy mercy; that we may rejoice and be glad all our days."—H.

THE PONY ENGINE

Once upon a time a little freight car loaded with coal stood upon a track in a coal-yard.

The little freight car waited for an engine to pull it up the hill and over the hill and down the hill on the other side.

Over the hill in the valley people needed the coal on the little freight car to keep them warm.

By and by a great big engine came along, the smokestack puffing smoke and the bell ringing, "Ding! Dong! Ding!"

"Oh, stop! Please stop, big engine!" said the little freight car. "Pull me up the hill and over the hill and down the hill to the people in the valley on the other side."

But the big engine said, "I can't, I'm too busy," and away it went—Choo! Choo! Choo! Choo!

The little freight car waited again a long time till a smaller engine came puffing by.

"Oh, stop! dear engine, please stop!" said the little freight car. But the engine puffed a big puff and said, "I can't, you're too heavy." Then away it went, too—Choo! Choo! Choo! Choo!

"Oh, dear!" said the little freight car, "what shall I do? The people in the valley on the other side will be so cold without any coal."

After a long time a little pony engine came along, puffing just as hard as a little engine could.

"Oh, stop! dear engine, please stop and take me up the hill and over the hill and down the hill to the people on the other side," said the patient little freight car.

The pony engine stopped right away and said, "You're very heavy and I'm not very big, but I think I can. I'll try. Hitch on!"

All the way up the hill the pony engine kept saying, "I

think I can, I think I can, I think I can, I think I can!" quite fast at first.

Then the hill was steeper and the pony engine had to pull harder and go slower, but all the time it kept saying: "I-think-I-can! I-think-I-can!" till it reached the very top with a long puff—"Sh-s-s-s-s!"

It was easy to go down the hill on the other side.

Away went the happy little pony engine saying very fast, "I thought I could! I thought I could! I thought I could! I thought I could!"

Don't forget the lesson, boys and girls. Think you can. Never think you can't.—H.

LESSONS FROM THE DANDELION

"The wind passeth over it and it is gone." Psa. 103:16.

Once upon a time in a tiny green camp by the roadside lived a soldier all alone. He had traveled a long way from a dark, underground country, and meant to see something of the world. The first thing that he saw was a broad field, full of waving banners, and he thought what a beautiful place he had discovered, and pitched his tent among the green grasses.

Soon the raindrop elves saw how tired and dusty he was from his journey, and they soothed him with their musical stories, and gave him a refreshing shower bath. Through the clouds came the sunbeam fairies, bringing him a beautiful uniform of green and gold, and a quiver of golden arrows. Then the soldier was very happy, and smiled out at passers-by, and cheered many a weary traveler with a glimpse of his sunny face. By and by spring went away over the hilltops, the birds had finished their nesting, and the butterflies came to herald summer. Then the soldier began to feel tired, and knew he was growing old. His gray uniform had faded, and the golden arrows had turned to silver, and the wind brownies shot them far away. So the soldier crept down among the grasses, and his green camp was left vacant. But everywhere his silvery arrows fell there blossomed bright, golden flowers, and the little children loved them,' and called them dandelions.

Some of the Indians tell to their boys and girls this story

about the Prairie Dandelion. In the Southland, the lazy old South Wind was resting on the ground. One day, as he looked across the prairie, he saw a beautiful girl with yellow hair. For days he saw the maiden, and every day he said, "To-morrow I will go and ask this beautiful girl to live with me." But the South Wind was lazy and put off going. One day he saw that the maiden's hair was as white as snow. "Oh, the strong North Wind has put his crown upon her head!" he sighed, for he thought he had lost her. But it was not an Indian maiden he saw. It was the Prairie Dandelion, and she vanished one windy day.

Let us do the good things we intend to do now. Opportunity passes. Life is fleeting. Be good now. Do good now.—H.

PART XXIX: COMMENCEMENT TEXTS AND THEMES

The Investment of Life: "Take ye away therefore the talent from him." Matt. 25:28.
Religious Education: "Learn to do well." Isa. 1:17.
The Indispensable Book: "If the foundations be destroyed, what can the righteous do?" Psa. 11:3.
Sent from God: "There was a man sent from God whose name was John." John 1:16.
Taking Aim: "This one thing I do." Phil. 3:13.
Starting Out: James 1:5.
The Voyage of Life: "There go the ships." Psa. 104:26.
To Understand Our Times: "The children of Issachar, men that had understanding of the times." 1 Chron. 12:32.
Growing to Know: "If any man think that he knoweth anything, he knoweth nothing yet as he ought to know." 1 Cor. 8:2.
Heart and Hand: "A wise man's heart is at his right hand, but a fool's heart is at his left." Eccl. 10:2.
The House of Wisdom: "Through wisdom is a house builded." Prov. 24:3.
Address to Graduating Class: "Who knoweth whether thou art come to the kingdom for such a time as this?" Esther 4:14.
The Teaching Book: "Nevertheless we have the more sure word of prophecy unto which ye do well that ye take heed." 2 Pet. 1:19.
The Teaching State: "All thy children shall be taught of the Lord and great shall be the peace of thy children." Isa. 54:13.
Education the Doorway to Service: 2 Tim. 2:15.
Pressing Toward the Mark: "Brethren, I count not myself to have apprehended," etc. Phil. 3:13.
Your Kingdom: "Who knoweth whether thou art come to the kingdom for such a time as this?" Esther 4:14.

PART XXX: COMMENCEMENT SERMON OUTLINES

PASSING DIVIDENDS

The other day the richest road in New England passed its semi-annual dividend. The president of the road reported that the road had made a large profit, but that the directors thought it wiser to use the money for improvements than to pay it to the stockholders. The stockholders and the public praised this action because they knew it was needed.

Every young student is passing his dividends. High school or college students may earn considerable money, and some of them do. They might pay it to those who have taken stock in them, their parents, but they are allowed to use it for improvements. When a student plays ball or joins a glee club or does anything else that is like play, while others of his own age are working, the people who are maintaining the schools are content, because they are expecting an improved, more capable manhood.

But passing dividends is an emergency step; it ought not to be made a habit. Those who have invested their money in a railroad have a right to the interest of their money. And so with the student. His parents may not need his money, but they have a right to expect his improvement. Those who sustain the schools and colleges by their gifts or their taxes have a right to find an improved product when school days are over, and to-day every educational institution is being tested and judged by this question. Last winter the New England college presidents and preparatory-school heads were discussing for two days whether a scientific test of their efficiency is possible. But whether the test be scientific or not it is being made. Our colleges and high schools are under fire. The people who help sustain them are asking if they are worth while, and they are getting their answers from the kind of young folks that are being turned out. To-day I am persuaded that unfortunate impressions about our schools are being produced by a very small minority of students who do foolish things, but every student has the reputation of his school very much in his own hands.

The best justification of any school of higher learning in the past has been that it has furnished leaders to the nation, and many an earnest student has been made brave during his days of struggle by the thought that he was being trained to be a man of authority. Figures show that the colleges have well met the expectation and that they send out ten times as many leaders as come from the uneducated group. But if they should fail to do this in the future, they ought at least to furnish graduates who do their work well. So when one who has had high school or college training neither leads nor does his work well, he is passing the dividends that the world has a right to share.—W. BYRON FORBUSH, D.D.

DEMOCRACY AND EDUCATION

Education without religion is merely a galvanized corpse.

I. Education is a function of religion. Moses began with education. We know that the development of Israel was the result of this education. Our Lord and Saviour was first of all called teacher. Go ye into all the world—not only evangelizing, but teaching them to observe all things I have commanded.

II. Education has been the conservation of religion. We do not know what Christianity might have become but for it. And we need to thank God for the scholarship of that day. There is no such thing as a "simple Gospel." Sometimes we drag the Gospel down to get a little popularity. We may talk about a simple ocean, but we can not talk of a simple God. The Gospel is not simple.

III. Every great revival of the world has been the result of education. Luther, John Knox, John Wesley, Jonathan Edwards, President Finney—all these came from the schools. The education came from the Church. It has been wrapped up with religion. Democracy itself will not be sufficient. Indeed, it is most dangerous, except with education.

TRUE EDUCATION

"And they taught in Judah, having the book of the law of the Lord with them; and they went about through all the cities of Judah, and taught among the people." 2 Chronicles 17:9.

1. It is the function of the state to furnish a general education. The church is the great teacher in the spiritual sphere, but cannot furnish an education of a general nature. Neither the church nor family possesses the authority or equipment for such an education.

2. The public school is the digestive organ of the body politic. It is the melting-pot. The Scandinavian and Slav become American.

3. Education is not complete without the moral element. Character is the great aim of education. It must contribute to the prosperity and permanence of the State. Mere mental development is insufficient.

4. The Bible is the only standard in the field of morality. The standard is not the mere dictum of the teacher, or the best literature, or the lives of our best men, or civil statutes, but the Word of God.

5. The Bible, therefore, should be taught in our public schools. It is not sectarian. The Bible as a book should be used in the school-room; not a book of mere selections.

6. The wide-spread and long-continued custom of Bible-reading in our schools, in connection with the foregoing considerations, is a strong argument for its retention. The Bible is read in many of the schools all over our land. Not long since the attitude of at least twenty-one States was distinctly favorable, and in only eight had opinions been rendered against it.—Rev. T. H. Acheson.

"PRESSING TOWARD THE MARK"

Young people of this class, let me lay upon your hearts the practical lessons of this hour.

I. You must have a worthy purpose, held on to with fingers of steel, if you are not to go wabbling and wavering through life as unstable as water, which adjusts itself to the bend and curvature of every shore.

II. You must have a worthy program, a definite plan of translating your purpose into deed.

III. You must have a prize to struggle for worthy of your manhood and womanhood. These three or failure. These three or oblivion. These three or cipherdom. These three, wisely and fearlessly chosen, and they will lift and glorify you and crown you with victory and honor.—ROBERT F. COYLE, D.D.

ADDRESS TO THE GRADUATING CLASS

"Who knoweth whether thou art come to the kingdom for such a time as this?" Esther 4:14.

I. The first fact of the message is the face of personality, "Thou art come." That I am, staggers me. There are times when I search for the reasons behind my birth. Value yourselves; I give you the supreme truth, Personality is eternal. You are here to-day at a commencement; you have finished, to begin.

II. The second fact of the message is the fact of place. "Thou art come to the kingdom." And the kingdom is the kingdom of the present. You are in the world; just now it may not be easy to realize it, but your feet are on the earth, and all about you are people with faults and follies as well as with smiles and congratulations. There is before you a humdrum business of bread-making and child-rearing, of harvesting and ship-building, of preaching and teaching, of suffering and dying, of service and of sacrifice. You have missed the message of this institution unless you go out from these halls to master practical affairs, to solve immediate problems, to meet the crisis of the moment, whether that crisis be a high circumstance such as Esther faced, or a small sum that wrinkles the brow of a child. We have not seen the beauties or caught the lessons of the radiant Jewess, whose soul was more exquisite than her form or face, until we have thrust her great ordeal into the life of our times, into the affairs of our generation.

Do not misunderstand me. God pity us when we lose our dreams or when we cease to see visions. We must never become so engrossed with ministries that we have no patience or time for musing, for prayer, and for communion. Eventually he runs in a circle who runs without rest. A business bankrupts itself when it becomes a mere counting machine. There is an efficiency that is inefficiency. We must cultivate the amenities of the heart; we must wait with friendship and tarry with God, if we are to see developed within ourselves that spiritual initiative that more than physical force and mechanical genius shapes the destiny of the world.

But we must bring this spiritual initiative, we must apply this moral fervor, this divine optimism, to the tasks of the kingdom. We must harness our dreams; we must put a sword into the hands of our visions; we must honor our friendships by rendering a service, and glorify our God by making a life.

The kingdom is your kingdom, yours to-day as it was Queen Esther's yesterday. Again the dignity of personality. Yours for years is the opportunity, and will you sulk because of one who seems by birth and environment to be more favored than you are?

The kingdom is your kingdom because yours is the responsibility. The kingdom is yours because the rewards are yours.

III. The third fact of the message is the fact of time. "For such a time as this." Already we have appreciated together the stupendous problems to which we are born, problems far more complex and appalling than those confronting the queen whose character is our real message to-day, but problems no less solvable, for they are human problems, and we are laborers together with God.

Let us analyze our time more closely.—REV. DANIEL A. POLING.

FOR SUCH A TIME

"And who knoweth whether thou art come to the kingdom for such a time as this?" Esther 4:14.

I. There is a wisdom for such a time as this. The problem may seem difficult. The path may be uncertain. There may be unrest and indecision on every hand. The nations of the world may have gotten themselves into a perplexing and an aggravating situation. The business of nations may be facing problems never faced before in all their history. Each person may have some difficulty in the life, that never has been there before. Everything and everybody may seem to be dazed and greatly puzzled. There is a Wisdom for such a time as this.

II. There is a patience for such a time as this. Everything seems to strike us the wrong way. We break a shoestring. We pull a button off our clothes. We spill some water at the breakfast table. We stub our toe on the walk and fall. Some friend of ours has not done for us what he or she promised to do. This keeps up for the entire day. Everything that we do or try to do goes wrong. It all gets on your nerves, and some call it "nerves," but there is a Patience for such a time as this.

III. There is a strength for such a time as this. We and our church are trying to put on a worthy program in the community. This requires equipment for doing what is desired. This requires workers to carry on the work. This requires money and interest to keep the work going. The closer we get to the task of the work before us, the more we stand back with horror at the great size of it. Then we look at ourselves and look again at the task before us. We exclaim, "It can't be done!" There is a Strength for such a time as this.

IV. There is a God for such a time as this. The great struggle between right and wrong was never greater than it is to-day. It would seem at times that everything right, just, and honorable, is being dragged down to defeat and dishonor. Civilized nations have been grasping at each other's throat in a death struggle. There has been a cessation in the hostilities, although the spirit of the war is still in the minds of the people. We stop and ask ourselves seriously, "Why must it be so?" There is a God for such a time as this.

V. There is a person for such a time as this. No great crisis has ever confronted the world, the nation, the state, the community or the organization, but that some person has stepped forward for such a time as this. God is preparing men and women to meet the needs of mankind. Are you using this Wisdom, this Patience, this Strength, and this God, so that you can be a person for such a time as this?—REV. W. E. RAFFERTY, D.D.

THE GARDEN OF LIFE

"Thou hast been in Eden, the garden of God." Ezek. 28:13.

All privileged conditions of life are gardens of God. The privileged conditions of modern life have far eclipsed those of any of the cities of the ancient world. Never has life afforded such channels for culture, influence and power as now. There are many more hundreds of millions of people outside of the garden than inside. The privileged people of the world are relatively few.

The second point is the fact that the garden of God is a place of opportunity. Even Adam had work to do in primitive Eden. He was put in the garden to dress it and keep it; he was not simply to lie down under the trees and have a good time.

If he had lived up to his privileges he would have had a tolerably strenuous life in trying to overtake his opportunity. You have been in Eden, the garden of God. You are there now. I tell you that Eden means work, that privilege means opportunity for service, that no man has the right to Eden who does not remember the people outside the garden gate.

One more truth, the garden of God is a place of temptation. The last place we should expect to find temptation is in God's garden. Ever since men began to think they have been asking why God allows men to be subjected to temptation. The only answer is that men would not be men did they not have the choice between good and evil.

We are wrestling in this country with the most tremendous problems which have ever confronted any nation—industrial problems, political problems, social problems, and, fundamental to all these, moral and religious problems. Around us on all sides is a seething mass of foreign born population, largely ignorant, sometimes degraded and generally quite unfamiliar with American ideals. Into this vortex of life you are now to pass from the pleasant placidness of your college days.

You will find it a very different kind of experience. If you are real men with red corpuscles in your blood and moral fiber in your soul you will not hug your cultured privileges to yourself and seek for some quiet corner where you can enjoy them, but, realizing that privilege means responsibility, you will fling yourselves into the rough and tumble of the battle, determined to give all that is in you for the good of your country and for the welfare of your fellow-men. Remember that only those who are above can help those who are below, and that unto whom much is given from him will much be required.—Rev. Paul F. Sutphen, D.D.

THE TEACHER AND HIS PUPIL

"The heart of the wise teacheth his mouth." Prov. 16:23.

The heart has been compared to many things—a citadel, a mirror, a temple. Here it is compared to a teacher.

I. The teacher of the lips. How much of evil does the heart of the wicked utter by means of the lips!

1. The heart of "the wise" is a powerful teacher. The head has never made the tongue so eloquent or effective. The heart of Paul made his stammering tongue to disturb voluptuous Felix, and confound cynical Athenians.
2. The heart of "the wise" is the only teacher of acceptable words. God hears none but such as are thus dictated.
3. Let it be a consecrated pupil. Say, "Lord, my mouth shall speak thy praise." Let your heart cause your lips—
   To speak the word of sympathy.
   To speak the word of prayer.
   To speak the word of thanksgiving.

TO YOUNG WOMEN GRADUATES

Some one has said that the best thing which cultivation can show—the fairest fruit of all its varied agencies—is a lady's parlor—of course with the lady in it. There is a very suggestive truth in this remark. To make the parlor possible, with its elegance, refinement, culture, and its gentle yet controlling influence, you must lay under tribute all the material, intellectual and moral forces of society.

The Church, the State, and the school, these three potent agents whereby society is informed, directed, and molded are intended by the economy of providence to be the chief auxiliaries by means of which the Christian home may be perfect and perpetuate itself, may furnish and seat within its parlor its succession of Christian women. When these homes are universal, when the entire human race on earth is gathered into households where purity, and wisdom, and peace are harmonious and complete, then neither school, nor state, nor church will have more than it can do.

Whether your power is to be exerted directly in the household, the sanctuary and selectest kingdom ordained of heaven for women, or whether you are to be employed about those ministries which are scarcely more remote from the center of our social life, as in teaching, in art, in literature, in works of active charity, the constant bearing of your best service will be to purify and strengthen and adorn the home.

It is not, believe me, in wealth or social position, or artificial accomplishments, that dwells the secret of a useful life. These are valuable accessories that no thoughtful man or woman will despise, but their value is in their being accessory to something of intrinsic excellence. It is in personal goodness—the incommunicable virtue of a noble and pure character, that must be found the spring of perennial beneficence, a spring that is fed by secret communication with the Fountain of Life, and that fertilizes and refreshes all its course with these healing waters. Happiness and usefulness are the flower and fruit of purity and goodness.

Knowledge is power; character is a greater power. It is your duty, to the world, to yourselves, to God, to be powerful in every form of virtue and holy activity. Keep your hearts with all diligence, for out of them are the issues of life. You have been called to the kingdom of woman's influence and obligation for such a time as this, a time of need, of boundless privilege, of opportunity for the highest and most enduring rewards. I cannot doubt that you will fill life with the ministry of thoughtful sympathy and Christian love, and pass at last from the earthly homes, which your presence has brightened and blessed, to the heavenly home, which has been made blessed and bright for you by One who has now gone to prepare for it, and who will then welcome and crown you at its threshold.—REV. LEMUEL MOSS.

PART XXXI: INDEPENDENCE DAY TEXTS AND THEMES

Mammon a Nation's Destroyer: "Thou shalt not covet." Ex. 20: 17.

The Bible and Christian Citizenship: "Except the Lord keep the city, the watchman waketh but in vain." Psa. 127: 1.

The Foundation of National Greatness: "The entrance of thy word giveth light." Psa. 119: 130.

Lest We Forget: "The wicked shall be turned into hell, and the nations that forget God." Psa. 9: 17.

Love of Country and Labor for the Church: "He loveth our nation, and himself built us our synagogue." Luke 7: 5.

The Patriotism of Jesus: "O Jerusalem, Jerusalem, that killeth the prophets, and stoneth them that are sent unto her! how often would I have gathered thy children together, even as a hen gathereth her chickens under her wings, and ye would not." Matt. 23: 37.

The Undismayed Christ: "He will not fail nor be discouraged." Isa. 42: 4.

The Unification of the Nation: "One law shall be to him that is home-born, and unto the stranger that sojourneth among you." Ex. 12: 49.

Why Nations Perish: "It is thy destruction, O Israel, that thou art against me." Hos. 13: 9.

Men Who Made America: "A man shall be as a hiding place from the wind, and a covert from the tempest, as rivers of water in a dry place, as the shadow of a great rock in a weary land." Isa. 32: 2.

Pure Patriotism: "And not for that nation only, but that also he should gather together in one the children of God that were scattered abroad." John 11: 52.

Twin Foes of the Republic: The Saloon and Mormonism: "They shall not hurt nor destroy in all my holy mountains; for the earth shall be full of the knowledge of the Lord, as the waters cover the sea." Isa. 11: 9.

Conquered with the Cross: "God forbid that I should glory, save in the cross of our Lord Jesus Christ." Gal. 6:14.

The Land We Love: "Blessed is the nation whose God is the Lord; and the people whom he has chosen for his own inheritance." Psa. 33:12.

True National Greatness: 1 Kings 10:1-9.

A Staunch Patriot: Neh. 2:1-8.

What Should be Our Attitude Toward Our National Sins? Neh. 1:6.

Our National Beginnings and Some Lessons from Them: "Surely there is no enchantment against Jacob, neither is there any divination against Israel. What hath God wrought!" Numbers 23:23.

The Song of the Patriot: Psa. 48.

Examples of Bible Patriots: Samuel, 1 Sam. 8; Eli, 1 Sam. 4:18; David, Psa. 33:12; Nehemiah, Neh. 1:3; Solomon, 1 Kings 3:9; Elisha, 2 Kings 13:17; The Lord Jesus Christ, Matt. 23:37, 38.

Genuine Patriotism: "He prophesied that Jesus should die for that nation and not for that nation only." John 11:51, 52.

An Exalted Nation: "Righteousness exalteth a nation; but sin is a reproach to any people." Prov. 14:34.

The Shame of a Nation: Prov. 14:34.

Attitude Toward Civic Conditions: Isa. 62:1.

Source of National Welfare: Psa. 147:12-14.

Value of Citizenship: Esther 4:13, 14.

Reproach of an Unpatriotic Citizen: Judges 5:17, 23.

The Patriotic Prayer: "Do good in thy good pleasure unto Zion; build thou the walls of Jerusalem." Psa. 51:18.

Prayer and Patriotism: "Pray for the peace of Jerusalem; they shall prosper that love thee. Peace be within thy walls, and prosperity within thy palaces." Psa. 122:6.

A Patriotic People: "Then sang Deborah and Barak the son of Abinoam on that day, saying, Praise ye the Lord for the avenging of Israel, when the people willingly offered themselves." Judges 5:1.

Being a Christian at the Ballot Box: Psa. 28:1-9.

God the Supreme Ruler: 1 Sam. 16:6-12.

Righteousness Paramount: Prov. 14:28-34.

INDEPENDENCE DAY TEXTS AND THEMES

Rulers Are of God: Num. 27: 21-23.
Obeying Rulers: Rom. 13: 1-7.
The Consent of the People: Ex. 24: 1-3.
Prayer as an Agency in Patriotism: "Pray for the peace of Jerusalem. They shall prosper that love thee." Psa. 122: 6. True patriotism puts prayer for one's country above every other agency for its progress and protection. God is the God of nations. "He putteth down one and setteth up another." If we would celebrate wisely our national Independence Day, earnest prayer for our country and for all who rule over us will fill a large portion of our time and thought for that day. Try this method of celebrating the "Glorious Fourth" this year, and you will find that patriotism is close akin to religion.
The Man Behind the Gun: "As a good soldier of Jesus Christ." 2 Tim. 2: 3.
The Munitions of War: "The whole armor of God." Eph. 6: 11.
On the Firing Line: "And there was war again, and David went out and fought . . . they fled before his face." 1 Sam. 19: 8.
The Base of Supplies: "My God shall supply all your need according to his riches . . . by Jesus Christ." Eph. 4: 19.
The Line of Communication: "Hereafter ye shall see . . . angels (messengers) ascending and descending upon the Son of man." John 1: 51.
The Reconnaissance: "Get thee down unto the host." Judges 7: 9.
Contraband of War: "No man that warreth entangleth himself." 2 Tim. 2: 4.

PART XXXII: INDEPENDENCE DAY SERMON OUTLINES

THE NATION'S GREATEST NEED

"Blessed is the nation whose God is the Lord." Psa. 33:12.

I. The Nation's greatest need to-day is to recognize the sovereignty of God. It will put iron into men's blood and strength into their resolve to do right. Yet, to-day there are many who have not time for God; they ignore his throne; they never mention his name; unless it be in some time of awful disaster and when all earthly things fail they turn to him in last resort. How much better to remember him all the way, allowing his throne to be set up in our hearts; giving place to his plan and looking forward to the consummation that shall be glorious and the victory eternal.

II. As we study the Scriptures we find it is a stormy book; there are battles and movement of things and while in places we see green pastures and feel the sweetness, yet these things are given amid convulsion in the social order, upheavals of kingdoms, the presence of enemies and terror, the marching of armed forces, the pestilence that walked in darkness, hurricanes of disaster that swept the land, rivers that have overflown their banks. But God is ever the King. He hath founded his kingdom upon the seas and established it upon the floods.

III. Multitudes turn to the wrong way, but in the thick of the fight and amidst the clamor of the world there is the voice of a great multitude amidst the mighty thunderings, saying, "Hallelujah, for the Lord God Omnipotent reigneth."

IV. God calls us to realize that he is on the throne and his voice is not meant as a lullaby, but intended to be clarion in tone. There are calls for rest of heart, but there is also the demand to tread the thorny steep ways that lead to holiness and if need be, to march without fear into the "Valley of the Shadow." The Lord reigns! Every man should then be at his task with both hands and consecrated soul, for he is on God's side and shall never meet defeat.—H. H.

THE BLESSING OF LIBERTY

"To proclaim liberty to the captive." Isa. 61:1.

I. One of the chief purposes of human governments is the bestowal of liberty upon all its subjects. No other word so thrills the patriotic heart. Liberty is loved more than life; men will roam sea and land to rest under the folds of the flag of liberty. Its waving leads legions onward to the battlefield, where soldiers die happily while liberty's banner is in the van of victory.

II. Liberty means the slave emancipated from his chains; it means freedom from the rack of torture, from the heel of tyrants, the rule of bigots, the bond binding the mind and the soul of manhood. Liberty means the banishment of the taskmaster of the oppressor, of the devil and his minions. Liberty stands under the stars and sings the song of freedom from the power of sin and from the crushing rule of despotism and militarism.

III. The great inheritance of a liberty-loving people is its memories of its heroes; its poets, historians, statesmen, legislators; its great givers and philanthropists. The organization of the nation may perish, but the influence of its mighty products will be garnered in the kingdom of God forever and ever. If we could hear the voice of the millions who have fallen on the battlefields of earth, would they not exclaim, "We died that liberty might live, that righteousness and truth might reign among all the peoples of the earth"?—Rev. E. W. Caswell, D.D.

THE BIBLE AND CHRISTIAN CITIZENSHIP

"Except Jehovah keep the city, the watchman waketh but in vain." Psa. 127:1.

There is an increasing tendency to relate the Bible to everyday life. No far-away mystic or theological interpretation of Scripture satisfies the modern man. We in these United States especially are a practical people, and we require from our religion, as from everything else, a serviceable aid in the matters nearest at hand.

I. Citizenship is a very practical and important matter at present, and there is much in the Bible regarding it. In the Old Testament, laws and procedure, politics and religion, were closely intermingled. Jehovah was the God of the nation as truly as of the individual.

II. It is taught in the Bible that good citizenship is a personal matter, a matter of honesty, paying one's debts, cultivating a keen conscience toward our neighbors, being unpartisan and developing the traits of mercy, peace and righteousness in all dealings. The old sexton at Amesbury, Mass., was asked his creed; he answered, "I try to shovel a straight path; I shovel it wide; I shovel it clean." A good citizen, whether he shovels snow or sells merchandise or builds bridges, is a man of conscience in his work. Citizenship is more than casting a ballot; it is a life of righteousness.

III. The Master taught that the Christian citizen was marked by serving. His was a ministry of washing his disciples' feet, of healing, of going the second mile. It was the democracy of service, and the constitution of the Christian state was written in love. A great citizen is one who makes his life not a career simply, but a mission. This was what the psalmist called, "Keeping the city."—C. S. E.

RIGHTEOUSNESS EXALTETH A NATION

"Righteousness exalteth a nation." Prov. 14:34.

I. Righteousness promotes the life of a nation. Good has in it the seeds of life. It is constantly reproducing itself. It has in it the potency of increased harvests of good. It produces thirty, sixty and a hundredfold. Evil has within itself the principle of decay. Its tendency is towards death, disintegration, destruction.

II. Righteousness promotes the prosperity of a nation. Evil does not pay. Good does pay. It is true of nations as of individuals that "Godliness is profitable unto all things, having promise of the life that now is, and of that which is to come." Queen Victoria was right when she handed a Bible to an ambassador from a heathen chief and said: "Tell your master that this is the secret of England's greatness." The best patriot is the man who loves his Bible best, tries hardest to live by it, and to get others to live by it.

III. Righteousness is the chief factor not only in the prosperity, but in the safety of any nation. The nation that lives by the Golden Rule will keep free from strife. It will not ignore the dictates of common sense. It will not lay down its arms and invite others to over-run and over-ride it. It will maintain its own strength and dignity. But it will maintain first of all righteousness of conduct. It will find its greatest strength after all in its character, its righteousness. A nation that is righteous is safe.

"But sin is a reproach to any people." It cannot be denied that in our times iniquity does most alarmingly abound.—H.

THE LAND WE LOVE

"Blessed is the nation whose God is the Lord; and the people whom he has chosen for his own inheritance." Psa. 33:12.

God has given us a pleasant land, a very fruitful land, a land blessed with intelligence, liberty and Christian faith. This country of ours is a goodly heritage. We believe it was wise forethought in our fathers which led them to set apart Independence Day for yearly observance, when the attention of all our people would be turned toward a review of our past history and toward a consideration of questions bearing upon our future national interests and welfare.

I. One of the facts the day should fix in our minds is that the founders of our Republic recognized God. The last sentence of the Declaration of Independence reads: "And for the support of this declaration, with a firm reliance on the protection of Divine Providence, we mutually pledge," etc.

II. We may learn also from this day something of the power of woman's influence. When Great Britain placed a tax on silk, the women of America said, "We will wear no silk." When a tax was placed on tea, they said, "We will drink no tea." While history speaks of the Warrens and the Jaspers let it not fail to mention also the women of the Revolution. And let us not forget the influence of women to-day upon the nation's welfare.

III. We may learn also from Independence Day the necessity for putting one's heart into one's work. The signers of the Declaration of Independence pledged their "lives, fortunes and sacred honor,"—all they had they threw into that movement for independence.

IV. Let us learn lastly, the importance of committing one's self publicly to the support of right principles. Fifty-six men put their names on the Declaration of Independence. Placing a name there meant victory or death. Had they not committed themselves thus publicly they would have been more likely to waver before the war ceased. But after the names were down there was no retreat. As Franklin said: "We must either hang together or hang separately."—H.

LOVE OF LIBERTY

"The small one shall become a strong nation." Isa. 60:22.

In 1608 an armistice was declared by Philip III, which closed a weary century of war. In that war Holland, with her insignificant three millions, had stood unswervingly against Spain for the inalienable rights of men two centuries before France wrote them in blood upon her walls or America sounded them forth in the clear notes of the Independence Bell.

The men of Holland had fought their campaign to a finish. Carlyle wrote: "The Dutch are a strong people. They raised their land out of a marsh and went on, for a long time, breeding cows and making cheese; and might have gone on with their cows and cheese until doomsday. But Spain came over and said, "We want you to believe in Saint Ignatius." "Very sorry," replied the Dutch, "but we can't." "Aye, but you must," said Spain. And they went about it with guns and swords to make them believe in Saint Ignatius. Never made them believe in him, but did succeed in breaking the own vertebral column and raising the Dutch into a great na n.

In our country's history three names emerge above all others as representative of the broad and vital principles on which the Republic rests, to wit: Washington, Lincoln and Roosevelt. Let Americans of English blood be proud of Washington; let those who trace their lineage to Scotland speak reverently of Lincoln; the sons and daughters of Holland on their part will ever be thanking God for their kinship with Theodore Roosevelt. His name alone, were there none other to show for the influence of the Dutch forefathers, would be ample proof that it had not "vanished into thin air."—Rev. David James Burrell, D.D.

FOES OF OUR COUNTRY

"A man's foes shall be they of his own household." Matt. 10:36.

I. With the state it is the same as with the individual, the worst enemies are those that are within. As a man's most deadly foes are his own passions, so a state's foes are a certain type of its own citizens.

The judge who misapplies the law, the official who takes bribes, the politician who uses his influence to liberate criminals, the big business man who crushes a weak opponent or oppresses his employees, the stock shark who gobbles up the public savings, and the host of others who profit from evildoing—these are the men who endanger America.

II. The battle is between the forces of disintegration and those of construction. It is an age-old battle, and it will last for years to come. We are but privates in a gigantic war of opposing forces headed by Christ on the one hand and Satan on the other.

III. The weapon we fight with is a Christlike life. Light overcomes darkness, therefore let us turn on the light. Good overcomes evil, therefore practice the good. Love vanquishes selfishness, therefore let us seek the love of Christ.

IV. Our victory is not that of force, but of divine ideas. The house of evil is crumbling faster than it can be built. The house of good cannot crumble; it is eternal.—R.

INFLUENCE OF THE DECLARATION

"With a great sum (price) obtained I this freedom." Acts 22:28.

While we celebrate on the 4th of each July the adoption of the Declaration of Independence, we perhaps do not reflect on the stupendous influence of that document on the world as a whole. It is safe to say that no political paper in all history has had so universal or radical an effect. Not only did its promulgation mark the beginning of the life of our nation, and not only was it the mother of the emancipation proclamation, but its advent started the wave of democracy and liberty now seen in every nation on the earth. Surely Americans have a right to be proud of a document that has literally inaugurated a new era of humanity.

Although it would hardly be within the truth to say that the Declaration of Independence had wrought all the marvelous political changes that have swept the world since July 4, 1776, it would be entirely within the truth to state that it has been the greatest single influence and therefore has the right to be considered the symbol of all the forces that have wrought these changes. And what a transformation it has been! Then liberty was nowhere. Now it is everywhere. Then England had sunk to well nigh her lowest stage of despotism. France was misgoverned and hopeless. Germany was a conglomeration of inchoate states, the Latin nations were in feudal bondage. Russia had scarcely emerged from semi-barbarism, all of Asia was as she had been for thousands of years. Africa and Australia were unknown and both North and South America were covered with fringes of colonies and vast savage interiors. To-day every land beneath the sun has been touched by the new life, the new aspiration, the new freedom.

France was the first to respond to the call, and with her own revolution drove the democratic wedge fashioned in America far into the heart of Europe. England, the very nation against which the American Revolution had been waged, was the next to be moved toward liberty by the new example, her two defeats by this country shocking her into sanity and her own thinkers forcing her to adopt reform bills, to take up a liberal colonial policy and to bring about a real revolution, although a peaceable one. Italy shook off the thralldom of centuries, united her states and joined the ranks of the progressive nations. One after another the states of Europe either became republics or constitutional monarchies. Even Russia could not escape the universal wave of democracy. Poor Spain has tried several times to adopt republicanism, but the reactionary forces have been too strong and have held her until all of her colonies and most of her ancient glory have been swept away.

Following the example of the United States, all of the Americans threw off the foreign yoke and became republics.

And Australasia, touched by it, has the most enlightened and progressive governments in the world. Truly the Declaration of Independence has done its work, and the story is only half told.—A. C. SQUIRES.

THE DUTIES OF AN AMERICAN CITIZEN

"The lines have fallen unto me in pleasant places; yea, I have a goodly heritage." Psa. 16:6.

On Friday, July 4th, begins the one hundred and forty-ninth year of independence of the United States. The day will furnish the occasion for sermons appropriate to the event commemorated from most of the more than one hundred thousand pulpits of our country; and from these discourses much will go forth to impress upon the public thought the fact that nothing becomes a nation so much as righteousness and true patriotism. There is much that is grand and noble in our history. There is much to inspire us to the realization of high ideals in the future. Every American citizen should do all in his power to perpetuate the civic and religious blessings which are his by birthright, and to hand down unimpaired to the latest posterity those free institutions under which it is his privilege to live.

I. It is the duty of an American citizen to love his country. Christ was a patriot; his mission was first to his own nation, and any religion which has not in it the elements of true patriotism is foreign to the religion of Christ.

II. It is the duty of an American citizen to reverence the laws of his land. Laws are necessary. They promote the well being of the people. Christianity does not destroy patriotism, but develops and sanctifies it. The Christian citizen should know the laws, reverence them, obey them. If laws are bad he may labor to change them; but true reverence for law should be one of the predominant traits of his character.

III. It is the duty of an American citizen to treat with respect those who are in office. It is written, "Thou shalt not speak evil of the rulers of my people." The speaking evil of those in authority is one of the most common sins of the American people. It is both a sin and a mistake. It is something all Christians should discountenance and discourage by word and example.

IV. It is the duty of an American citizen to exercise the elective franchise according to the best light and judgment he has. It is one of the charges of Mr. Kidd, in his stimulating work, "Social Evolution," against Americans, that they lack civic self-sacrifice. He says that they prefer self and party to the town or city, the state or nation. Some prefer self to the extent that they do not even take the trouble to vote at all. It is the citizen's duty to vote, and to vote intelligently and honestly. Those who stand aloof because of the bad repute of politics only help to make the matter worse.

V. It is the duty of an American citizen to aid in the general diffusion of sound knowledge throughout the land. A republic cannot exist where the people are ignorant. The ignorant cannot understand their duties and rights as citizens. In America the people are the rulers. We are all kings. It is our duty to be intelligent and to promote intelligence throughout the whole land. That means among the foreigners that come, in the slums of our cities, in the frontier regions of the country, among white and black, red and yellow, and people of all conditions.

VI. It is the duty of an American citizen to do all in his power to elevate the moral character of the people. The heart as well as the head needs cultivation. "Righteousness exalteth a nation." The holders of the destiny of a nation like ours should be moral as well as intelligent. They should be Christian. They should recognize the God who gave us our nation and has guided our history.

During perilous times in ancient Rome there were two aspirants for the throne, Constantine, a professed Christian, and Maxentius, a fierce fanatical pagan. The conflict appeared to be between Christianity and paganism, between Christ and the devil. Constantine relates that about noon, when in prayer, on his march, a flaming cross appeared in the sky, with the words, "In This Conquer." He henceforth displayed the standard of the cross in his army and fought in the name of Christ. In his name, we shall conquer and reach the highest and holiest destiny. In Christ's name, in the sign of the cross, we shall be ever victorious. It is the duty of an American citizen to recognize the God of nations, who has given us our "goodly heritage," and to exalt the banner of true Christianity.—H.

WHAT THE LIBERTY BELL SAID: TALK TO CHILDREN

Don't you always feel glad that it was a boy who helped send out the news that our Congress in the State-house in Philadelphia had decided that our country was to be free? On the morning of that fourth day of July the old bell-ringer of the State-house had been up in the steeple waiting to ring his bell if Congress should adopt the Declaration of Independence. He had put a boy down at the door to send him up word as soon as there should be any news.

Hour after hour went by, and no news came, for our statesmen were thinking very soberly before they could really make up their minds to say that we should break away from England for all time. The old bell-ringer said, "They will never do it; they will never do it!" and then suddenly there was a great shout from below, and there stood the boy clapping his hands, and crying, "Ring! Ring!" The old man caught the clapper of the bell in his hands and swung it back and forth a hundred times, and every time the bell called out "Free! Free! Free!"

There is a strange thing about the words engraved on that bell. They say: "Proclaim liberty throughout all the land and to the inhabitants thereof," and yet those words were put there when the bell was cast in 1753, which was more than twenty years before we ever thought of being free from England and an independent country.

The splendid old bell did its work and stands now in Independence Hall at Philadelphia, where we can see it when we go to that city.

Little silver Liberty Bells have been made. There is a school in New York that has one, and on the last day of school they ring it once for every year of our independence. How many is that this year?

PART XXXIII: TEXTS AND THEMES CONCERNING VACATION

The Ethics of Holidays: "Come ye yourselves apart into a desert place and rest a while." Mark 6:31.

Purpose in Taking a Vacation: John 4:36.

Some Pleasures in Vacation Time: Luke 24:13-15. I. Christians can commune together. II. Jesus draws near. III. Have "good report" of others.

The Spirit in Which We Should View God's Works: Psa. 104:24. Admiring God's wisdom and riches and goodness. See adaptation and design in them. Worship the Designer.

Work, Then Vacation: Mark 6:30. The apostles had been engaged in work for Christ that must have taxed their strength and their sympathies much as it doubtless delighted them. The best preparation for enjoying a vacation rest is to have done with one's might work that is worth while.

Christ's Consideration: Mark 6:31. Christ did not spare himself, but he knew the weakness of his followers' flesh, and it was at his call only that they sought quiet and rest. He was mindful of their need even although there was still no lack of opportunity for service, all the more because they were so crowded.

Serving Others During Vacation: John 4:4-10, 25, 26. "As ye go preach." Speak to others as did Jesus by the well in Samaria.

Vacation Dangers: 1 John 2:15-17. 1. Of over-love of the world. 2. Of forgetfulness of its God. 3. Of uselessness.

Results of a Well-Spent Vacation: Isa. 40:31. Renewal. 1. Physical. 2. Mental. 3. Spiritual.

Perils of the Summer: "There came a viper out of the heat." Acts 28:3.

Holiday Rest: "In quiet resting places." Isa. 32:18.

The Religious Side of Rest: "Come ye yourselves apart into a desert place and rest a while." Mark 6:31.

Vacation Benefits and Dangers: "Then they that were scattered abroad everywhere preaching the word." Acts 8:4. Preach the word, teach the word, live the word, while on your vacation.

The Holiness of Holidays: "I will give you rest." Matt. 11:28.

Learning of God in Vacation: Psa. 19:1-7. By studying Nature, and seeing God's wisdom, love and design in creation.

Sermons in Shoes: "As ye go preach." Matt. 10:7.

Studying Nature: Psa. 65:5-13.

Summer Sojourners: 1 Pet. 2:9-11.

Choosing the Best: Phil. 4:8-9.

Appreciation and Contentment: Psa. 16:5-9.

Religion When We Rest: Mark 6:30-44.

Purpose in Taking a Vacation: John 4:36. To "finish our work." Rest in order to work. Like horses on a hill. They stop at the "Thank-you-mams" and rest to make a stronger pull up the hill.

Choice of Vacation Pleasures: 1 Cor. 8:13. Don't offend others by foolish indulgences. Don't weaken our own principles or theirs. Examples—Sabbath breaking, card-playing, dancing.

Dangers in Excess of Pleasures: 1 John 2:15-17. I. Overlove of the world. II. Forgetfulness of God. III. Usefulness. IV. Even harmfulness.

We should rest, not for dreams, but for to be and to do.

PART XXXIV: SERMON OUTLINES CONCERNING VACATIONS

VACATION REST

"Come ye yourselves apart into a desert place, and rest a while." Mark 6:31.

At this season of the year how much we hear about vacation. The winter, with its cold, invigorating weather, the time for hard exercise, bodily and mental, has given way to springtime, with its balmy air, its buds and flowers, to lure us on toward the time, when, with aching brow and tired frames, we turn from the busy throng in life's mad rush for a livelihood, toward the coolness and the quietness and the rest of a summer vacation.

Shall it be spent by the seashore, on the mountain's height, in an ever-changing sight-seeing, at a fashionable resort, or in the quiet of the country? Where and how shall we spend our vacation? At this season these are the questions asked, and which must be answered. We regret that many have but a short rest-time. Perhaps some, only the legal holidays. I never hear the word vacation, or rest-time, but I recall those words of Jesus, "Come ye yourselves apart into a desert place, and rest a while." Though he be foot-sore and weary, he is ever thoughtful of his loving followers.

I like to study those words of Jesus.

I. First. It is an invitation, come. How many times the Blessed Master uttered that sweet word, "come." "Come unto me, all ye that labor and are heavy laden, and I will give you rest." "Come, take up thy cross and follow me." "Come, ye blessed of my Father, inherit the kingdom prepared for you from the foundation of the world." Not go, a command, but come, an invitation. Come with him for rest. Come to him to rest.

II. Second. "Apart." Separate from the multitude.

There is inspiration and strength in numbers, when a battle must be fought or heavy task performed, but the tired body and mind require quiet, to be alone, apart from those who would disturb and annoy. Jesus, when worn in body and sad in spirit, went alone, on the mount, or in the wilderness, and spent a night in prayer. Again we find him alone in the Garden of Gethsemane.

III. Third. "Into a desert place," separate from the multitude, they are to retire to a desert place. No noise, no confusion, no crowds, alone with nature and Jesus. "And rest a while." When the day is far spent, his disciples return to work. We see here Jesus only bids them rest when weary. They tell him all things, both what they had done and taught. They needed rest. A lesson for us—we should rest when tired, for then and then only can we do our best work. There is some rest and refreshment in a change of scene from one place of life to another, but if one is to get the most good from a rest-time, it must be spent in quiet. What a wonderful power to quiet and soothe has nature, the cooling air, the beauty of stream, of tree, of flower, the changing sky or singing bird.

Those can truly appreciate the rest and quiet of nature who through the long winter and springtime have been confined within the walls of a heated, noisy city.

In nature's quiet is the opportunity for communion with God. As Jesus went alone on the mount and in the garden, so we need go alone with Jesus; for rest in the fullest, sweetest sense of the word means the quiet place where one can meet with nature and with God.—E. Y.

COME YE APART

"Come ye yourselves apart into a desert place and rest a while." Mark 6:31.

Every human body needs the recuperation of physical rest. When Daniel Webster made his last visit to John Adams, the aged ex-president said: "I am as well as any man of nearly ninety years could expect to be. I find I am afflicted with an incurable disease called old age. My spirit is occupying a very shaky tenement. And as far as I can make out, sir, the Landlord does not intend to make any more repairs." That statement of John Adams was figuratively right, and yet literally wrong. The human body, which was once created out of dust, is being re-created up to the very brink of the grave. We eat and drink and rest in order to give nourishment and strength to the bones, the muscles, and the flesh. And rest is just as essential for the physical re-creation as food and water and light.

The purpose of this sermon is to show that every hard-working Christian, at least once a year, should go out into the country and take a vacation, a prayerful rest, the same as Jesus' disciples, who left their work to take a rest. It is every Christian's duty at least once a year to leave the home, the store, the factory, and have a complete change of scene and food. When Phœbe Cary came to die, looking up at her physician, she said, "Doctor, you can do nothing for me. The reason I am dying is because for years I would never take a rest. Even when I went off into the country I always took my books and pen and worked." Thousands and tens of thousands of the best brains and hearts of the pulpit, the bar, the medical office, and of all the Christian departments of life, have simply killed themselves in their young manhood and womanhood because they would not obey Christ's command and take a rest.—REV. FRANK DEWITT TALMAGE, D.D.

PERILS OF THE SUMMER

"Then came a viper out of the heat." Acts 28:3.

The ship which carried Paul, the prisoner, had been wrecked on the rocks of Melita. The rescued crew, passengers and soldiers, wet to the skin from the sea water and the cold rain, gathered shivering around a fire made by the hospitable islanders. Paul, as usual doing his part, collected a bundle of drift wood. No sooner had this new fuel become ignited than a viper, made dormant by the winter cold, was warmed to life with uncomfortable suddenness. Indignantly leaping from its fiery bed, it lit upon the chilled hands of the apostle, stretched out over the fire. How astonished the natives were at this apparently divine judgment upon a criminal escaped from a watery grave. How much greater their astonishment when, casting the viper off into the fire, contrary to all previous experience with such deadly snakes, the arm neither swelled with the poison nor did Paul fall over suddenly, dead.

Every year the summer exodus becomes greater, from the city to the country, from man-made streets to God-made fields, from the derived to the original. Every year the health of the nation is becoming better, the strain of living easier to bear.

The occasional Christian duty of absolute cessation from routine work is obvious. Too little guarded against are the vipers which are animated by the heat of this bending the vacation season to fearful activity. Fastening upon our souls, the poison of their bite sickens and kills unless we are inoculated with the same virus which saved Paul. They are myriad.

I. Idleness is the name of one. Very old and very true is the proverb: "Satan finds some mischief still for idle hands to do." Vacation means a mind vacant of its ordinary routine, as well as a body vacant from its usual place. But the mind, like the body, should be somewhere else—never nowhere. Now, get away far enough to gain a bird's-eye-view of the year you have lived so feverishly, to take a mental and spiritual inventory, to see the mistakes you have made, to measure the successes you have won. Such retrospect and prospect are the opposite of idleness. They have no viper sting.

II. Inconsistency is a viper with a deadly summer-bite. With the thermometer at ninety it is not so easy to be conscientious as when it is at zero. Is it not just as binding? The best capital I have is my good name. Conveniences from which you are deprived in a boarding-house may make it hard for you to have your prayer time with God. Nothing should make it impossible. Excursions, baseball games, outings, boats, fishing tackle, reduced railroad fare, the stifling heat of the city, the need of being at work early Monday morning, all induce you to forget the sacredness of the Lord's Day. Companions urge you to go with them here, there and everywhere, except where you can draw near to God. Insidiously, coaxingly, that viper of Sunday Desecration whispers in your ear, "Don't be a Puritan."

III. How the viper of Irresponsibility shoots out its poisonous fangs in the heated term! If every city Christian who visits the country during the summer would let his light shine instead of putting it under a bushel, what a change for good there would be among our farmer boys, instead of an awkward aping of city vices so laughable were it not so bad. You and I have no right to let it be a conundrum whether we are Christians or not. We should take a rest from routine religious duties; never from religion.

IV. Another vicious viper is Indifference. Summer discomfort is peculiarly conducive to selfishness. Rudely we jostle each other for the best seat, most secluded nook, as we would never think of doing at other seasons. If some one else needs it more than I do why should I demand the best, although I am on a vacation? Gentleness to the awkward, the poor, the sick, the over-burdened, is a privilege in the sunshine as well as in the snow-storm. To bear one another's burdens is a law of Christ not abrogated by a rise in the mercury.

And these vipers are dangerous to those who stay as well as to those who go away. They glide into city homes and the seashore cottages. It is a truism that the Devil puts in his busiest time while the Church is most quiescent. There is no season when the soldier of the Cross is free to fraternize with any one of the forces of evil. When from the fire of these torrid days crawl out these evil serpents of Idleness, Inconsistency, Irresponsibility and Indifference, take not Eve as your pattern. Listen not to their pleadings to yield—and fall! Rather with Paul the shipwrecked, strong in the power of God, shake the foul viper from your soul.—REV. EDWARD NILES.

THE VALUE OF AN EDDY IN THE STREAM OF LIFE

"Come ye yourselves apart into a desert place and rest a while." Mark 6: 30.

Jesus proclaims the value of an eddy in the stream of life.

I. There are times when the worker should forsake the crowds and take to the desert; when he should let the work go; when he should forget that there are people tired and hungry and sick; when he should turn his back on the throngs of eager, interested, insistent, needy humanity, and sink himself for a while, beyond the reach of publicity, in some serene solitude.

II. There are occasions when what we need is not to be prodded, to be told to be more energetic, more diligent and assiduous, to rise earlier and work longer and be instant in season and out of season; times when we do not greatly need a fresh dissertation on the charms and virtues of the strenuous life. God knows we have heard enough about "the strenuous life." The trouble with the average life to-day is, it is a little too strenuous. Humanity swarms in ceaseless activities.

III. We need the solitude and quiet of the eddy for rest. One may be so absorbed in his work as to be oblivious of physical exhaustion. Christ's keen eye detected that his disciples were weary and he said to them: "You must rest. Your work is important. Come apart and rest a while." It was to be just for "a while." It was not to be permanent. Rest is not the regular program for life. Work is the regular program. But Christ knew the value of a pause in the music of life. He would have these men rest long enough to give their worn bodies and weary brains a chance to recover; until they could get themselves in hand and made ready for a fresh campaign.

People sometimes need rest. We are made of the sort of stuff that gets tired. We are not made of iron and stone and steel, but of flesh and blood, and these are no match for machinery in a long race. The failure to observe the need of rest is often accompanied by disastrous consequences.

IV. There are times when rest is as much a divine command as work; when it is as much one's duty to quit as to go on; when the place where God wants us is there where there are no tools and no audience; nothing but desert and solitude. "Rest a while!" O thou blessed human Christ, who didst take our tired and weary human nature up into thine own; who at Jacob's well didst rest thyself and by that act didst consecrate all human rest; thou dost look with tender interest on those who are jaded and worn with toil and dost thrust in between them and exacting duties and say to the thronging crowds, "Stand back"; to insolent industry and noisy machinery and roaring tumultuous trade, "Stand back! Give blood and brain and muscle a chance."—REV. JAMES I. VANCE, D.D.

PART XXXV: TEXTS AND THEMES ON THE SABBATH

Guarding the Sabbath: "Remember the Sabbath day to keep it holy." Ex. 20:8.
The Lord's Day: "I was in the spirit on the Lord's Day." Rev. 1:10.
The Sabbath a Day of Witnessing: Acts 17:1-4.
The Sabbath a Day for Doing Good: Luke 13:16.
The Lord's Day the Best Day: Neh. 13:15-22.
The Sabbath a Day of Worship: Isa. 58:13, 14.
A Day of Holy Memories: John 20:19-23.
Jesus Kept the Sabbath: Luke 4:16-24.
A Day of Vision: Rev. 1:9-13.
Periodicity as a Law of Nature: "Remember the Sabbath day to keep it holy. Six days shalt thou labor and do all thy work." Ex. 20:8, 9.
Cutting from the Loaf: "Render therefore unto Cæsar the things which are Cæsar's." Matt. 22:21.
The Consecration of One Day in Seven: Jer. 17:19-27.
The Sabbath: I. Day of rest. II. Day of liberty. III. Day for necessary work. IV. Day for communion with Christ. V. Day for worship in God's house. VI. Day for doing good, "Keep your Sundays for the great things of the soul."
The Sacred Sabbath: Matt. 12:1-13.
How Can We Enrich Our Sabbaths? Mark 2:23-28. I. By churchgoing. II. By the Bible study. III. By kindly deeds. IV. By visitation. James 1:26, 27. V. By restfulness. Ex. 20:8-11. VI. By service. Mark 6:1-6.
Sabbath Worship: He went into their synagogue, "as his custom was, . . . on the Sabbath." Luke 4:16. In the midst of the Assembly. Psa. 22:22. "The day that Jehovah hath made." Psa. 118:24.
The True Principle of Sabbath Keeping: Matt. 12:5-8.
A Holy Keepsake: "Remember the Sabbath day to keep it holy." Ex. 20:8.

Doing Good on the Sabbath: "Wherefore it is lawful to do well on the Sabbath day." Matt. 12:12.
Promises to Those Who Gather in God's House: Matt. 18:19, 20.
Our Need of the Lord's Day: Jer. 17:21-27. 1. For physical rest. 2. For mental refreshment. 3. For spiritual uplift. 4. For the far look.
The Holy Man and the Holy Day: Rev. 1:1-10.
The Pearl of Days: Mark 16:2.
The Sabbath a Necessity: Mark 2:27. It meets our (1) Physical need; (2) Moral need; (3) Social need; (4) Intellectual need; (5) Spiritual need.

PART XXXVI: OUTLINES OF SERMONS ON THE SABBATH

SUNDAY REST IN THE TWENTIETH CENTURY

"Remember the Sabbath day to keep it holy. Six days shalt thou labor," etc. Ex. 20:8-11.
1. Physical, mental and moral relations of Sunday rest.
2. Industrial relations of Sunday rest.
3. Domestic and social relations of Sunday rest.
4. Civic and national relations of Sunday rest.
5. Religious relations of Sunday rest.
6. Sunday rest in different countries.
7. Sunday rest in twentieth century civilization.

SABBATH BENEFITS

"The Sabbath was made for man." Mark 2:27.
Sabbath benefits:
1. To the body.
2. To business, by resting the workers. Mention the people who must work even now on Sundays.
3. To the working men. (How should we like to work on Sundays?)
4. To the mind. (Rest, worship.)
5. To the rich, because it forces them to think of better things than dollars.
6. To the nation. (Only Sabbath-keeping nations are really great. Why?)
7. To the home. (Sketch a home without a Sabbath.)

OUR NEED OF THE LORD'S DAY

Jeremiah 17:21-27.
Every Sabbath may be the Lord's Day—if we observe some fundamental things. We need it for:

I. Physical rest. Think of the heavy burden of labor, the daily grind. We need the one day in seven for the sake of our bodies. Our animals need it; aye, strange to say, machinery lasts longer, does better work, when one day a week is given for freedom. Seven days' work kills the body.

II. Mental refreshment. Don't read the common books of the week. Do not read anything that continues the same mental processes through the Sabbath. Don't study your school day lessons; and, of course, don't wrap yourself round with the big Sunday newspaper. Read that which gives the mind a change as well as a rest.

III. Spiritual uplift. The world has yet to come to a sensible appreciation of the worth of worship. Even the church people do not fully appreciate it. It is one of the greatest things in our life. We need the day, we need the worship, we need to realize the blessing from "communion with saints." There is no fellowship on this earth like the fellowship of people who come together to worship God.

IV. The long look. This is perhaps the greatest of all. The world is swallowed up of the time-spirit. What is called the "zeitgeist" is the dominant thing in all our working. We tire after a while of the mechanics of life, and often long for the "dynamics" of life. Sunday gives this to us. It is not the peculiar day, touched by a peculiar law, bound by a peculiar penalty. A thousand times no. That is so unworthy of my thought of our Father that I cannot mention it in the same breath with his name. But the great expanding vision, the subtle suggestion of the eternal, the emphasis on the great truth we are so apt to forget—that man's life consisteth not in the abundance of things; and, flashing before my heart the thought of the Eternal, who is our Father—all this makes the Sabbath a delight to us.—REV. W. H. GEISTWEIT, D.D.

SANCTIFY THE SABBATH: HOW?

Ex. 31: 12-14.

To sanctify this day, we should consider it—

1. A day of rest; not, indeed, to exclude works of mercy and charity, but a cessation from all labor and care.

2. As a day of remembrance—of creation, preservation and redemption.

3. As a day of meditation and prayer, in which we should cultivate communion with God. Rev. 1:10.

4. As a day of public worship. Acts 20:7; John 20:19.

5. As a day of joy. Isa. 56:2; Psa. 118:24.

6. As a day of praise. Psa. 116:12-14.

7. As a day of anticipation—looking forward to that holy, happy and eternal Sabbath that remains for the people of God.—W. M. ANDERSON, D.D.

THE SABBATH A NECESSITY

"The Sabbath was made for man and not man for the Sabbath." Mark 2:27.

I. The Sabbath is a physical necessity.
II. The Sabbath is a social necessity.
III. The Sabbath is a religious necessity.

THE SABBATH A DELIGHT

"Remember the Sabbath day to keep it holy." Ex. 20:8.

Surely the Lord knew that we needed a Sabbath to develop the better parts of our natures. The Intellectual, the Moral and the Spiritual part of man must have some cultivation, if the man is to be fully developed in every part of his nature. Those parts of a man's faculties which most resemble God are the noblest, and no man should neglect the cultivation of them. No man who takes just pride in himself will do so.

For every noble man will want to be something more than a brute. Yet who neglects his better nature, cultivates only his brute part, and the grosser elements of his nature. The Sabbath was made for man, because he needed it, for the good of both his physical and spiritual natures. He needs it to develop the best part of himself and to prepare to meet his God. Man is capable of a high order of delight. This the Sabbath generates. Thus the Sabbath contributes delight, not only because it affords rest from exhausting toil, but also because its proper observance develops the more noble parts of man's nature. No nation, or family, or individual who

neglects the Sabbath will stand the peer of those who keep it sacredly.
  I. How should the Sabbath be kept?
    1. By abstinence. From sin. From business. From diversion. From journeying and unnecessary engagements, idle visiting, etc.
    2. By attendance on public worship of God.
    3. By cleaving afresh to the Lord.
    4. By prayer and meditation.
    5. By family associations.
  II. Why it should be kept.
    1. Because the cares of life tend to make us forget God.
    2. Because we are commanded by God to keep it.
    3. Because there are promises to those who do observe it.—S.

MADE FOR MAN

"The Sabbath was made for man." Mark 2:27.

1. "The Sabbath is made for man." It is an institution given of God. It is a boon and not a burden.
2. The maintenance of the Sabbath is essential to the success of the gospel, and hence to the well-being of the race.
3. There is just now in our country an amazing disregard and desecration of the Sabbath.
4. The Christian church itself has very largely fallen into this sin of Sabbath desecration.
5. The remedy for the evil lies primarily with the church.
6. If the church cannot save the Sabbath, it can neither save itself nor the world.—Rev. James Brand, D.D.

THE NEED FOR THE SABBATH

"Remember the Sabbath day to keep it holy." Exodus 20:9.
  I. The physical need.
  II. The moral need.
  III. The social need.
  IV. The intellectual need.
  V. The spiritual need.—H.

THE SABBATH A REMINDER

Deut. 5:12-15.

The Sabbath is really a memorial occasion. It reminded the Jews of their deliverance from Egyptian bondage by the mighty arm of God, in recognition of which mercy he commanded them to keep the Sabbath holy.

I. For their own good they could not afford to forget that deliverance, including the fact that he made of them a great nation, and that their first and highest allegiance was to their Deliverer.

II. Through that same deliverance and development of life, individual and national, he provided a Saviour for the world of mankind, his own Son, through whom we have deliverance from sin.

III. To keep us in grateful remembrance of these facts, let us observe the Sabbath day, to keep it holy.

CIVIL STEWARDSHIP

"Render therefore unto Cæsar the things which are Cæsar's." Matt. 22:21.

Our duty to civil government is set before us in a general way by these words of Jesus to the politicians of his day who sought to entrap him in his talk. Cæsar represented the civil government of that time, and the things to be rendered unto him were the taxes imposed by the Roman emperor and represented by the tribute money.

The Cæsar of our day in the United States to which we as followers of Jesus Christ are expected to pay tribute, is not an individual or an emperor, but in an important sense ourselves. Being "a government of the people, for the people, by the people," we are our own Cæsar, and to ourselves we render tribute. Christ, therefore, commands us to support this government in accordance with the laws we have made. And something more is implied for we are not only Cæsar to whom tribute is paid, but also Cæsar who lays the tribute. For what then do we demand this tribute? How much of it goes into the pockets of those to whom it does not belong, just because of our indifference and neglect? How much of it supports our law courts, alms houses and jails just because of iniquitous legislation, affording license to sin? In other words, can we, as Cæsar, give account of our stewardship with joy?

What vital questions these are for consideration at this time.

HOW WE SHOULD KEEP THE SABBATH

"And he said unto them, the Sabbath was made for man." Mark 2:27.

I. Why made for man? The body needs the holiday and the soul needs the holy day. "Keep the Sabbath holy," because man needs rest and the soul needs to be refreshed.

II. If man needs the Sabbath how should he observe it? 1. As a day of joy: (1) joy in the sense of respite; the Psalmist says, "Let us be glad and rejoice in it"; (2) because it reminds us of the resurrection; (3) joy in the privilege of grace and fellowship. 2. The day should be kept as a day of spiritual absorption and refitting for representation: (1) by attendance upon divine worship—Christ went to church on the Sabbath; (2) by works of charity, Bible school work, teaching the word; (3) by meditation in the word and prayer; (4) by renewing the family altar fires and by rekindling the zeal of home religion about the family circle.—REV. C. A. TERHUNE.

SABBATH KEEPING IN CHRIST'S WAY

"The Son of man is Lord even of the Sabbath Day." Matt. 12:8.

I. Christ did good to others on the Sabbath. A selfish Sunday is not a Christian Sabbath.

II. Christ "went to church" on the Sabbath. An habitually churchless Sunday is not a Christian Sabbath.

III. Christ read the Bible on the Sabbath. A Sunday on which we seldom read the Bible is a poor Christian Sabbath.

IV. Christ kept the Sabbath by doing all he could that day to please God. Can a Christian do better—dare he do worse?

V. Christ taught at the "church" on the Sabbath. A

person unwilling, as he is able, to teach in the Sunday School scarcely is keeping the Sabbath.

VI. Christ was careful to set a good example on the Sabbath—as every other day. Setting a good Christian example on Sunday honors the Christian Sabbath.—REV. P. P. FARIS.

THE SPIRIT OF SABBATH-KEEPING

"Remember the Sabbath Day to keep it holy." Ex. 20:8.

I. All our secular cares are to be laid aside on the Lord's day. The Sabbath is a short voyage every week between two continents of toil. But "rest is not quitting the busy career; rest is the fitting of self to one's sphere." For right-thinking people, Sunday should be the busiest day of the week. Our Lord's Sabbaths were his busiest days. They were spent alone in prayer, or in attendance at the synagogue; or in "going about doing good." Not a few of his most wonderful works of healing were wrought on that day. "My Father worketh hitherto," he said, "and I work." There was no idle rest for him.

II. This is a Christian land. At its birth it was christened San Salvador, "Land of the Saviour." It was nurtured in prayer and has prospered under the special favor of God. Whether we shall so continue remains to be seen. One thing, however, is sure; if we are recreant to our trust we shall, sooner or later, join the procession of empires that have risen, one by one, flourished and tottered to their fall. The Sabbath is "a seal of the covenant" between the Lord and his people.

III. And with that sign goes a promise that spans our future like a rainbow: "If thou turn away thy foot from doing thy pleasure on my Holy Day; and call the Sabbath a delight, the holy of the Lord, honorable; and shall honor him, not doing thine own ways, nor finding thine own pleasure nor speaking thine own words: then shalt thou delight thyself in the Lord; and I will cause thee to ride upon the high places of the earth."—REV. DAVID JAMES BURRELL, D.D.

HOW TO ENJOY SUNDAY

I. "Man's chief end is to glorify God and to enjoy him forever." If it were not for sin, all men would enjoy Sunday. Sunday is made for the rest of man and the glorifying of God. It should be remembered. If men were holy, it would be enjoyed. Its themes are the most inspiring. Its duties are the most inspiring. Its privileges are the most enjoyable.

II. The word "Sabbath" means rest. It is made in the wisdom of God for the rest, elevation and education of man. The Sabbath law runs through nature. Man cannot displace it. He cannot substitute another day for it. It just fits man's needs and nature. The rest which he may get on Sunday fits for the work which he is to do for the other six days.

III. It fits man's needs in home building. He has time to worship with his family. Parents have a good opportunity to teach their children to know about God and to do special work with them for their own improvement. The family has time for study and meditation which they would not have during the busy week days.

IV. Too frequently Sunday is made a holiday. The children gather the impression that the religious duties are burdensome and unpleasant. They soon come to think that the only pleasures of Sunday are picnics, pleasure rides, picture shows, excursions, and such like. All of this is degrading to the Sabbath day and ruinous to the character of the children.

V. The Sabbath law was not temporal or local or optional; but it is a great, continual, binding law upon all men everywhere. If ever our nation is the prey of revolutionists, it would be found to have entered through the rent of Sabbath desecration. Sunday should be the happiest day in the week. Sunday can be made the happiest day in the week. God intends us to enjoy Sunday.—W. M. ANDERSON, D.D.

PART XXXVII: LABOR DAY TEXTS AND THEMES

The Divine Toilers: "My Father worketh even until now, and I work." John 5:17.

The Limitation of Ambition: "Seekest thou great things for thyself? Seek them not." Jer. 45:5.

A Man's Job: "Quit you like men, be strong." 1 Cor. 16:13.

A Personal Providence: "I am poor and needy, yet the Lord thinketh upon me." Psa. 40:17.

Triumphant Trudging: "They shall walk, and not faint." Isa. 40:31.

Unnecessary Burdens: "It seemed good to lay upon you no greater burden than these necessary ones." Acts 15:28.

A Choice of Masters: "Being made free from sin, ye became servants of righteousness." Rom. 6:18.

The Sin of Indifference: "And by chance a certain priest was going down that way; and when he saw him, he passed by the other side." Luke 10:31.

The Base Line: "Beginning from Jerusalem." Luke 24:47.

The Christianizing of Commerce: "Her merchandise and her hire shall be holiness to the Lord." Isa. 23:18.

A Life for a Life: "I came that they may have life . . . I lay down my life for the sheep." John 10:10, 15.

The Peril of Prosperity: "After they had rest, they did evil again before thee." Neh. 9:28.

The Dog in the Manger: "Ye extend not in yourselves and them that were entering in ye hindered." Luke 11:52.

A Man and His Brother's Burden: "And it came to pass in those days, when Moses was grown up, that he went out unto his brethren, and looked on their burdens." Ex. 2:11.

Glorifying the Commonplace: "And the King shall answer

and say unto them, Verily I say unto you, inasmuch as ye did it unto one of the least of these, ye did it unto me." Matt. 25:40.

The Tragedy of Success: "For what shall a man be profited, if he shall gain the whole world, and forfeit his life?" Matt. 16:26.

God Requires Our Best: "But whatsoever hath a blemish, that shall ye not offer; for it shall not be acceptable for you," etc. Lev. 22:20-25.

Christian Socialism: "Not looking each of you on his own things, but each of you also to the things of others." Phil. 2:4.

The Ministry of Helps: "And God hath set some in the church, first apostles . . . then . . . helps." 1 Cor. 12:28.

Our Individual Ministry: "And Jesus went about all the cities and villages, teaching in their synagogues, and preaching the gospel of the kingdom, and healing every sickness and every disease among the people." Matt. 9:35.

The Higher Selfishness: "Take heed to thyself." 1 Tim. 4:16.

The Plea of Impotence: "Sir, I have no man, when the water is troubled, to put me into the pool." John 5:7.

The Vindicated Sacrifice: "To what purpose is this waste?" Matt. 26:8.

The Call is Power: "And he said unto him, Stretch forth thy hand." Luke 6:10.

The Shame of Standing Aloof: "In the day that thou stoodest on the other side (aloof), in the day that strangers carried away his substance, and foreigners entered into his gates, and cast lots upon Jerusalem, even thou wast as one of them." Obadiah 1:11.

The Christ of To-day: "Who is this?" Matt. 21:10.

Preparedness for Progress: "Let your loins be girded about, and your lamps burning." Luke 12:35.

Causes of Poverty: "The destruction of the poor is their poverty." Prov. 15:10.

The Dignity of Service: "I am among you as he that serveth." Luke 22:27.

The Industrial Conflict: "What hath a man for all his labors?" Eccl. 2:22.

The Church and the Workingman: "Is not this the carpenter's son?" Matt. 13:55.

Labor's Great Champion: "I have called you friends." John 15:15.

Resource and Responsibility: "How many loaves have ye?" Matt. 15:34.

Sweat and Bread: "In the sweat of thy face shalt thou eat bread." Gen. 3:19.

The Life of Working People: 1. Social. 2. Domestic. 3. Intemperance. 4. "Anti-poverty" societies. 5. Principles of relief. 6. The Church and charity. 7. Historical charity. 8. Modern charity.

Historical Charity and Modern Charity: "Now abideth faith, hope, charity, these three, but the greatest of these is charity." 1 Cor. 13:13.

The Unbrotherly Question: "Am I my brother's keeper?" Gen. 4:9.

Tears for the City: Luke 19:41-46.

The Way Downward: Prov. 1:20-23.

Work Heartily Done: "Whatsoever thy hand findest to do, do it with thy might." Eccl. 9:10.

Labor Day in Eden: "And the Lord took the man and put him in the Garden of Eden, to dress it and to keep it." Gen. 2:15.

The Labor and Liquor Problems: "Our inheritance is turned to strangers, our house to aliens, we are orphans and fatherless, our mothers are widows," etc. Lam. 5:2-5.

A Servant Who Was Dear: Luke 7:1-10.

Prodigals in the Slums: "To each one his work." Mark 13:14.

The Labor Principle: "To each one his work." Mark 13:34.

Greatness Through Service: "Whosoever will be chief among you, let him be your servant." Matt. 20:27.

Resource and Responsibility: "How many loaves have ye?" Matt. 15:34.

Immigration: 1. Character of. 2. Peril of. 3. Restriction of. 4. Distribution of. 5. Assimilation of. 6. Immigrant centers. 7. Protective societies. 8. Religious opportunity.

PART XXXVIII: OUTLINES OF LABOR DAY SERMONS

THE MEETING-PLACE OF MANHOOD

"The rich and the poor meet together." Prov. 22:2.

The most difficult problem of modern labor questions is to find a meeting-place where labor and capital, manhood and money, can come together "on the level" and settle differences in the spirit of actual brotherhood.

God's word will furnish that meeting-place. "The rich and the poor meet together; the Lord is the maker of them all." Our common humanity in the presence of our common God and Maker gives the meeting-place of manhood.

I. The rich and the poor do meet on the level of common humanity. In our human nature we are all alike. Birth and motherhood are the same, be that mother queen or peasant. The primary necessities are the same. Rich and poor meet together in the necessity for food and drink. Hunger and thirst know no social distinctions. Pain, sorrow, suffering, make all mankind of kin. Emperor and beggar alike bow the head to the earth to creep into the grave, for death recognizes no exemptions.

II. The rich and the poor must meet together on the level of supreme soul interests. They must meet at the foot of the Cross for salvation. They must meet on exactly the same footing at the Judgment Seat of God. "For there is no difference." If saved, they must meet in heaven on perfect equality. If lost, they meet in hell, neither claiming the preeminence!

III. Therefore, the rich and the poor ought to meet on a perfect equality in the church of Jesus Christ if both be Christians. "Who maketh thee to differ?" "One is your Master, even Christ."

The Duke of Wellington was kneeling at the altar rail to receive the sacrament when a laborer knelt beside him. A church official would have removed the intruder, as he considered the laboring man. But the great Duke said firmly: "No, we are all alike here!"

IV. Surely, then, the rich and the poor, the laborer and the capitalist, meeting together on the level of common human necessities and experiences, meeting together on the level of common soul interests and destinies, meeting together as children of One Father in his house; these ought to be able to meet together as brothers in fraternal conference, around the council table, to settle all questions that pertain to their common interests in business.

The Word of God will show the meeting-place for manhood.—R. C. HALLOCK, D.D.

THE BATTLE FOR BREAD

"In the sweat of thy face shalt thou eat bread." Gen. 3:19.

Man must have bread. He has a material nature which can only be supported by the material. Man has to provide for himself his food, and raiment, and home. In doing this he experiences great difficulty. He has laws of society to observe, which regulate his conduct towards his fellows. He has also men of different dispositions to deal with. It is in facing and contending with these conditions that the struggle for bread consists.

I. The beginning of this struggle. God placed our first parents in Eden as their home. He furnished it to please their taste and satisfy their appetite. But he set a limitation. He allowed them to eat of all the trees therein but one; and to the eating of this tree he attached penalty. In the difficulties of procuring the needs of life outside the gates of Eden began that struggle for sustenance that has been going on ever since.

II. While the struggle for bread is a consequence of sin, God has ordered that it result in blessing. In man's fallen condition it is good for him that he has to toil and battle against difficulties for his bread. No man can give careful attention to the subject without seeing that God has made labor a blessing to man. The powers of his mind have been awakened and developed by it. Advancement in invention, discovery, arts and science, is attributable to it.

III. Though this struggle was occasioned by sin it is honorable to be engaged in it. When man was expelled from Eden he was not pauperized. God did not hand out three meals a day. He told him to earn it; to wrest it from untoward conditions. Thus did he tend to develop in him a spirit of noble independence.

God honors work. When he sent his Son into the world to save it, he did not send him to reside amid the affluence and ease of the rich man's place; but he sent him to Joseph the carpenter's home. Work is the fashion of heaven.

IV. This struggle may be severer than was ever intended. With many it is deplorably severe. Why is this? There is more than one reason. 1. Competition in prices. 2. Avarice. The undue love of money is largely responsible for making the battle for bread as severe to large numbers as it is. 3. Inhumanness. Man was made to love his fellowman. The cruelty perpetrated on toilers by some employers chills the very blood even to think of it. 4. Extravagant living of employers.

Other reasons might be given, but let these suffice.

V. The religion of Jesus has done much for those engaged in this struggle and will do more. 1. To it men are indebted for the higher views they have of the dignity of their own nature. 2. These higher views of themselves are appearing in their efforts to assert their rights and gain recognition of their manhood. 3. Religion is leading employers to recognize the rights of their employees. And this shall be increasingly the case as it controls the consciences of men. 4. It also comforts the heart of the toiler who possesses it. It makes his home, however humble it may be, a place of happiness; it helps him to bear up under life's burdens.—D.

GOD'S LAW OF LABOR

"In the sweat of thy face shalt thou eat bread!" Gen. 3:19.

At the very beginning of history, among the first established rules of human conduct we find a compendium of political economy and industrial science. "In the sweat of thy face shalt thou eat bread." Whether this be precept or penalty, whether the narrative be literal or symbolic, its teachings are the same, and well worth our notice. Observe:

1. The universality of labor. In Adam, the Federal Head, or representative of the human family, it is addressed to each one of his posterity. Being personal to him, it is personal to each of them. If an exception can be allowed in the case of A, B can claim a similar exception. So also C and so on; and the law is nullified. Hence the command is universal. Compare Ex. 20:9.

2. The necessity of labor. Without food life must cease. Without labor there is no food. The command to labor being universal, he who eats bread in the sweat of some other man's face is a highway robber among men, and a traitor before God.

3. The dignity of labor. Labor is, by virtue of its divine appointment, an act of worship rendered to God. We have made it an act of sacrifice to Mammon by engaging in it that we may increase our wealth, or consume it upon our lusts. Labor is degrading only, and always, when prompted by a selfish motive.

4. The reward of labor. "To eat bread" is to live. Thus the divine scale of wages is established once for all. Existence on God's earth is the only and all sufficient reward of labor. Every man has a right to this, and no man has a right to any more. To this also agrees the teaching of natural religion. In the words of the Hebrew poet, Job 1:21, "Naked came I ... and naked shall I return." Or St. Paul, 1 Tim. 6:7, 8, "We brought nothing into the world, and we can carry nothing out." "Having food and raiment," the divinely appointed wage, "let us be therewith content."

5. The equality of labor. If all labor is alike honorable and alike rewarded, all distinctions are at once done away with. The king and the peasant, the general-in-chief and the high private, the philosopher and the coal miner, the merchant prince and the plowman, all stand side by side in the grand array of workers. This is the only true democracy. A complete recognition of this equality will go far toward introducing an industrial millennium.—JOHN G. OSBORN.

WORK AS A MEANS OF GRACE

"And because he was of the same craft, he abode with them and wrought, for by occupation they were tent-makers." Acts 18:3.

Among the Jews in early times, it was customary to teach all their children the full details of some useful calling. It is recorded as a saying of one of the wisest of the rabbis that "he who would not bring his son to a trade was as if he forced him to be a thief." Christ's disciples were workingmen. Christ himself was a carpenter. Here we see that Paul was a tent-maker. Work is honorable. It may also be very wholesome for us and usually is.

I. Consider, first, some facts in regard to Paul's conduct as a worker.
1. Paul chose a decent and reputable calling. No one can doubt that tent-making was above reproach as a business. Some occupations in which men engage today are neither decent nor honorable—saloon-keeping, etc.
2. Paul sought consistent companionship in his business. Aquila and Priscilla were intelligent, high-minded and companionable to this man of God. Bad companionships, ill-mated partnerships, have wrecked many a business.
3. Paul found opportunities to do good when hardest at work. Probably he was the means of the conversion of Aquila and Priscilla, and we know that they became so spiritually intelligent that afterwards he sent the young and eloquent Apollos to them to be "instructed more perfectly in these things," before he was to start out to preach.

II. Note, secondly, some advantages growing out of the fact of Paul's laboring with his hands.
1. It put him alongside the people and in sympathy with them.
2. This contact with the people enabled Paul to appreciate their needs and how to meet them. It is not always the fault of the poor that they do not get along better. They do not know how. They can be

taught by those who will take the necessary steps to learn and appreciate their needs.

3. Paul's work in Corinth evidently brought cure for the despondency he was in when he came there. Work is wholesome for an individual. It is wholesome also for a Church. There is nothing like exercise to keep people warm and well.

4. Paul's work deepened his personal love for Christ. This was because he did his business for Christ and in his name. Business is a means of grace when the underlying motive for doing is love of Christ and a purpose to do his will in the spot where he has placed us. "Prayer and provender hinder no man's journey."—H.

PART XXXIX: ARMISTICE DAY TEXTS AND THEMES

Promises of Peace: Psa. 29:11; Prov. 3:17; Isa. 26:3; Isa. 54:13.
The Duty of Living in Peace: Mark 9:50.
Peace on Earth: Luke 2:8-18.
Peace Among Nations: Isa. 2:4.
The Reign of Peace: Rev. 21:1-8.
Seek Peace and Pursue It: 1 Pet. 3:8-18.
The Peace of God: Phil. 4:1-17.
Why Should All Nations be Peace Lovers?
Warring Elements in Society and the World To-day.
Why is War Wrong?
First Peaceable: James 3:17.
Ruled by Peace: Col. 3:15.
Peace with Men: Rom. 12:9, 10.
What is the Connection Between Prayer and Peace?
Why is Christ Called the "Prince of Peace"?
Arbitration: How Does it Promote Peace?
How to Get Peace: 1. Religion of Christ. 2. Spirit of Christ. 3. Love the great solvent.
Warring Elements: 1. Men's selfishness. 2. Nations' jealousies. 3. Contests between class and class, and capital and labor.
War Forbidden: "Thus saith the Lord, Ye shall not go up, nor fight against your brethren." 2 Chron. 11:4.
War Averted: Joshua 22:11-34.
God Uses War as a Judgment: Leviticus 26:17.
War Repugnant to God: 1 Chron. 22:8.
Evils of War: 2 Sam. 2:26.
War to Cease: Psalm 46:9.
The Higher Heroism: Micah 4:3.
The Meaning of Peace: 1. The Greek word appears to mean "to bind," implying severance and union. 2. The Eng-

lish word implies a pact, compact, an agreement. 3. The Hebrew word includes the ideas of friendliness, rest, security, completeness. Note the order of experience: union; agreement; friendship; rest; security; completeness.

The Need of Peace: 1. Peace of conscience in pardon and acceptance, Isa. 48:22; Rom. 3:17; Psa. 120:6. 2. Peace of heart in rest and fellowship, Num. 6:26; 25:12; Psa. 4:8; 29:11.

The Provision of Peace: 1. "Peace with God," Rom. 5:1. Barriers removed. 2. "The peace of God," Phil. 4:7. Burdens relieved. These are distinguished in John 20:19, 21 (see context); also in John 14:27, peace as a legacy and as a gift.

The Source of Peace: 1. "Of God," Phil. 4:7. Col. 3:15 R.V. 2. "The God of peace," Rom. 15:33; 16:20; 1 Cor. 14:33; 2 Cor. 13:11; Phil. 4:9; 1 Thess. 5:23; Heb. 13:20.

The Medium of Peace: 1. Christ's person, Eph. 2:14; Isa. 9:6; prince, 2 Thess. 3:16; Heb. 7:2. 2. Christ's work, Eph. 2:15; Col. 1:20. Cf. Isa. 53:5. 3. Christ's preaching, Eph. 2:17; Acts 10:36. 4. Christ's gift, John 14:27.

The Sphere of Peace: 1. In Christ, John 16:33. 2. In the Holy Spirit, Rom. 14:17.

PART XL: ARMISTICE DAY SERMON OUTLINES

ARMISTICE DAY INSTITUTED

In the great city of Paris, in front of the famous Hotel des Invalides, stands a big railroad car. Across its broad side are the words, "The car in which the armistice was signed, November 11, 1918."

This car is the most historic railroad car in the world. For around that big table, by men seated in those strong chairs, was signed the significant document which ended the most terrific combat recorded in the history of mankind.

The story of Armistice Day began when those mighty war leaders, grave and worn, and holding the happiness of humanity in their hands, signed that memorable compact. The thrill of relief which went around the world has never died out. Throbs of joy and thankfulness fill every heart on the anniversary of that great day.

Armistice Day began spontaneously. Nobody waited for decree or proclamation. The news that the war was over flashed around the globe. And a new holiday was born.

Armistice Day was born in joy and gladness. There have been other days of thanksgiving and festivity at the ending of big wars, but never one like Armistice Day. For never before in human history has practically the whole world been involved in war.

The first Armistice Day celebration set the pace for those which have followed. The second and the third were repetitions of the various features of festivity, with parades, patriotic exercises, and devotional services of prayer and praise.

In its later development Armistice Day has risen into greater prominence. In 1921 the Belgian Parliament put November 11 into the place at first occupied by August 4 on their calendar, because that day, November 11, was "the day of liberation from the war and from the enemy."

The United States Congress the same year made November 11 a national holiday for 1921. Urging its observance as a mark of respect for the unknown dead, President Harding in his proclamation referred feelingly to the solemn services which were scheduled for that day. In Arlington Cemetery the body of an unknown soldier was buried with every honor. This single unknown hero was the representative of the many interred in European cemeteries, whose identification-marks had been destroyed in the battles. That year many hundreds of those buried in Europe were brought back for burial in the home land. And Armistice Day took on even stronger resemblance to Memorial Day.

The movement to make Armistice Day a legal holiday in the United States has sprung up as spontaneously as the birth of the day itself. Legislators in the United States Congress and in state legislatures have introduced bills to this effect. And the day has been recognized as one deserving of a permanent place as a national holiday here as well as in European lands. Governors now annually issue calls, and the two-minute prayer at noon has become nation-wide in the United States of America as in Great Britain, for there also the date is enshrined in the hearts of the people.

The American Legion and the British, French, Italian, and Belgian veterans have naturally assumed the chief charge of Armistice Day. Schools and churches in various lands use it impressively in their efforts to combat the war spirit and to promote brotherhood and good will among all the people. The war mothers everywhere meet for mutual comfort and solace. Thoughtful men and women have united to perpetuate the lessons of the war, as witness the effective movements for the practice of economy and thrift, for arbitration, for the study of war's terrible results, for a wider use of good music, and for the enforcement of our prohibition laws.

PART XLI: PRISON SUNDAY TEXTS AND THEMES

Prison Reform: "I was in prison and ye came unto me." Matt. 25:36.

Grinding in the Prison-house: Judges 16:21.

The Sighing of the Prisoners: Psa. 79:11.

To Hear the Groaning of the Prisoner: Psa. 102:20.

Loosing the Prisoners: "The Lord looseth the prisoners." Psa. 146:7.

Prisoners Visited by Friends: Matt. 11:2; Acts 24:22.

Prisoners Required to Labor: Judges 16:21.

Peter in Prison: Acts 12:3-19.

Joseph a Prisoner: Gen. 39:20-23.

Kindness to Prisoners: Jer. 38:7-28.

Duty to Prisoners: "Remember them that are in bonds, as bound with them." Heb. 13:8.

Blessing the Prisoners: "The prisoners heard them." Acts 16:25.

An Apostolic Prisoner: "In prisons more frequent." 2 Cor. 11:23.

PART XLII: PRISON SUNDAY SERMON OUTLINES

THE SIGHING OF THE PRISONER

"Let the sighing of the prisoner come before thee." Psa. 79:11.

The sighing of the prisoner is heard to-day. He has good reason to sigh:
I. Because he has brought himself within prison walls.
II. Because he has awakened to the forfeit he pays.
III. Because his friends are few.
IV. Because he feels his need of God. A deep sigh reaches high.—REV. S. B. DUNN, D.D.

OUR DUTY TOWARD PRISONERS

"I was in prison, and ye came unto me." Matt. 25:36.

In describing the judgment scene in the last day Jesus gives a graphic picture of the separation of the evil from the good, the sheep from the goats. One of the reasons assigned for the separation was: "I was in prison, and ye came unto me"; and "I was . . . sick and in prison, and ye visited me not." When those who were assigned to his left hand asked in surprise, "Lord, when saw we thee . . . sick and in prison and did not minister unto thee?" Jesus said, "Inasmuch as ye did it not to one of the least of these, ye did it not to me." If Christian people to-day should be judged by this test which Jesus mentioned, would we be wholly guiltless in the sight of our Lord? There is a duty which pastors and Christian people owe to those who are imprisoned in our penal institutions. In many cities and towns Christian people have joined together for the holding of religious services in prisons, and many a criminal has thus been turned toward a better life.—C.

CHRISTIANITY AND THE PRISONER

"To proclaim liberty to the captives, and the opening of the prison to them that are bound." Isa. 61: 1.

There is more or less general sentiment sweeping the country at present embodying a larger justice and a more humane point of view toward the prisoner. It is as though we had heard afresh the word of the psalmist: "Let the sighing of the prisoner come before thee!"

Perhaps we have not stopped to consider how truly Christian is this attitude, or how it falls in line with the mission of Jesus to this earth, as that mission is outlined in the great words of our text.

Recently I spent an afternoon in a great factory where there are five hundred ex-convicts working side by side with other employees; but it has been so planned that no one knows who these ex-convicts are; no one points them out and keeps them conscious of their shame. As a result they are becoming trustworthy, efficient, and the makers of good homes.

One man was pointed out as a successful and able workman, who had been in prison for years before he came to his present employment. The police, he said, had followed him and watched him so that it was impossible to get or to keep a job. "My wife is the only person who has ever been decent to me," he explained. The department manager told the man to come around to the factory and he would give him work. After a few weeks he wrote the man a letter, saying he had noticed his good work and sent him a little book. The next day the man appeared at the manager's office, and he could hardly speak. "You know," he said, "you are the only gentleman who ever spoke to me that way. No one ever sent me a book before. When I took it home last night, Mary and I couldn't eat any supper. I'm going to stick and make good." And he did. Was this not preaching good tidings?—C. S. C.

A MORAL EARTHQUAKE

Acts 16: 25-34.

A prison is not a very likely place in which to establish a church. It is often a place of hard hearts; hearts calloused even in prisons. God can find a way to speak to every soul of man; and the way he found in Philippi was the earthquake method. People are usually ready to listen to God when an earthquake takes place in their lives.—REV. R. P. ANDERSON.

A SAINT IN PRISON

Acts 12: 1-10.

When a saint is sent to prison he carries the gospel with him. It is impossible for prison walls to confine an idea, or for tyrants to kill it. The saint finds work to do for God within prison cells. Angels come to him. Opportunities for testimony come to him. Bunyan in prison spoke to the world, to the ages. In doing work in prison we may be speaking from a platform that will reach wide circles.

PART XLIII: GOOD CITIZENSHIP DAY, TEXTS AND THEMES

Is America Christian? "And lo, the beam is in thine own eye." Matt. 7:4.
Citizenship that is Christian: Isa. 62:1-17.
Putting Religion into Politics: Isa. 1:1-17.
To Cleanse the Nation: Isa. 1:10-17.
The Ballot-Scourge: John 2:13-22.
On the Lord's Side: Ex. 32:19-22.
Diseases of the Body Politic: I. Social. II. Moral. III. Industrial. IV. Political.
National Recognition of God: "And when we cried unto the Lord God of our fathers, the Lord heard our voices." Deut. 26:7.
Poultices that Do Not Heal: "For they have healed the hurt of the daughter of my people slightly, saying, Peace, Peace: when there is no peace." Jer. 8:11.
The Patriotism of Our Ancestors: "Turn thou us unto thee, O Lord, and we shall be turned; renew our days as of old." Lam. 5:21.
The Lord Speaking Peace: "I will hear what the Lord will speak; for he will speak peace unto his people, and to his saints; but let them not turn again unto folly." Psa. 85:8.
Civic Pride: Acts 21:37-39.
Cleansing a City: Matt. 4:1-6.
Passion for Civic Purity: Jer. 33:1-9.
Love of the People: Rom. 11:13-36.
High-Minded Officials: 2 Sam. 23:1-7.
Cleaning Up Wrongs: Mark 11:15-19.
The Coming City: Rev. 21:10-27.
A City Redeemed: Isa. 52:1-15.
A Prophet in Politics: Amos. 6:1-11.
God the Supreme Ruler: 1 Sam. 16:6-12.
Righteousness Paramount: Prov. 14:28-34.

True National Greatness: 1 Kings 10: 1-9.
Prosperity and Religion: 2 Chron. 34: 1-8.
A Staunch Patriot: Neh. 2: 1-8.
A Christian at the Ballot Box: Psa. 28: 1-9.
The Sort of Citizens Our Country Needs.
Patriotism Falsely So-Called.
Why a Christian is the Most Efficient Patriot.
Individual Efficiency as Citizens: Phil. 4: 8.
Consecration to Country: Acts 13: 36.
Our National Sins: Neh. 1: 6.
The Source of National Prosperity: Psa. 147: 12-14, 20.

PART XLIV: GOOD CITIZENSHIP DAY SERMON OUTLINES

PUTTING RELIGION INTO POLITICS

Isa. 1:10-17.

I. The prophets were good citizens. They had much to say about politics. They knew that the welfare of the Church was wrapped up in the welfare of the government. We live in a better day, having more light on the questions of life and duty. It may be that the evils of life to-day are as bad as they were in olden time; but it is doubtless true that there is more emphasis laid upon good and duty than in former times.

II. But we know that the forms of religion are worthless without the spirit, both then and now. One reason that these are better than former times is that the people now are beginning to see their obligation to the state and to society. The call of to-day for righteousness is the same, but it is a louder call than formerly. The call of Isaiah is the call for the present time: "Wash you, make you clean; put away the evil of your doings from before mine eyes; cease to do evil; learn to do well; seek judgment, relieve the oppressed, judge the fatherless, plead for the widow."

III. It will be well if all the social and civic duties taught by the prophets shall be studied again by modern teachers. If there was need for righteousness then, there is, if possible, greater need for it now. The Church will never fill its highest mission until its influence shall permeate society, and influence politics.

IV. The aim and purpose of democracy has been defined as "The diffusion of happiness, through the development of character, by a process of gradual growth, the secret of which is the indwelling of God in humanity, the end of which is the brotherhood of man."

V. There are only two kinds of government in the world: One where the individual is the subject; and the other where the individual is the citizen. This second kind of government is increasing, and the first kind is losing. The citizen idea shall be victorious, and the subject shall fail.—REV. W. H. ANDERSON, D.D.

THE CHRISTIAN AND HIS BALLOT

Luke 19: 41-48.
Once during Christ's ministry, the Herodians approached him and asked him, saying: "Teacher, what thinkest thou? Is it lawful to give tribute to Cæsar or not?" Back of that apparently simple and reasonable question was a malignant design: they desired to ensnare him in his talk. Jesus saw their wicked purpose, yet he never flinched in the face of it. "Render unto Cæsar the things that are Cæsar's, and unto God the things that are God's," was his candid reply. This answer is the wisest ever given to a perplexing question, and contains the true theory of Church and State in a nutshell. Both are of divine origin and authority. The Church is concerned with the eternal welfare of men; the State with their temporal relations.

The November election is at hand. Every man and woman ought to vote.

I. Wherever the right to vote is given, it ought to be exercised. To fail to do so is almost a crime.

II. The next and most important thing to do is to vote right. The duty and privilege of every elector is to vote for good men and measures, so that the welfare of the community and nation, the public and private weal of each individual citizen, may be promoted.

III. The privilege of the franchise includes a grave responsibility. Public policies and private interests are shaped and fostered by its influence. The ballot is the maker of men and nations. It should be used at every election, especially when great moral and economic issues are pending, but not without care and prayer, that the right may have the benefit of its power.—R. T.

CHRISTIAN CITIZENSHIP

A Christian man is Christian in every place and moment and department of his life. He is just as much a Christian man when he is asleep and unconscious as when he is awake and active; just as a profane and infidel man is infidel and profane and wicked even in the silent watches of the night.

The Christian man is Christian when he eats and when he drinks and in whatsoever he does, for he lives unto the Lord, and whatever he does he seeks to do it just as God would have him to do it, and so for the honor and glory of God.

It follows, as the night the day, that such a man will discharge his public duties as a citizen conscientiously, and in love and fear and loyalty to his country as God would have him do. He will be concerned with the well-being of the land in which he lives, and will pray and work for its true advancement.

I. One conception of good citizenship is that of living a blameless life, in integrity and obedience to the laws. Of course, one is not a good citizen if he is a law breaker and criminal; if he is dishonest and a disturber of the peace.

II. But one may go much further than this in the promotion of his country's welfare. He may seek to have evil things rooted out of society and the life of the community. He may seek for true reforms. He may work for better conditions in the life and work of the people. He may make himself felt as a moral and uplifting force.

III. But one may go still further than this, in trying to make the people better. The work of enlightening and educating the people is a very important department of good citizenship. The promotion of public schools and of other educational influences and institutions is greatly desirable in the general uplift of the entire community.

IV. There is a higher manifestation for our citizenship than even seeking for education and intellectual enlightenment and information. This is in the promotion of true religion. In religion is the true safety, uplift and well-being of a people or nation, as well as of an individual. He who would befriend and save his nation must see that the influences of true religion are diffused among the people.

It was said by George Washington that the man who ignored morality and religion could lay no claim to being a true patriot.

CHRISTIAN DEMOCRACY

"One is your Teacher, and all ye are brethren." Matt. 23:8.

When America went to war the habits of thousands of people were revolutionized. Girls who had spent most of their time in social frivolities suddenly found themselves doing Red Cross work, going to the front as nurses, serving in heroic ways for the relief of distress at home and "over there."

One of these transformations occurred in a young woman who had been a butterfly of fashion, living in a town near one of the great military camps. With other girls of her set she ministered to the social needs of the soldier boys, inviting them to her home for Sunday dinner, entertaining them at the Rota Club, and entertaining them as social equals. Many of these boys were college-bred and were handsome and attractive in their uniforms.

After the armistice was signed, a wave of reaction swept over many hearts and the tension of suspense was followed by a return to old selfish habits. Many of the boys in the camp came into the town, after their discharge from military service, seeking work.

One young woman who had nobly served others during her brief apprenticeship in unselfishness one day came out of the kitchen where she had gone to give an order to a servant, and said to her mother, "What do you think, mother! I found Lieutenant B— delivering our groceries! He said he had worked his way through college before he enlisted for the officers' training camp, and he took the first job he could find! I invited him to come to dinner next Sunday."

"You must not do that!" the mother said sharply. "Go back and excuse yourself from such an invitation. He is not in our set."

"But we had him here several times, mother! He is in every way worthy."

"It is not the same," said the mother.

"You mean, mother, that the overalls are not as good as the uniform?"

Alas for our boasted American democracy! The boy in overalls did not dine next Sunday with the American family. Of what use is all this talk about making the world safe for democracy if we have none of it ourselves! "For all ye are brethren," said the Master.—Rev. Charles M. Sheldon, D.D.

CHRISTIAN PRINCIPLES IN POLITICS

Luke 22:24-27.

I. The day of the "ring" and the "machine" is gone. Now a candidate for office not only must outline his platform before election but must "make good" after election. The real "political power" of our land is not the party elected to office but those who do the electing. There is no more powerful instrument in the hands of the people than the ballot. Your vote is more than a "scrap of paper"; it can spell anything you wish. Use it intelligently and you build a Christian nation. Abuse it ignorantly, and you help ruin your country.

II. Study current events. Be conversant with politics. Determine to know the record of the men who are seeking office. Insist that they represent your best interests; it is your right and privilege as a citizen so to do. Vote as you pray in order to make righteousness supreme. Begin in your town.

III. One of the great evils of to-day is neutrality. Not to take a stand, not to put yourself on record concerning the burning issues of the day is treason. No voice or life spent in good is in vain. Inertia is worse to battle against than open opposition. The number of people who will do right at all costs and wrong at all costs is not the majority of the population of the country. Christ's party and the devil's party are both comparatively small, but in the nature of things, negative forces gain and positive forces lose by mere neutrality. The man who wants something wants everybody to say "yes" to his demand, but his opponent does not say "yes." To refuse to say "yes" for practical purposes amounts to saying "no."

THE BEST GOVERNMENT

1 Tim. 2:2.

The Apostle Paul refers to the best government when in 1 Tim. 2:2 he pleads for a government where it will be possible for the people to "lead a tranquil and quiet life in all godliness and gravity."

I. The best government is the one that has the least necessity for law, where the people are intelligent, and know how to govern themselves, where they are righteous and control their actions, where they are just in their treatment of their fellowmen.

Mr. Gladstone laid down a most important Christian principle for the regulation of social and political life when he said, "We must make it as easy as possible to do right, and as hard as possible to do wrong." When moral conditions are not what they should be in a community the people find it difficult to do right and easy to do wrong.

II. We should be influenced in our voting by the character of the men who are to be chosen for office and the principles for which they stand rather than any mere partisanship. Politics has gotten to be a business, the ring and the machine rule. Men are asked to what party they belong instead of being asked for what principles they stand. As in late years many college presidents have been chosen because of their ability to raise money for the institution, so, to-day, many political leaders are chosen because they can be made the tools of their party leaders. If they "break away" from their party leaders they have a hard road to travel.

Democracy is one of the great words to-day. Nations are banishing autocrats and making experiments in government of the people, by the people, for the people.

III. The needs of the people for peace, justice, righteousness can only be met as the principles of democracy prevail. But the principles of democracy must be permeated with the spirit of Jesus Christ if they are to furnish a basis for happiness and progress.

The early Christian Church was the first real democracy. Jesus laid down the only principles that will establish right human relations and make them permanent. The Christian Church should reveal to the world the fruits of democracy, and it should be the great force for the promotion of democracy in the world.—REV. A. DURYEA.

PART XLV: ELECTION DAY TEXTS AND THEMES

God the Supreme Ruler: 1 Sam. 16:6-12.
Righteousness Paramount: Prov. 14:28-34.
True National Greatness: 1 Kings 10:1-9.
Prosperity and Religion: 2 Chron. 34:1-8.
A Christian at the Ballot Box: Psa. 28:1-9.
The Sort of Citizens our Country Needs.
Patriotism Falsely So-Called.
Why a Christian is the Most Efficient Patriot.
Individual Efficiency as Citizens: Phil. 4:8.
Consecration to Country: Acts 13:36.
Our National Sins: Neh. 1:6.
The Source of National Prosperity: Psa. 147:12-14, 20.
Our Civic Conditions: Isa. 62:1.
Compromise: Psa. 28:3.
How May One Help to Remedy the Evils in Our Land? Neh. 2:17-18.
In What Spirit Should the Christian Perform His Civic Duties? 2 Tim. 8:15.
What is the True Glory of a Nation? Psa. 33:12.
The Reproach on a Citizen Who Fails to Do His Duty: Judges 5:17-23.
The Christian's Vote: Prov. 19:2, 4, 8.
Value Your Citizenship: Esther 4:13, 14.
The Source of National Prosperity: Psa. 147:12-14, 20.
Our Civic Conditions: Isa. 62:1.

PART XLVI: ELECTION DAY SERMON OUTLINES

THE DIVINE ELECTION

"Knowing, brethren beloved of God, your election." 1 Thess. 1:4.

November 7 will be a most important day to the American people. The choosing of a President of the United States is always significant; but many believe that the choice made on that day will be of unusual significance to the republic and to the world. Is it not an auspicious hour to consider what we may call the divine election, or, the higher politics? Our subject, therefore, embraces three steps.

I. First, the Candidacy. Upon what is it based? What are the issues? In the campaign drawing to a close there has been a free discussion of vital, living issues. Yet they are not one whit more essential than the issues involved in the divine election. What are these? What are all of us candidates for, whether we will or not? What are the issues of human life which refuse to be ignored? Just these: Righteousness, peace, joy, hope, eternal life. These are some of the age-long issues upon which the candidacy of each life is based. Every soul has been divinely nominated for office in these finer regions.

II. Second, the Voters. Now every candidate must submit his cause to the voters. Nor is it otherwise in Paul's divine election. Who, then, are the voters? They are two, and the first—let it be said reverently but emphatically—is God. Every candidate for office in the higher realms should remember this: the good God had already voted for you. God is so profoundly interested in your soul's election to the office of noble living here and to boundless felicity hereafter, that he hath sent his only begotten Son to declare this truth throughout the length and breadth of the world. The other voter in the divine election is you yourself without embarrassment, but with deep satisfaction. Moreover, you must vote for yourself, and with decision. No man can be coerced into goodness any more than he can be forced into heaven. God and the universe seem to have great respect for the rights of suffrage in these august things.

III. Third, the Inauguration. In the largest sense, the choice of the voters on November 7 will not have been fully realized until he is inaugurated on the 5th of March. A similar principle holds in the divine election also. Although your candidacy be based upon the highest truths, and although God votes for you and you vote for yourself, such is the majesty of the high office to which you are chosen that you will not exhaust its honors and meaning in this world. You will have to be inducted into the happier climes of immortality before the entire significance of your election is fully appreciated.

Should not one be careful to vote right for destiny?—F. E. SHANNON.

PART XLVII: THANKSGIVING DAY TEXTS AND THEMES

King David's Thanksgiving Proclamation: "O give thanks unto the Lord; for he is good; for his mercy endureth forever. Enter into his gates with thanksgiving and into his courts with praise. Be thankful unto him, and bless his holy name. Praise the Lord, O Jerusalem; praise thy God, O Zion; for he hath strengthened the bars of thy gates, he hath blessed thy children within thee; he maketh peace in thy borders; he filleth thee with the finest of the wheat. Let the people praise thee, O Lord; let all the people praise thee." Psalms.

The Unreaped Corner: "And when ye reap the harvest of your land, thou shalt not wholly reap the corners of thy field, neither shalt thou gather the gleanings of the harvest." Lev. 19:9.

The Crowning of the Year: "Thou crownest the year with thy goodness; and thy paths drop fatness." Psa. 65:11.

Soul-Husbandry: "And when he saw a fig-tree in the way he came to it, and found nothing thereon, but leaves," etc. Matt. 21:19.

God's Call to Joy: Luke 10:21.

Thankful for What? Psa. 33:1-22. For his word: Psa. 119:105-112. For his work: Jer. 10:12, 13. For his loving kindness. Psa. 119:57-64. For his watchfulness: Job 36:1-7. For his deliverance: Acts 12:6-11.

The Beauty and Utility of Gratitude: Psa. 111:1-10.

God's Wonderful Works: Psa. 40:1-11.

How Does God Want to be Thanked? Psa. 100:1-5.

Praise is Comely: Psa. 33:1.

Why We Give Thanks: "Our fathers trusted in thee." Psa. 22:4.

The Praising Habit: "Oh, that men would praise the Lord." Psa. 107:8.

Thanksgiving Proclamation: Psa. 100.

A Thanksgiver: Luke 17: 11-19.
A Backward Glance: Isa. 63: 7-9.
Eternal Thanksgiving: Rev. 7: 9-17.
Daily Thanksgiving: Phil. 4: 6.
Expressing Our Gratitude: "Let the redeemed of the Lord say so." Psa. 107: 2.
The Blessing of a Thankful Heart: Neh. 8: 10. "The joy of the Lord is your strength." "The joy of the Lord" is joy in the Lord, rejoicing in the goodness and wisdom and power and beauty of our God. No life is strong without this, and every life that has it is a mighty life.
Tidings for the King's Household: 2 Kings 7: 9.
The Brimming Cup: "My cup runneth over." Psa. 23: 5.
Thankfulness and Courage: "When Paul saw, he thanked God and took courage." Acts 28: 15.
Songs of the Heart: Psa. 103: 1-22.
Thanksgiving that Never Ceases: Psa. 146: 1-10.
The Loaded Table: "Come and dine." John 21: 12.
Reasons for Thanksgiving: "The earth is the Lord's." Psa. 24: 1.
Causes of Thanksgiving: Joel 2: 21-27.
God's Open Hand: "Thou openest thine hand." Psa. 145: 16.
The Thanksgiving Feast: "Go your way; eat the fat." Neh. 8: 10.
God's Overflowing Goodness: "Thou art good." Psa. 119: 68.
Forgetting to be Thankful: "When thou shalt have eaten and be full; then beware lest thou forget God." Deut. 6: 11, 12.
Daily Marvels: "Blessed be the Lord, who daily loadeth us with his benefits." Psa. 68: 19.
A Cheerful Temper: "He that is of a merry heart hath a continual feast." Prov. 15: 15.
Happy Mediocrity: "Give me neither poverty nor riches." Prov. 30: 7-9.
In Everything Give Thanks: 1 Thess. 5: 18.
Thanksgiving for Mercies: Psa. 107: 1.
The Joy of Harvest: "They joy before thee according to the joy in harvest." Isa. 9: 3.

THANKSGIVING DAY TEXTS AND THEMES

The Full Table of the Year: "Oh, that men would praise the Lord for his goodness, and for his wonderful works to the children of men." Psa. 107:8.

The Eternal Praise Service: Rev. 5:8-14.

The National Doxology: "Oh, praise the Lord all ye nations." Psa. 117:1, 2.

Thanksgiving of the Past: "Our fathers trusted in thee." Psa. 22:4.

Thanksgiving Joy: "This day is holy unto the Lord your God," etc. Neh. 8:9, 10.

The Giver and the Gifts: Jas. 1:17.

The Benefits to a Nation of Giving Thanks: Psa. 50:14.

Thankfulness as a Habit: "I will bless the Lord at all times, his praise shall continually be in my mouth." Psa. 14:1.

Universal Thanksgiving: "Let everything that hath breath praise the Lord." Psa. 150:6.

The Sin of Thoughtlessness: "And when he thought thereon, he wept." Mark 14:72. Thoughtlessness is a sin and thanklessness is a sin.

The Supreme Claims of God: "And the best of the oil and all the best of the wine, and of the wheat, the first fruits of them they shall offer unto the Lord." Num. 18:12.

PART XLVIII: THANKSGIVING DAY SERMON OUTLINES

GRATITUDE FOR GOD'S REMEMBRANCE

"How precious also are thy thoughts unto me, O God." Psa. 139:17.

The sense of loneliness is always saddening. In such an hour how consoling to feel that we are remembered by at least one human being. How much more consoling to know that we are thought of with loving interest by a goodly number of friends! Yet what are either of these assurances to the supreme consciousness that God remembers us, and that we share in all his benevolent plans!

1. His thoughts of us are loving thoughts. He is our Father, and lovingly thoughtful of all his dear children.
2. His thoughts of us are constant. He never forgets. In all places, times, circumstances, he thinks of us.
3. His thoughts of us are personal thoughts. He does not think of us as indefinite parts of some multitude. "The Lord thinketh upon thee."
4. His thoughts of us are wise thoughts. His plans for us are the best possible plans.
5. His thoughts of us are thoughts of helpfulness. We may think of a person without any disposition or desire to help him. But God has disposition to help, ability to help, and thinks of us on purpose to help.

THANKSGIVING DAY

Neh. 8:9, 10.

This records an early Thanksgiving day which began with solemnity and which ended in joy.

I. Profound meditation precedes true thankfulness. It must reach down to the "law of God" (v. 8) in order to rise to the heights of joy.

II. Thanksgiving need not be postponed until all is perfect or prosperous; but it must discern the divine plan. "You have as much material prosperity as is good for you."—AMBASSADOR BRYCE.

III. Highest joy is the joy of sharing our blessings; through the Church—the channel of helpfulness to all the world.

THANKSGIVING

"Abounding in thanksgiving." Col. 2:7.

I. Thanksgiving as a duty. See text and Col. 3:15 to end.

II. Thanksgiving as a privilege. Illustration, returning thanks for a gift from a friend. One wants to do it.

III. Thanksgiving should be continuous. Not simply one day in a year, but each day should be a thanksgiving day.

IV. Thanksgiving should have a prominent part in the life, especially of the Christian—"Abounding in thanksgiving."

V. In thanksgiving we should always recognize the supreme importance of spiritual gifts.—E. H. KNIGHT, D.D.

SPECIAL REASONS FOR THANKSGIVING

"Give thanks unto him." Psa. 100:4.

I. That the harvests of the year are so bountiful. Note the facts as to the crops of corn, wheat, cotton, hay, etc., for the year. Then consider the relation of these harvests to the business of the whole country.

II. That we are American citizens. Contrast our condition with that of the inhabitants of any other land.

III. That there is in progress a rising tide of interest in civic righteousness. Gather facts in proof of this statement.

IV. That in our religious life we have the privilege of service. Estimate the influence of the "Men and Religion" movement in this direction.—E. H. KNIGHT, D.D.

JOYFUL THANKSGIVING

Isa. 42:1-13; Psalm 146.

These verses of prophet and psalmist are filled with wonful promises and many reasons for thanksgiving on the part of the ancient Jews. Our reasons for thanksgiving, personal and national, are as many. Without following closely the verses let us in their spirit think of some of our own reasons for joyful thanksgiving.

I. Thank God for life. Carlyle has somewhere said: "Every man should put himself at zero, and then reckon every degree ascending from that point as an occasion for thanks." That is the true standard. Precisely on this scale does the Bible compute our mercies. Every step we take from where conscious unworthiness would consign us should call for our offering of gratitude. "It is of the Lord's mercies that we are not consumed." "Why should a living man complain?" So begins the anthem of thanks. It starts at the lowest note of all: "We are alive. We are not consumed." Whatever we may think of our hardships and deprivations, we are all far above the extreme point, and therefore have much occasion for thanksgiving. A writer in the Quiver well expresses this thought. He says: "I felt most ill-used because a slight accident had disabled my right hand. Taking a walk through crowded streets, I met one man with one leg only, another without the usual number of arms, a blind woman, a girl with her face terribly disfigured, two deaf and dumb men, an old man with a 'church-yard cough,' two funerals, and a van of prisoners. Having passed these, and come to a lunatic asylum, I made up my mind that I should be very thankful that I was not as badly off as thousands of more deserving people."

II. Not only are we alive, but what a wondrous life it is we are permitted to live! It is not the life of an animal. A man alive! Can you find in all the works of God a being which surpasses him? He stands upon the earth, but his eyes need not be earthward bent. His is the upward look, the onward march, the glorious future. It is a grand, a glorious, a divine gift, this pulsing, throbbing, mastering, glowing life we live. To live, to be conscious, to think, to solve problems, to read the pages of nature and to reverently turn over the pages that reveal God, to believe that this is not all of life, but that above things animate and inanimate it is to endure forever, the immortal spark never to be quenched, the immortal world never to disappear, for all this, included in the one fact of life, shall we not evermore give thanks?

III. Our gratitude is due also because of the age in which we live. The mists of superstition have almost disappeared. The darkness of ignorance no longer envelops us. We have got out of the Egyptian night into the clear, crisp morning of liberty.

And this liberty includes liberty to worship, and liberty of the Church to foster and educate and cultivate in men the spirit of worship. When compared with her condition in many years of the past the Church of Christ has much to be thankful for. Now and then we hear rumors of the decadence of the Church. We are told that she is losing her influence and vitality. But this rumor, far more the expression of a wish than the statement of a fact, is not true. The fact is that the Church never did better work than it is doing to-day. The pulpit never more honestly declared the truth than it is declaring it to-day; and the Church is getting at the mind and the heart of the world as never before.

Fifty years ago a Christian gentleman paid advertising rates for space in the *Commercial Advertiser* of New York to fill with religious reading matter. When at the end of the year the man came to renew his contract the editor told him that the religious matter had proved so interesting to his readers that he would furnish the space free. Fifty years ago one must pay advertising rates to get religious matter into a secular newspaper. To-day the great dailies print column after column of sermons, and International Sunday School lessons, and reports about missions and missionaries and of the church life and work. No, the world is not losing interest in the Christian religion, and for this fact let the Church be thankful.

Let us cultivate more the spirit of thankfulness. Archbishop Trench speaks of a tribe in Brazil in whose language there is neither the word nor the idea of "thanks." God forbid that a like fact should ever come to pass in our language. As Spurgeon in his quaint way puts it: "Even the little chick never takes a drink of water without looking up and giving thanks!" Let us not fail to look up and recognize God as the giver of every good.

Get the habit of thanksgiving. There is a beautiful legend of a golden organ in an ancient monastery. Once the monastery was besieged by robbers who desired to carry off its treasures. The monks took the organ to the river which flowed close by and sank it in the deep water in order to keep it from the hands of the robbers. And the legend is that though buried thus in the river, the organ still continued to give forth sweet enchanting music, which was heard by those who came near.

Every Christian life should be like this golden organ. Nothing should ever silence its music. Even when the floods of sorrow or disappointment flow over it, it should still continue to rejoice and sing. We should have the habit of thanksgiving. We should cultivate the habit. Some people are never grateful to God. Some are grateful when things go well. But God is always good and his dealings with us are good. To be grateful one day in the year cannot make up for three hundred and sixty-four days of ingratitude. Every day should be a Thanksgiving Day.

It is said that in Africa there is a fruit called the "taste berry," because it changes a person's tastes so that even if eaten several hours after the "taste berry," becomes sweet and delicious. Gratitude is the "taste berry" of Christianity, and when our hearts are filled with gratitude, nothing that God sends us seems unpleasant to us. Sorrowing heart, sweeten your grief with gratitude. Burdened soul, lighten your burden by singing God's praises. Disappointed one, make your disappointment his appointment by a thankful spirit. Lonely one, dispel your loneliness by making others grateful. Sick one, grow strong in soul thanking God that he loves you enough to chasten you. Keep the "taste berry" of gratitude in your hearts, and it will do for you what the "taste berry" of Africa does for the African.

Oh, that the grumbler, the pessimist, the chronic complainer might acquire the "thank you habit"! The "thank you" spirit should girdle the globe and ascend towards heaven. Earth bends with its burden of blessings to enrich grateful hearts.—H.

VOLCANIC THANKSGIVING

"Blessed be the God and Father of our Lord Jesus Christ," etc. 1 Pet. 1:3-5.

An eruption of the soul in fiery lava of gratitude, remarkable alike for the affection expressed and the favors enumerated.

I. We are rich in God. Such a God, "Father of our Lord Jesus Christ," and "abundant in mercy."

II. We are rich in experience. "Begotten again unto a lively hope." "Kept" in a fortress. "A salvation ready to be revealed."

III. We are rich in heirship. To a "resurrection" like Christ's. To an "inheritance" "incorruptible" and "unfading" and "reserved." To a daybreak ready to be "revealed."

FEAST OF INGATHERING

"And thou shalt observe . . . the feast of ingathering at the year's end." Ex. 34:22.

Thanksgiving, our feast of ingathering—memento of God's goodness.

I. Its educational value—aids reflection; stimulates piety; tends to national virtue.

II. Its epochal character. "At the year's end."—Sacred seasons, punctuation marks.

III. Its joyous phenomena. Joy of gathering; joy of using; joy of celebrating.—REV. S. B. DUNN, D.D.

REAL THANKSGIVING

1 Thess. 5:14-24.

I. Thanksgiving.

It is very strange that we are not constantly and thoroughly grateful to God for all his mercies to us. Look how dependent we are, and see how much we have and when we realize that it all comes from the hand of God, we ought to be thanking God all the time.

Gratitude is a mark of culture. The more delicate and intense the sense of gratitude, the more surely we may know that those who give it are cultured and refined. They who show no appreciation for any kindness or service are base indeed.

Gratitude is a pleasing exercise of the mind. It produces a pleasant effect on the feelings. You feel better if you feel grateful. It does not have a humiliating effect. It does not depreciate your own worth in your own estimation.

II. Thankspaying.

Gratitude is really a debt. We owe something, and thanksgiving is the paying of that debt. While this is one of our greatest obligations, it is one of the easiest paid. As soon as we become conscious of the debt, it is paid. The trouble with many is that they are slow to see that they have any blessings to be grateful for. One time the writer was requested to call by a certain good woman, and when he came she said: "I want to tell you my troubles." He took out his watch and said, "If you will spend fifteen minutes in telling me of your blessings, I will listen to your troubles thirty minutes." She looked rather surprised and said: "I had not thought of that before, I will not tell you my troubles, but let us talk about my blessings."

III. Thanksliving.

Real gratitude will be constant in its flow. We need not think to be grateful spasmodically. It is correct to feel like saying, "Praise the Lord," all the time. That gratitude which shows itself in the life is the best sort.

A Thanksgiving life will be a life void of selfishness. Higher ideals than selfish ones will fill the mind and heart. Many are selfish without knowing or thinking of it.

A Thanksliving life will be a life of service. Serving is the best way of showing gratitude. Whenever you are conscious that some one has done you a favor, your first thought is, What can I do in return?—W. M. ANDERSON, D.D.

THE DOWER OF A NATION

"And I will make of thee a great nation," etc. Gen. 12:2. Thanksgiving Day sums up the nation's dower:

I. Blest of God. "I will bless thee."
II. Nursed to greatness. "Make thy name great."

VI. Ministers to sister nations. "Thou shalt be a blessing."—Rev. S. B. Dunn, D.D.

THE GOODNESS OF GOD

"They shall abundantly utter the memory of thy great goodness," etc. Psa. 145:7.

Thanksgiving, observatory from which to level telescope upon goodness of God.

I. What is revealed. A goodness possessed; a goodness shown; a goodness impressive.

II. What is felt. A "memory"—of the God who is good; of its personal realizations; of a sense of gratitude, so apt to fade.

III. What is done. "Uttered"; statedly; without stint; in unison; with reverence; "sing of," etc. To-day unveil a tablet to the goodness of God.—Rev. S. B. Dunn, D.D.

EXCELLENT LOVING-KINDNESS

"How excellent is thy loving-kindness, O God!" Psa. 36:7.

The late Dr. Howard Osgood, of Rochester, maintained that in every instance in which we find the term "loving-kindness" in the Old Testament, we are at liberty to substitute the word "grace" and in every instance in which we find the word "grace" in the New Testament we do not go far astray if we substitute for it the word "loving-kindness." Doubtless there is a doctrine of grace in the Old Testament.

I. God's grace is eternal. He loved us before the world was, and chose us from before the world's foundation. He will love us until the world's last hour of doom. God's lovingkindness is excellent because of its eternity. Human lovingkindness has a time limit, but God's has not. Moreover, God's grace is excellent because of its pure benevolence. Who of us deserves salvation? What man ever earned it? "God commendeth his love to us in that, while we were yet sinners, Christ died for us."

II. Then God's loving-kindness is excellent because of its methods. Many an act of human kindness is wrought so tactlessly that it gives offense without meaning to do so. How gentle is God's approach to human life! With more than a father's pity and more than a mother's love the Eternal touches and teaches us in order that he may lead us into the way of life everlasting.

It is the testimony of practically all the students who sat under a certain college professor recently gone to his coronation that he never was impatient with even the most stupid. Only rarely did he indulge in words that left a sting. The willful and the vicious he could reprove with words that fairly blistered, but his tenderness to the timid, his care not to wound the feelings of the sensitive, earned for him the title "saint," by which he was affectionately known to many. He had learned patience in the school of Christ, and his loving-kindness was excellent because it was derived from God.—REV. C. C. ALBERTSON, D.D.

PRAISE GOD

"Blessed are they that dwell in thy house: they will be still praising thee." Psa. 84:4.

I. Praise God for a home. Tens of thousands of boys and girls will go to sleep to-night without a mother to tuck them into bed, and without any one of the pleasures of home about them.

II. Praise God for food and clothes. Millions of persons are hungry to-day, and many of them are suffering for want of clothing.

III. Praise God that you do not lift blind eyes to a sky you have never seen. Be grateful for your sight, through which so many of your pleasures come. Praise the kind Father in heaven, too, for your hearing and speech. Are not the sun, the moon, the stars, the air, the water, the rain, the snow, the trees, the flowers, worth a word of praise? Yet how seldom do we thank God for these common blessings?

IV. Praise God for books and for the pleasure and power which come from reading and education.

V. Praise God for the wonderful inventions and progressive spirit which made to-day the best time in all the world's history to be alive. The comforts, the conveniences, the pleasures and the blessings that are possible to all of us in these modern days are surely worth a "Thank you!" to the Giver of them all.

VI. Praise God, most of all, for the blessed Bible and the loving Saviour. Jesus is the theme of the praises that are sung in heaven; shall he not be our chiefest cause for praise here?

How shall we do all this praising? With our lips. In our hearts. By our lives. Just to be glad and grateful is praise that pleases God. Then, to give another person reason to be glad and grateful is still a better way of praising God.

OLDEN TIME APPRECIATION

"Destroy not the ancient landmarks which the fathers have set." Prov. 22:28.

We never become so far advanced that we are independent of the "days of old." Some moments of thanksgiving may well be given to an appreciation of the "ancient landmarks."

I. Old-time virtues:
  1. Hospitality.
  2. Courtesy.
  3. Citizenship.
  4. Patriotism.
II. Old-time institutions.
  1. Educational.
  2. Domestic.
  3. Civic.
  4. Religious.
III. Old-time character: plain, straightforward, humble, godly.—REV. C. R. SHAVER.

WHY GIVE THANKS?

"Thou crownest the year with thy goodness, and thy paths drop fatness." Psa. 65:11.

This day is for thanksgiving. It is not appointed for a fast but a feast. We may appropriately consider how the gifts we acknowledge as a nation may be preserved and increased. But it is not observing the day for national thanksgiving to concentrate attention on the sins confessed and unconfessed of which we are guilty, or to magnify the perils which threaten society and endanger the stability of government. There are times fit for that duty, but Thanksgiving Day is the one day of the year appointed for a different purpose. What then are the chief causes why all the people should praise God as this year draws to its close?

I. Prosperity. It is the greatest of any year in our history. Never before were farms so fruitful, mines yielding such stores of wealth, employed labor so abundantly rewarded.

> "Praise waiteth for thee, O God . . .
> Thou crownest the year with thy goodness;
> And thy paths drop fatness."

II. Peace. There is no strife within our borders. Our national flag is as much honored in one part of the country as in another.

III. Power. Our nation is recognized to-day as a mighty leader among all nations. It has come into a place of power which its people in the last century hardly dreamed of, and which, even in this year, is a surprise to mankind. It has preserved the integrity of the Chinese Empire, and has reversed the policy of mighty kingdoms; and its power has been exercised, not for its own aggrandizement, but for the welfare of all mankind. Oppressed peoples turn to us for deliverance, and those greedy for spoil halt at our word.

IV. Patriotism. This year is witnessing a moral renewal, an awakening sensitiveness to honor in business, integrity in government and a new consciousness of civic responsibility, which has found expression at the polls as well as in pulpits and on platforms. Bosses have been overthrown, combinations of thieves and plunderers broken up, forces of intemperance have been overcome in cities all over the land. The people are rallying around honest and self-sacrificing leaders, are striving for higher ideals in government, are moving to protect the weak and promote the nobler interests of their fellowmen.

V. Piety. There are prayers for religious quickening, and signs of its coming, in so many places that those who are watching for new revelations from God are persuaded that we are entering on a new era of national reaching after spiritual ideals. Christians of all names are coming into closer fellowship for united effort to impart the blessings of the gospel of Christ to all men.

Our material wealth is great and growing, but our greatest cause for thanksgiving is that this wealth does not satisfy; that there is abroad in the land an unsatisfied longing for the things that fulfill divine ideals in man. The number is multiplying of the poor in spirit, the meek, the merciful, the peacemakers, those who hunger and thirst after righteousness, those who are persecuted for righteousness' sake—whose is the kingdom of heaven, who shall be called sons of God.

PART XLIX: OUTLINES OF SERMONS ON SPECIAL OCCASIONS AND TO FRATERNITIES

A PASTOR'S INSTALLATION SERMON

"Therefore came I unto you without gainsaying, as soon as I was sent for; I ask therefore for what intent ye have sent for me?" Acts 10:92.

There is a whispering-gallery from the lip of the needy to the ear of God. It is recorded of the elder Dionysius of Syracuse, that he ordered a cave to be constructed for his prisoners in the form of an ear, so that every word they uttered was conveyed to one common tympanum, close to which he sat. The world is such a cave; every cry, however feeble, is heard by him who inclines his ear to hear "the groanings of the prisoners."

Cornelius had preferred his request, and left it with God. There was some delay in gratifying it, for God was training Peter by various methods so that he might overcome his prejudices, and engage in the work so distasteful to him. When that was done, the prayer of Cornelius was fully answered. Four days elapsed, and then a scene of most significant import is beheld; there stands Simon, the rigid Jew, in the house of a Gentile, and not only so, but he stands there to tell of privileges common, alike, to Jew and Gentile. He does not stand alone; six of his countrymen are spectators of his zeal. He displays neither pride nor indifference; he gives them to understand he has come without reluctance, at their request, to render the service they desire.

I. Notice, first, his commendable silence. "Without gainsaying."
   1. He was silent, although his mission was foreign to his prejudices. If we would do anything for God, we must stifle our prejudices.
   2. He was silent, although he doubted, perhaps, his own

qualifications for the mission. If he did not doubt, it is certain he was strongly tempted thereto, verse 20. Doubts will invade the mind, but we should never encourage or utter them. If lions are said to be in the way of duty, put the finger of faith in your ear, and you will never hear their roaring.

Every word we utter of "gainsaying" is a strand, of which the devil makes a rope to bind the hands of usefulness.

3. He was silent, although the commission was sudden and surprising.

The wise man said there was a time to keep silence. We may be assured that time has come when God commands us to do or suffer.

II. Notice, secondly, his eager diligence. "As soon as I was sent for." He came with all promptness. We believe earnestness is as much an ordained means for the success of the gospel as prayer or faith. In the case of Peter we have this earnestness exemplified.

1. He did not hesitate on account of his stained character. Had not the command been explicit, he might have said, I will wait before I go forth as an apostle to the Gentiles, and, by an exemplary and holy life, strive to regain my reputation, at least, in the eyes of the brethren. For I believe the thought of his denial and abandonment of the crucified Lord never was out of his mind for an hour. Many are held back from usefulness by fear lest men should taunt them with their former character. Their fear, however, not their history, is the real barrier to usefulness. Like Artemon, who was so afraid lest anything should fall on him, that he had two slaves to carry a brazen shield over him constantly; his precaution placed him in jeopardy, for the shield was the most likely thing to fall on him.

2. He was not tardy on account of his inexperience. It was the first time of his going as a missionary to the Gentiles. But he was courageous. He knew he had a sermon in his heart, and trusted in God to bring it to his lips.

The young pastor may ask with anxious concern, as he looks forward to years of labor and considers his own inexperience, "Where are all my sermons to come from?" He need not fear; if he faithfully place the ordained trumpet to his lips, God shall make a variety of melody.

Each one of us is called to some service. The finger of God points to some Cæsarea; first of all let us know where it lies, and then eagerly hasten thither.

III. Notice, thirdly, his pointed question: "I ask, therefore, for what intent ye have sent for me?" Like a physician, he wastes no time in idle formalities; he goes straight to the patient, and inquires why he is sent for. It is well for the Christian pastor to start fairly; to have his mission fully understood; to know the expectations of his charge, so that neither they nor himself may be disappointed afterward.

We may suppose some answers to the question, as given by modern congregations, and state the fitting rejoinders.

1. To be a censor of others. No, the preacher's position is that of a shepherd, not a sheep-dog.
2. To be a caterer for our intellectual wants. No, the preacher should strive to improve the minds of his people, but his chief mission is to the heart.
3. To be a boon companion. No, a preacher should rejoice to share the joys of his hearers, but his first business has to do with the poor and sorrowful.
4. To repeat the particular creed of his hearers. The preacher's duty is to deal with God's word, and not with the systems manufactured therefrom.

Let the answer to the question of Peter, when repeated by preachers now, be such as this, "We have sent for you to expound and enforce the Word of our Master; to admonish the erring, and encourage the faint; to teach men their danger, and proclaim the Deliverer." Then shall our preachers be more like Peter, their sermons more like his, and their success something after the sort recorded in the 44th verse.

THE CHRISTIAN'S CONFIDENCE

"He knoweth the way that I take." Job 23: 10.

Job was like a poor traveler on a lonely road. The devil

had been permitted to intercept his course, and bruise, and lame, and strip him of all he had. Now, these so-called friends weave elaborate arguments to prove that, because he is in such a sorry plight, therefore he must be in the wrong road. So Job virtually says, "It does not matter what you think, God knows all about me, and if he thought it was wrong for me to be as I am, he would tell me!"

I may take this as the language of every tried child of God, and paraphrase it thus:

I. "He knoweth the way I take," for he directed me. God ordained even his footsteps. The greatest comfort we can have in time of affliction is to know God ordains it; to know we are not responsible for our sufferings.

II. "He knoweth the way I take," for he visited me. I have had communion with him. He would not be false to me. He would not strengthen me in a wrong course.

Let the afflicted soul in his darkest hours say: "God must know my state, for I have felt him to be near."

III. "He knoweth the way that I take," although it is almost trackless. I walk alone, and can hardly find my way, but I am sure of going right, because God is looking on. This is walking by faith.

IV. "He knoweth the way that I take," although I have sometimes doubted it. God's guidance is not dependent on our faith. He is true to us, however skeptical we may be. It is not always that the afflicted can feel all is right.

V. "He knoweth the way that I take," so I conclude he will never abandon me. His past mercy is a pledge of future grace. He never yet left the soul he engaged to guide.

VI. "He knoweth the way that I take," so I do not mind its horns. "It is very rough and perilous," says the soul; "I grow weary, and am wounded at almost every step, but if a gracious God keep his eye on me I cannot perish."

VII. "He knoweth the way that I take," therefore I must reach home. It must lead to final and blessed rest, for he has promised eternal life and felicity to those who put their trust in him. He knows the snares, the perils, the trials of the way, and will guard and deliver and succor me. It does not matter, then, what the road is, nor how we feel therein—it leads up to heaven.

FREEMASONRY TRIUMPHANT

Text: "And they sing the song of Moses, the servant of God, and the song of the Lamb." Rev. 15:3.

When we pass from the narrow confines of the room which represents to us some of the features of King Solomon's temple to that Temple "not made with hands, eternal in the heavens" what song shall we sing? Our text is the answer: "The song of Moses and the song of the Lamb."

I. The song of Moses: What was that?

1. The song of patriotism. You will find its exact wording in Exodus 15. The song of the redeemed yonder is the song of every true Mason here. It is a fact that many of earth's greatest patriots have been Freemasons.

Some foolishly think that our secrecy is incompatible with patriotism. As well suppose that a private meeting of directors of a corporation means bankruptcy, or a Vatican conclave the horrors of the Inquisition. Individuals, families, societies, have secret matters that it is not necessary or expedient to publish on the housetops. If the publication of our secrets would enhance the interests of justice or the happiness of the world, or were they of a base or reprehensible nature, there might be no excuse for their retention; but since they are not of this class we do not feel we should be blamed for putting a seal on our lips, and politely asking outsiders to mind their own business.

Of this we are sure, that no Mason has ever absorbed the poison of disloyalty to our country, its flag, its constitution, or its rulers, from the principles and precepts he has acquired in the lodge rooms of his Order.

If it ever comes to a trial of strength in this country between anarchy and law, it will soon be discovered where every true Mason stands.

2. The song of law. Examine the constitutions of nations, the Magna Charta written in the blood of martyrs, the decisions of great law courts, and what name do you find between and under the lines? Moses. He rises in isolated grandeur above the law givers of all time. The moral law as enunciated by him is as obligatory to-day as on the day he uttered it. This, too, is a Masonic song. At no communi-

cation are our members permitted to forget the laws that circumscribe them.

What is the furniture of our lodges? No matter where they be situated, in New York or Hong Kong, Berlin or Oklahoma. It is the Bible, the Square, and the Compass. What does the Bible mean? Law. The Square? Law. The Compass? Law. The Bible is on every Masonic altar, and its teachings underlie our principles. Go into any lodge-room in the wide world, and you will find the Book. We sadly fail in our efforts, I am aware, to shape our lives to the model it presents, but the fault is all our own, and not the Order's to which, with all our unworthiness, we belong. The Square? That needs no explanation. Like the Decalogue, the Shepherd Psalm, the Beatitudes, it is self-explanatory. He is a "square" man! Did you ever go to a dictionary for a definition of the term? No; instinct told you. A man whose word is enough. No oath or bond could strengthen it.

The Compass? Law still. That no man is a law unto himself. That others have rights he no more dares to invade than one star to transgress the orbit of another. With the Compass he says: "Passion, outside that circle thou canst not go! Selfishness, thus far and no farther!" Whenever you see a brother permitting himself to trample over fences hallowed by sacred pledges, and wandering into forbidden grounds, show him the Compass, and he will stand reproved in the presence of its mute eloquence. Whenever you discover in yourself a tendency, however faint, to violate the line that all morality and religion sanction, whisper the meaning of the Compass to your soul, and strengthen your will to obey its high behest.

3. The song of prophecy. Not permitted himself to go over into the Promised Land, Moses predicted the fulfillment of God's promises for his people. Within the scope of his prophetic vision he saw the Land entered, conquered, occupied, a kingdom established, a Temple erected, all the glittering splendors of David's and Solomon's reign, and the everlasting rule of David's greater Son. Masonry is embodied optimism, the incarnation of hope and good will. She believes in the capabilities of human nature, the willingness of Divine to reinforce the human, the betterment of the world by the coöperation of God and man. She looks upon the past,

gathers from hoary antiquity all that it has to teach, but keeps her eyes steadily fixed on a future brighter than all the golden days of the past.

My brethren, we stand for the betterment of the world. We do not believe the world is going from bad to worse, but from better to best.

4. *The song of immortality.* At the head of the 90th Psalm are these words: "A Song of Moses." I am not sure that he wrote it, but I am positive that he believed in immortality, that when on Mount Nebo he put his head on God's soft hand, he did so in the firm conviction that the ravishment of eternity was about to open before him. So God gave to his beloved sleep, and death was swallowed up in victory.

There is inspiration in the funeral of a Mason. There is sadness, of course, over the loss of a brother dearly beloved, a grief which finds fitting expression in the exclamation: "Alas, my brother!" But I never see the acacia dropped upon the casket without hearing an echo of St. Paul's superb challenge: "O death! where is thy sting? O grave! where is thy victory!"

I have had time to touch on one stanza only of heaven's song. But there is another.

II. *The song of redemption:* "And the Song of the Lamb." Moses was the schoolmaster to bring us to the greater Prophet he foretold. "The law was given to Moses, but grace and truth came by Jesus Christ."

We turn from Sinai, enshrouded with the smoke of the Divine presence to the little town of Bethlehem, where the Babe is cradled who is to change the face of history, and to a place called Calvary, where he wins the world by sacrifice.

The holy Saints John are deeply reverenced by every Mason. The Song of Redemption was precious to both of them. One said: "Behold the Lamb of God that taketh away the sin of the world." The other declared: "These things are written that ye might believe that Jesus is the Christ, the Saviour of the world."

We, like the choir invisible, must sing both stanzas of the Song.

The Song of Moses, the servant of God, for that is the song of patriotism, law, prophecy, and immortality.

"And the Song of the Lamb," for that is the song of our personal redemption and the world's salvation.—Rev. A. E. Barnett.

THE THREE LINKS OF THE INDEPENDENT ORDER OF ODD FELLOWS

I. First, Fellowship. There is implanted in the human heart a desire for fellowship. Life is absolutely lonely without it. Joy is always multiplied by sharing it and trouble is always lightened by dividing the burden. As the tear-drops in a child's eyes are hung with rainbows by kind words, so in the life of manhood, where larger feelings meet. No man has mourned for a hermit's life. Such a life is absolutely unnatural. Every one of us is absolutely a creature of society.

For these reasons men organize, and among the organizations the Odd Fellows stand among the first. The Order is founded upon Friendship, Love, and Truth, a trinity of forces which makes a chain hard to break.

True friendship always shines brighter in trouble, and this is its test. Trouble is to friendship what acid is to the gold. Are you aware of the fact that true friendships do much toward character? It is a rare thing in the journey of life that a man climbs to a summit of fame without willing hands to help him up.

II. The second link. You recall the familiar story of the sculptor whose touch seemed endowed with magic, and who, when a little girl marveled at the beauty of an angel he had wrought and referred to it as having been carved by him, declared that the angel was already in the marble, and that he had only cut away the stone around it, allowing it to escape.

Happy is that man in an organization who looks to men all around and discovers the angel of their nature, for every man has a better angel; and happy that Order, no matter what it is, that cuts away the marble and lets the angel out of the man. It is the grandest work in all the world.

You not only have the financial interest, but the entire interest of a brother at heart. You will not think me harsh if I say to-day that he is not a good Odd Fellow who looks to the financial benefits that accrue from the Order, and forgets the moral obligations that bind him to a brother.

And he is not worthy of the name of Odd Fellow who simply enters into it as an insurance organization.

Love is embraced in friendship. Ah, what a power is love! Love puts a new face upon this old world of ours.

III. The third link. But I want to dwell more extensively on that third link in the chain—Truth. Do you know it is our business as charitable men and women to learn the truth? And it is our business as Odd Fellows to learn the truth about God and the great hereafter.

Are you aware that a man is only great as he appropriates what God has provided for him? A butterfly came into my study one day and bathed its wings in the sunshine, and then lighted on the Word of God on my desk, spread its wings, fluttered a while, walked across the page, and then flew out of the window forever. And the thought struck me that I am greater than that butterfly. A world of wisdom was under its feet, a world of revelation was beneath it, and it did not see it; but I do understand it, I do appropriate it to myself. That brilliant flower is brilliant simply because it appropriates to itself the brilliant colors that are around it. That bird sings sweeter than that other bird on the top of the tree simply because it appropriates the music; and he is greatest in the journey of life who appropriates to himself what God Almighty has provided for us. We are to learn to love him and serve him, and we are to learn one more lesson, and that is the lesson of help.

Friends, there is nothing that endears us to our fellowmen like the practice of the virtues of Friendship, Love, and Truth.

Grandly all these years has this old Order pursued her way. The blessings of hundreds of widows and orphans have been heaped upon her. "If every blessing were a flower, she would be hidden from sight beneath a wilderness of blossoms." Her cheeks are ruddy with the hues of health, her eyes are limpid with love, and her stalwart form cheerfully bears the burden she so cheerfully assumes.

May you be Odd Fellows indeed! Odd to those who are sinful and worldly, odd to the stingy and mean, odd to all that is depraved and unholy and material, but thoroughly in harmony with God and with your brethren dwelling in tents down here and in the palace of the King hereafter.—Rev. V. W. Teves.

ROYAL ARCANUM FELLOWSHIP

Text: "He that maketh many friends doeth it to his own destruction; but there is a friend that sticketh closer than a brother." Prov. 18:24.

In all ages—since history records the aspirations of men, their efforts along different lines of endeavor, their accomplishments and conclusions—a definition comprehensive enough to embrace the full meaning of Friendship or Fellowship has been sought after, alike by pagan and Christian, learned and unlearned. Seneca, the Stoic, urged, "If you wish to gain affection, bestow it," while Ovid added his poetic sentiment to the philosopher's convictions, "The way to be loved is to be lovely." Emerson blended both in a sentence, "The only way to have a friend is to be one."

The Bible, however, does not amuse with sparkling epigrams when it can better instruct by profound principles. We find choice suggestion concerning active friendship, or fellowship, implied in the Golden Rule. There is a longing for kindly favor in most hearts, and the Golden Rule would suggest that such favor be secured by guarding our way, step by step, by being kind and friendly, and thus show ourselves worthy of "fellowship."

Following out this clew to fellowship, we find numerous passages in the Bible which give valuable suggestions and deep meaning; as, "A companion of fools shall sweat for it." "A companion of harlots wasteth his substance." "Make no friendship with an angry man, and with a furious man thou shalt not go."

The word translated friends, in the text, means to delight in, to have mutual delight. It is the same word used to show the attachment of Jacob and Joseph, Jonathan and David. It may, consequently, be viewed in the light of companion. But here, too, we find a word of warning: "A man of companions breaks himself up, but there is a Friend more attached than a brother."

The meaning, in all these cases cited, is to suggest a true basis for friendship. And it indicates that such can only exist where both are true and upright. Otherwise, the results must be disappointing and disastrous.

In order to avoid disaster, certain safeguards may be of value, and certain fundamentals are suggested, which declare that more than mere natural endowments are necessary to true "fellowship."

I. First, The Safeguards: As the lighthouse suggests and implies the dangerous coast, so the thought of safeguards in fellowship suggests the perils of society.

1. Indiscriminate companionship may lead to many dangers. Many people go into society with the best intentions, but are prone to forget the true basis and worth of society and life.

There must be an Exemplar; and the true model of all worthy society and fellowship is he who "went about doing good." True society is neither recluse nor ascetic, but is the mingling of men with men to do each other good. Who can estimate the good that is flowing into society from the multiplied combines of Christian "Fellowship," courtesy, cheer, and charity? A safeguard should consequently be placed against all questionable approaches, lest this influx of good be disturbed and hindered by "fellowship" and fraternity.

In order to accomplish this guarding of society, God has inaugurated, organized, united effort against evil. One of these organizations is the Church, which must be ever regarded as the mother of society and all true "fellowship" and fraternity.

This is one of the great principles of our noble Order, and of which we need not be ashamed; for this principle, combined with other high and noble strivings which are the natural outgrowth of this deep, broad, profound fundamental—such as Fraternity, relief to the sick and distressed, aid to widows and orphans of deceased members, and in many ways active in works of "Mercy and Charity," sympathy and brotherhood—may, I think, be safely applied to the Royal Arcanum, in that it brings men into close fellowship and cherishes those feelings that thrive and put forth blossoms in each other's welfare.

They are calculated to make men thoughtful and helpful.

Expanding the sentiments of "Virtue, Charity, and Mercy," they remind us of the principles of the Gospel, which does good to all men, by "breaking bread to the hungry, giving a cup of water to the thirsty, watching at the bedside of the sick, visiting the imprisoned"—duties which are, alas, too often neglected in ordinary friendships. Every one of the principles of the Royal Arcanum is useful as a guard or signal against evil, and proudly raises the banner covered with the inscription of "Virtue, Mercy and Charity."

These principles will help any thoughtful, sincere man to live up to the true standard of the Church of Christ, which is the greatest of all Orders of Fellowship—for it is a "World-wide Brotherhood."

We are told in the text, "But there is a friend that sticketh closer than a brother." The secrect of this close cleavage and unbreakable union is to be found in the strong, firm foundation upon which it rests. It is for a worthier purpose than mere natural kinship, and the attachment is consequently more close and durable.

2. Fellowship inspires to high purposes. Emerson vividly displays this principle when he says, "Our chief want is somebody who can make us do what we are able. This is the service of a true friend. How he flings wide the doors of existence, what questions we ask of him, what an understanding we have. It is the only real society."

3. Again, "Fellowship" gives impulse to unselfish relationship. Brotherly love and human Brotherhood are conceptions now held in deservedly high esteem, but they come to us through the Gospel and the Church.

II. And now, in conclusion, let us think of that "Friend that sticketh closer than a brother," in imitation of whom we have found possibilities of "Fellowship," and whom ages of Christian thought have recognized as the source of all that is noblest and most beautiful in human character.

If ever fellowship aroused enthusiasm for truth and imparted peaceful blessings, the burning and shining lights in the history of reforms, revivals and missions may be used as means by which to measure the power for good of Christian fellowship.

But ideas need organization, and this involves fellowship.

Wiclif said, "Jesus chose twelve men that they might have fellowship with him." This gives us a conception of true fellowship. But what is most surprising is, that such a fellowship as Christ gave an example of could ever be compared with modern society. Should we not, then, stop and reflect, and ascertain how much we come short of this model, even the Christ, for that alone is true fellowship? The Church is the true organization of hallowed and blessed friendship.—Rev. Noah E. Yeiser.

FRATERNAL LIFE INSURANCE

Text: "Set thine house in order." 2 Kings 20:1.

In presenting to you the question of insurance, it becomes necessary to lay down three propositions, or unfold to you a condition, the remedy, and the result. First, we are in a lamentable condition. This condition is a stubborn fact, presenting itself to every intelligent brain. It is not the creation of a pessimistic mind. The stubborn fact confronts the optimist and the pessimist alike, and the part of wisdom is to comprehend it and apply an adequate remedy.

The condition is one of extravagance, recklessness, and carelessness. This is the most extravagant, reckless, and careless age of the world, in one sense of the word. It costs you more to live to-day than ever before. The combined forces are demanding all that a man possesses and all that a man is.

This is the age of uncertainties. The wealthy man of to-day is the pauper of to-morrow, because of the rapidly changing circumstances. The heat and passion in which business is conducted preclude meditation, consideration, and deliberation; and with electric rapidity the man makes his money, the man spends his money, the man rises, and the man falls.

These things being true, the question that agitates the honest man is—How can I provide for my family, provide against encroachments upon their bounty and their future safety? He spends his time laboring for them. But little can be made and saved by any one man to-day. Men by honest labor make very little and save very little.

I present to you this thought: I believe the remedy is to be found in a safe insurance policy. The brainy business man of the country, the wealthiest man of the land, side by side with the prudent, careful, honest toiler, have each and all arrived at the conclusion that the safest investment and provision for their wives and children is a well-protected insurance policy. They are taking out these policies—policies that cannot be attacked by law; policies that cannot be affected by the changing conditions; policies that cannot be stained by politics; policies free, pure, heaven's blessings and earth's benedictions, handed direct to the orphaned children and to the widowed wife.

The statement in my first proposition being true, it then becomes a man's duty to provide for his family. In fact no man has a right to take unto himself a wife unless he can see that in the natural course of events he can provide for her beyond her wants and suffering. No man has a right to bring into this world a child and lay it in the lap of the State and demand that the Sheriff become its nurse, the jail its nursery, and the public treasury its benefactor. No man has a right to bring into this world a child unless he has made an honest provision for its support, its deportment, and its education. In the course of business events it may be impossible for him to absolutely secure to this child all the comforts and blessings he would like to bestow upon it, but it is possible for him to insure his life, and thereby secure to his wife comfort and happiness. It is possible for him to insure his life and make absolutely safe the comfort and protection of his dependent children. An insurance policy is a bridge across this yawning chasm of extravagance, recklessness, carelessness, and uncertainty. It becomes an honest man's duty to bridge this chasm in order that his dependent wife and suffering children may cross it in security and peace.

Again, I call your attention to fraternal insurance. I believe in it. I believe in anything that will righteously draw men together and teach the great idea of brotherhood, humanity, helpfulness, and divine kindness. I believe in old-line insurance. I have policies in the best old-line companies. So I have policies in several fraternal orders; and I took policies in fraternal insurance because they teach the idea of brotherhood, of friendship, of charity, of confidence, of kindness, and love; of personal, hand-to-hand contact with a man in his suffering and in his sorrows. I am in these fraternal insurance orders and many other fraternal orders because they bring to my personal attention and lay upon my personal heart the woes, sorrows, and pains of the individual man, the individual woman, the individual child.—REV. MARK A. MATTHEWS, D.D.

LOVE AND THE MYSTERIES: SERMON FOR FRATERNAL ORGANIZATIONS

Text: "Though I understand all mysteries and have not love, I am nothing." 1 Cor. 13:2.

When St. Paul's Corinthian audience heard the word "mysteries" there was conjured up in their minds an entirely different picture from that which springs in the modern American mind. They did not think of the mysteries of science, or the mysteries of the stars, or even the mysteries of a haunted house. On the contrary the Corinthian would think of the Elusinian Mysteries, that were regularly celebrated on the road from Athens to Corinth, or the Orphic Mysteries, which kept alive the memory of the great singer Orpheus, or the mystery of Samothrace, or of Ephesus.

These secret cults were so common at the time that it is very possible some of the heathen converts in the Corinthian Church had been initiated into one or more of them and could say, I understand the Elusinian, or the Orphic, or the Ephesian Mystery. Probably Paul knew that some who would read his words would recall the sort of miracle-play which had been enacted before their eyes when they were initiated into the Elusinian Mystery. They would recall how Cora had been snatched before their eyes by Pluto, the god of the underworld; how her mother Ceres, the goddess of agriculture, had mournfully searched for her while all growing things withered under her neglect. They had seen the daughter restored after the mother had gone to the underworld to beg for her and had witnessed the gift of agriculture to the world as a final result.

Others there were who had not been initiated but who knew that the candidate was purified by a sacrifice and then led, after prayer and fasting, through dark passages confusing with terrifying sights and sounds, but was at last allowed to return to the light and given a view of their goddess.

Some of the members of the church had probably met on the wharves of Corinth sailors who feared no storms at sea, for they knew the Mystery of Samothrace and its protecting secrets. Others had encountered the superior air of members of the Orphic Mystery who had learned secrets guaranteed to give them peace in the life to come.

Recalling that this is the original meaning of the word "mysteries," we can easily paraphrase the text to read: "Though I understand all the secrets of all the fraternal societies and have not love, I am nothing." For any one at all familiar with the rituals of our great secret societies will see a strong resemblance between the "mystery" of the first century and the lodges of the twentieth.

To be perfectly frank with St. Paul we must explain that he himself, in using the word, was not thinking of the cult at all. He was using the word in a secondary sense, namely, that of some hidden truth, the guardian of which could impart it only to those who earnestly sought it and under the most favorable circumstances. It is in this sense that he speaks of "the mystery of godliness," the mystery of the transformed body at the resurrection, or the mystery of salvation.

But we will do no violence to the meaning of the writer if we substitute the word "lodge" for "mysteries," and read it as we have suggested: "Though I understand all the inner meaning of the ritual of my lodge and have not caught the spirit of love, I have no right to be considered a member."

In fact, we can win some practical inspiration by translating the entire chapter into the vernacular of the lodge: "Though I speak with heavenly eloquence in the lodge room, if I have not love I will make no more impression than a sounding brass or a tinkling cymbal. And though I understand all the ritual of the lodge and have such faith in its worth that I can move mountains of opposition, and have not love, I have no standing as a member. Though I bestow my entire fortune to feed the poor of the lodge, and though I give my last ounce of strength to carry on its work, it can bring me no satisfaction unless I have a loving spirit in the task."

Here, then, is a test by which any brother may decide whether he is a credit to his lodge or not. By studying these words he may learn whether he has caught the true spirit of fraternalism or whether he has been carried away by less important features. If he feels that he has not been wielding the influence he should in his organization, he may find the answer here. If he feels that he is not getting enough satisfaction out of his lodge work, perhaps he can find the explanation here. Never has the true inwardness of fraternalism, as well as of religion, been so clearly and powerfully expressed.

Paul was one of the most practical men the world ever saw. He never allowed mere emotion to carry him away. Always he came back to the sober realities of life. So he does in this chapter. He drops suddenly from his rhapsody on Love to a dozen practical tests, lest any man plume himself falsely on having this great essential in his heart. He has no wish to encourage sentimental people whose energies are expended in words. To such he sets a severe heart-searching: "Have you," he asks, "the drab negative quality of patience as well as the bright positive quality of kindness? Can you endure without complaint, as Lincoln did, slights, insults, open wrong, in the constant hope that the erring brother may come back to your friendship again? Do you, on the other hand, make it a constant practice to fill the lives of those about you with thoughtful deeds of love? If you do not you cannot claim to have this supreme quality."

These are his first two tests. The next two deal with our relations to inferiors and superiors respectively. "Can you," he asks, "look without envy upon a brother who has received honors and gifts that you believe to be your due? Can you, on the other hand, endure sudden prosperity or unlooked-for honors without a desire to strike envy into the hearts of your former equals?"

Then he passes on to life within the lodge room itself: "Do you injure the feelings of your brothers by rude and unseemly conduct or by heedless scramblings after privileges that you think are your due? Love does neither of these. Or if others forget themselves to commit these faults, are you easily aroused to resent their conduct? Love is not easily provoked."

How have you dealt with erring members? Have you endured all manner of wrongs from them? Have you persistently turned a deaf ear to unpleasant rumors, believing only that which was good about them, and hoping ever that they would mend their ways to win the love and respect of all? Have you been the last to censure and the first to forgive?

If you have done these things, then your life is crowned with the greatest and most enduring of all graces.—REV. J. B. BURKHARDT.

INDEPENDENT ORDER OF FORESTERS

"O, give thanks unto the Lord, for he is gracious, and his mercy endureth forever." Psalm 136:1.

We are assembled to-day in compliance with the order of the Supreme Chief Ranger. It is surely our duty, as it is our privilege, to assemble together as Foresters and give our most hearty thanks to our heavenly Father for the great blessings we have enjoyed and the many mercies he has given us.

This beautiful Psalm is a continual flow of thanksgiving for several specific mercies, such as the deliverance from Og, King of Bashan.

When Israel was marching northward, out of its desert sojourn, there must have been many a quaking heart when the vast and warlike preparations of the enemies were known. Og was a giant—one of the remnants of a fierce race, who had in the past lorded it over a large part of Western Asia. His kingdom was extensive and rich—full of cities and people, with strong natural fortresses.

But full of faith in God, right up to the frowning walls of the great fortress the aged Moses led the army of Israel. He did not wait for Og to come out against him, but marched forward to the giant's capital and by the suddenness and determination of his attack made havoc of the city and gained a glorious victory. The old domination of Bashan was wiped out, and the land became the inheritance of the tribe of Manasseh.

In all the memories of Israel's wonderful history this victory held a conspicuous place. The story of Og was told from father to son through all the generations of the national life; and history shows that it was introduced into the religious service as a subject of their thanksgiving and a lesson for their faith. This was a psalm for public service, to be engaged in by all. The nation felt its ancient victory to be a present blessing and regarded it as a pledge of God's future care.

I. Let us, brethren, apply the lesson to ourselves and strive to profit by their example. As I speak of this great worldwide Order of the Independent Order of Foresters and the marvelous blessings God has granted us, we shall see, I am sure, cause for thanksgiving and grounds for rejoicing, as well as hope for the future. The position the Independent Order of Foresters holds to-day is a most remarkable one. As we look back to 1881 and see it in its infant and helpless struggle for life, and now look at it in its giant manhood and prosperity, is it, I say, not remarkable? What a blessing this has been. How many widows have been helped? How many fatherless children have been provided for through this agency? Christian brethren, it is surely some privilege to be a co-worker in making provision for the afflicted and needy around us. It is one of the grandest objects in which we may be united. Next to the spiritual work of the Church there is nothing more noble, more elevating, more unselfish, more in keeping with the spirit of the Christian religion than the grand work this noble Order is doing.

II. Test the work of the Order by the commands laid down in the inspired Book of God. In Galatians 6:10 it is written: "As we have opportunity, let us do good unto all men." In James 1:27 we read: "Pure religion and undefiled before God and the Father is this to visit the fatherless and widows in their affliction and to keep himself unspotted from the world." And what does our Lord Jesus Christ teach us in the story of the Good Samaritan? Oh! for more of that spirit! May God open such hearts and touch and move them by his love and grace. Pure love towards humanity can only spring from love to God. Only he who loves God with all his heart and soul and strength can for God's sake love his neighbor as himself. Oh! what love and compassion we see in the life and work of Jesus Christ. He loved us, he died for us. Thank God for every institution which encourages and helps on this work, which was, and is, so dear to him. I am proud to belong to an Order which is engaged in this Christ-like work. Brethren, in every man behold a brother and do him all the good you can. I thank God for what has been accomplished, and I pray the work may go on and prosper.

The record of this Order is such that its members may be proud. Much of the success is due to the master mind of our Supreme Chief Ranger, whose genius, worth, and energy have placed the Independent Order of Foresters in the foremost rank of fraternal institutions. We thank God for this work for our race. We thank God for all the Order has done to dry the orphan's tears and soothe the widow's breast. It has comforted broken hearts and brightened human homes. Shall we not resolve here and now that, God helping us, we will strive to help on every cause whose aim is to benefit society? Let us have unwavering faith in and sincere love for Jesus Christ, the Saviour of men. As "he went about doing good," so let us follow that bright example. For all the good work done by our noble Order let God be praised. Let each and every member help on the good work, and feel it a privilege as well as a duty to coöperate with the Supreme Chief Ranger and his officers in advancing the interests of the Order, which has done so much good in the world. May God be glorified and man blessed.

This great fraternal society has now been planted in nearly every country in the world by the persevering energy of the Supreme Chief Ranger, and it has enrolled in its membership the leading men of all professions—men capable of examining its principles and scrutinizing its workings. In its private meetings it encourages friendship and brotherly love. It looks after the sick and makes provision for the permanently disabled, whether from sickness or accident, and in old age, when man especially needs a helping hand, it comes to his assistance in the provision it makes him. Thus it works for man during his life, as well as making provision for the family after his death. For all these benefits give God thanks and pray for his continued favors. The spirit of harmony and good-will which prevails in the Order is another cause for thanksgiving. But enough has been said, I trust, to call forth the thankfulness of our very souls, and from the past we gather hope for the future.

Remember, brethren, we are here not for excursions and worldly pleasure, but to give thanks to Almighty God for his mercies. May our conduct be such as not to rob our service of all merit. Let our prayers be not from the lips alone, but from the heart. And may the constancy of our lives show forth the sincerity of our hearts that we may be accepted of God, and when this life be over may we each, through the mercy of God and the merits of our Lord Jesus Christ, receive the "well done, good and faithful servant, enter thou into the joy of thy Lord." I will say no more. May God bless you all and make us each to abound in every good word and work to the honor and glory of his holy name, and to the well-being to all around us.—REV. E. DAVIS, A.M.

THE SUPREMACY OF LOVE: SERMON TO ODD FELLOWS

Text: "The greatest of these is Love." 1 Cor. 13:13.

The ultimate analysis of Christianity, its peculiar crown and discriminating royalty, is explained in a single word—Love. Love is not only the master passion in man, to which all other passions do homage, it is the master passion of God; it is also the master principle of the universe. Nations, peoples, systems are all distinguished by some predominating spirit. The genius of England is practical, that of Germany is speculative, that of France is sensational, that of Italy is esthetic, that of India is idealistic, while that of America is cosmopolitan. So of religions: they are separated from each other by some marked distinguishing features. Thus the genius of Judaism is ceremonial, that of Hindooism is mystical, that of Mohammedanism is fanatical, and that of Christianity is expressed by "Love."

Romance and poetry through all past ages have never wearied in picturing the sorrows and joys or in singing the glories and triumphs of Love. Its tragedies, its sufferings, and its victories represent all that is greatest in history and most thrilling in literature. But in Christian literature Love is regnant, the most beneficent influence and the mightiest force in the world. And in Christianity only is it enthroned and sceptered as monarch ruling by divine right. It is the pearl of great price; the jewel of priceless worth.

The jewel of society is "pleasure," and the casket which holds it is "good form." The jewel of business is "gold," and its casket is "commerce." The jewel of science is "wisdom," and "mind" is its casket; but the supreme jewel of fraternity and Christianity is "Love," and its casket is the "heart." In the Bible heart is a word that abounds. Brain, I believe, is not mentioned in Scripture, but as the world goes, "brain counts for a good deal more than heart does." It will win more applause and earn a larger salary. The current demand is for ideas. A cold and unfeeling judgment, a crude, half barbaric and wholly selfish commercialism may place a premium upon keenness of intellect and shrewdness of mind in a materialistic age, but the conclusion of all history supports the high vision of Bourdillon in the sweetest sonnet ever written:

> "The night hath a thousand eyes,
>   The day but one,
> But the light of the whole world dies
>   When the sun is gone.
> The mind hath a thousand eyes,
>   The heart but one,
> Yet the light of the whole life dies
>   When love is done."

One of the brightest flower-clusters of Holy Writ is the chapter from which our text is taken. It is the Swan-song of the great Apostle. This golden chapter contains Paul's estimate of the worth of love. In the first three verses he gives a statement of its value by a most "striking contrast which seems an exaggeration." Four things were held in supreme favor in the Christian Church. First, the gift of tongues. Paul himself had heard, in heavenly rapture, angelic language impossible for him to re-utter, but he places love in contrast with that, saying: "Though I speak with the tongues of men and of angels and have not love, I am become as sounding brass and tinkling cymbal." Gifted with eloquence which melts into muteness even angelic harps and lyres, my utterances are but the soulless clanging of cymbal, if "this heavenly virtue makes not musical and fragrant all I say." To the Greeks knowledge was the supreme possession—valued above jewels. But there were exalted souls in this Corinthian church divinely favored with that deeper insight which comes of inspiration. Both are placed in contrast with love when he says: "And though I have the gift of prophecy and understand all mysteries and all knowledge and have not love, I am nothing." "The sage and prophet are nothing, without love." Again, the power to work wonders, a mark of peculiar favor, had been bestowed upon some. "Though I have all faith so that I could remove mountains and have not love, it profiteth me nothing." Finally, the Apostle arrays in imagination the glorious army of heroes and martyrs of self-sacrifice, and the benefactors and philanthropists of that early church, whose liberality was so lavish that it seems an insanity to the world, and he puts all this in contrast with love: "Though I bestow all my goods to feed the poor, and though I give my body to be burned, and have not love, I am nothing." Behold the character portrayed in these sublime sentences—this glorious composite!

For the justice and validity of this judgment three irrefragable reasons are assigned.

First, he resolves love into its constituent elements. Or, as Drummond has so happily stated it, he "gives an amazing analysis of what this supreme thing is. It is like light. As you have seen a man of science take a beam of light and pass it through a crystal prism; as you have seen it come out on the other side of the prism all broken up into its component colors —red, and blue, and yellow, and violet, and orange, and all the colors of the rainbow—so Paul passes this thing, Love, through the magnificent prism of his inspired intellect, and it comes out on the other side broken into its elements. And in these few words we have what might be called the spectrum of Love."

The spectrum takes the beam of that light, which no one can really define, and throws it into seven hues. But the spectrum of Love has nine ingredients. They are patience, kindness, generosity, humility, courtesy, unselfishness, good temper, guilelessness, sincerity—these make up the supreme gift.

These great qualities indicate the effect of love upon character and conduct. The Apostle, by a few master strokes, describes love in the concrete. He presents a character in which love is the regnant principle, the dominating passion.

"Love suffereth long." Love is patient, calm, passive. It is equal to any strain. It "understands and therefore waits."

"Love is kind." Kindness is love made visible, turned inside out. It speaks only gentle, tender, helpful words and does only kindly deeds to weary pilgrims along life's rugged pathway. It is the spirit of the old philosopher who said: "I shall not pass this way but once. Any good thing, therefore, that I can do, or any kindness that I can show to any human being, let me do it now. Let me not defer it or neglect it, for I shall not pass this way again." Better still, it is the sublime thought of "Him who went about doing good."

"Love envieth not." It hath no hateful, jealous feeling for one who may be doing the same work you are doing, but better. Love is generous.

"Love vaunteth not itself, is not puffed up." It is humble. It is careful to "think no more highly of itself than it ought to think." It rejoices in lowliest tasks.

"Love does not behave itself unseemly." This is love in relation to etiquette. It furnishes and finishes the true gentleman. It communicates grace and dignity to character and winsomeness to the life.

"Love is not easily provoked." Its temper is always sweet. It brings with it the angels of content, peace, and delight.

"Love thinketh no evil." It is pure, and can think purity only. But it thinks. Love is ever thoughtful, ever inspired. What a man thinks is determined largely by his ruling love. Those who are pure in thought and life will not, because they cannot, think evil of others. Love is guileless. "Love rejoiceth not in iniquity, but rejoiceth in the truth." Love, too, warms and inspires. Truth instructs and directs. Truth rejoices in the quickening influences of love, while love rejoices in the illuminating power of truth. Love is always sincere. It sees truth in a new light such as "never fell on land or sea," and it rejoiceth in it evermore. How love quickens human wits! How it strengthens human weakness! What burdens it has enabled drooping shoulders to carry! What toils it has enabled human hands to accomplish! What prodigies weak women and tender children have performed while they were nerved and braced and upheld by the animating inspirations of love! What power doth it possess to transform the life! How it elevates and sublimates the soul!

Paul's second reason is that love is a mark of manhood in Christ. Growth toward love, and into love, had been the law of his own life. "When I was a child I spake as a child, I thought as a child, I understood as a child; but when I became a man I put away childish things." Love, indeed, is the great end towards which all creation is tending. The discovery of that thought has been of inconceivable comfort to me, for I have seen the human race, beginning in the lowest state of animalism, grasping, cruel—the shark, the leopard, and the lion regnant, as though destructiveness was the original creative design. Out of it I have seen emerging, little by little, other qualities—love of cubs and whelps, then I have seen the animal creation reach to the level of the human family, and that family, under some mystic influence which we cannot call nature at every step, steadily unfolding toward intelligence, toward refinement, toward imagination, toward sympathy, toward love, and in love evermore, sphere by sphere. The law of unfolding sets the whole creation upon a march from the lower form of organized matter up through every variation of organization, through every form of passion, seeking the highest, holiest thing in the universe—the star around which the whole creation is revolving. The name of that star is Love.

But Paul's chief reason for extolling love as the great passion of life is that "love never dies." To emphasize his great thought the Apostle enumerates these great things in the catalogue of imperishables in the estimation of his day. The greatest thinkers of his age believed that prophecies would endure whatever else might fail. "But," said he, "whether there be prophecies, they shall fail." This book is full of prophecies. One by one they have been fulfilled, and so failed —their work is finished. "Whether there be tongues, they shall cease." The Hebrew tongue in which he spoke has passed away. The Greek tongue, so mellifluous and facile, is spoken by the few only, and is passing away. The Latin is obsolete. The Indian language perished long ago.

"And whether there be knowledge, it shall vanish away." What has become of the wisdom of the ancient Egyptians, the knowledge of the old Greeks? It has all vanished away. "Now we know in part." "We see through a glass darkly." All that we see of commerce and government and institutions is passing away. "The fashion of this world passeth away." Love survives by might supernal and by right eternal, for "God is love."

I felicitate myself that I am speaking to-day to representatives of a great fraternal order, whose beneficent sway is world-wide, which is bound together by a golden chain with three jeweled links—Friendship, Love, and Truth. What a glorious trinity of principles! I am sure that it is not by accident that you place Love at the center of the motto. Securely there it holds friends together in truth. It would refuse to hold friends together in falsehood. The temper of every link in your charmed chain is practical. It will stand the test of use. Yours is not ideal only, but embodied friendship; not visionary, but real truth; not abstract, but incarnate love—love that transforms sorrow into joy, pain into pleasure, loss into gain. Yours is a love that makes a paradise of a wilderness, and a feast in the house of poverty. Its highest delight is in giving pleasure to those beloved. During the last seventy years it relieved 250,000 widows by an expenditure of over $91,000,000. It realizes most gloriously the sublime stanza of Schiller:

> "Have love—not love alone for one,
>   But man as man thy brother call,
>   And scatter like the circling sun,
>   Thy charities on all."

May each new day, fraught with deeds of love like those which passed between David and Jonathan, knitting their souls together in a true friendship, beam upon your glorious Order, as upon the pathway of the just, which "shineth more and more unto the perfect day."—REV. H. O. BREEDEN, D.D.

www.ingramcontent.com/pod-product-compliance
Lightning Source LLC
Chambersburg PA
CBHW032001220426
43664CB00005B/97